1979

Infinite Jest: Wit and Humor
in Italian Renaissance Art

"The Discovery of Honey" (detail), Piero di Cosimo

Infinite Jest
Wit and Humor in Italian Renaissance Art

Let's laugh. And how?
With the mouth, the nose,
the chin, the throat, and with all
of our five natural senses. But
it isn't worth anything if you
don't laugh from the heart ...

Bonaventure Des Périers, *Nouvelles*
Récréations et Joyeux Devis, Lyon, 1558

Paul Barolsky

University of Missouri Press

Columbia & London

1978

Copyright © 1978
by The Curators of the
University of Missouri
University of Missouri Press,
Columbia, Missouri 65201
Library of Congress
Catalog Card Number 77-15843
Printed and bound in the
United States of America

Library of Congress
Cataloging in Publication Data

Barolsky, Paul, 1941–
  Infinite jest.

  Bibliography: p.
  Includes index.
  1. Wit and humor, Pictorial
—Renaissance, 1450–1600—
Italy. 2. Italian
wit and humor,
Pictorial. I. Title.
NC1523.B37   709'.45   77-15843
ISBN 0-8262-0241-1

The illustrations are reproduced through the courtesy of the following institutions.

Alinari-Scala: photos by Alinari—Figures 2-1 through 2-4, 2-11, 3-1, 3-5, 3-8, 4-5, 4-8, 4-9, 4-10, 5-2, 5-4, 5-8, 5-19, 6-7, 6-8, 6-9, 7-7, 7-9, 7-10, 7-13, 8-2, 8-5, 8-7, 8-10, 8-12, 8-13, 8-15; photos by Anderson—Figures 1-2, 2-5, 2-6, 2-9, 3-3, 3-10, 4-1, 4-2, 5-11, 5-15, 7-2 through 7-6, 7-11, 7-12; photo by Brogi—Figure 6-6.

Royal Library, Windsor Castle, copyright reserved, Figures 3-1, 3-2.

Kunsthistorisches Museum, Vienna, Figures 1-4, 4-12, 5-12, 5-14, 8-4.

The Metropolitan Museum of Art, New York: The Jules Bache Collection, 1949, Figure 1-5; Rogers Fund, 1952, Figure 5-3; bequest of Mrs. H. O. Havemeyer, 1929, The H. O. Havemeyer Collection, Figure 6-1; Rogers Fund 1905, Figure 8-1.

Reproduced by courtesy of the Trustees of the British Museum, London, Figures 2-7, 2-8, 5-5, 5-13, 7-8.

Gabinetto Fotografico della Soprintendenze alle Gallerie di Firenze, Florence, Figures 2-10, 3-6, 5-1, 5-9, 5-10, 6-2.

Reproduced by courtesy of the Trustees, The National Gallery, London, Figures 2-12, 3-4, 6-3, 8-3.

Gemäldegalerie, Staatliche Museen Preussischer Kulturbesitz, Berlin, Figures 2-13, 8-14.

Worcester Art Museum, Worcester, Mass., Figures 2-14, 2-15.

Bibliotheca Hertziana, Rome, Figures 4-3, 4-6.

Les Musées Nationaux, Paris, Figures 4-7, 5-6, 5-7, 6-5, 8-9.

Staatliche Kunstsammlungen, Dresden, Figure 4-11.

National Gallery of Art, Washington, D. C., Ailsa Mellon Bruce Fund, Figure 6-4; Widener Collection, Figure 7-1.

By permission of the Trustees of the Chatsworth Settlement, photograph by courtesy of the Courtauld Institute of Art, Figure 1-1.

The Fogg Art Museum, Harvard University, purchase by Alpheus Hyatt Fund and Friends of Art, Archaeology, and Music, Figure 2-16.

Ashmolean Museum, Oxford, Figure 3-7.

Städelsches Kunstinstitut, Frankfurt, Figure 3-9.

Hermitage, Leningrad, Figure 5-16.

Gabinetto Fotografico Nazionale, Rome, Figure 5-17.

The Frick Art Reference Library, New York, Figure 5-18.

Herzog Anton Ulrich-Museum, Braunschweig, photograph by Museumfoto B. P. Keiser, Figure 8-6.

The Art Museum, Princeton University, Figure 8-8.

Christ Church Picture Gallery, Oxford, Figure 8-11.

Acknowledgments

Despite the brevity of this book, my debts are enormous. I owe a great deal to Sydney J. Freedberg, whose teaching and writings have influenced my approach to Italian Renaissance art. His stringent criticism of several chapters in the penultimate draft of this book was helpful. Konrad Oberhuber, who read two versions of this work, has been exceedingly generous; he has offered much sympathetic criticism and several ideas that have been assimilated in the text. In addition, both Frederick Hartt and James S. Ackerman have read different versions of the text and have offered valuable and kind advice. I owe a special debt to Ulrich Middeldorf, who encouraged me when I first undertook this study; he also made countless and delightful bibliographical suggestions. I am grateful to David Winter, Robert Sanoff, and Nora Wiseman, who read my essay, offering helpful and extensive criticism of its form and content. Robert Kellogg and Mary McKinley also made some useful suggestions, as did my *lettori anonomi*. My graduate students at the University of Virginia have made various points during our discussions of Renaissance art and literature, which are indicated in the notes. The University of Virginia has kindly facilitated my research by awarding me both research grants and a Sesquicentennial Fellowship in the fall of 1973. Both the Fiske Kimball Library and Alderman Library made special efforts to procure materials necessary for my research.

Finally, it is harder for me to estimate the impact of my two *putti*, Deborah and Daniel. If they occasionally slowed the progress of my work, they almost always reminded me (in their way) that the subject of my book is by no means abstract. Most of all, I owe to my wife, Ruth, the good-humored wisdom that this book would be written after all. The extent of her support has been immeasurable.

P. B.
August 1977
Charlottesville, Virginia

For Ruth,
Deborah,
and Daniel

Contents

I. *The Place of Humor in Renaissance Art*

Now you must follow this dog's example, and be wise in smelling out, sampling and relishing these fine and most juicy books, which are easy to run down but hard to bring to bay. Then by diligent reading and frequent meditation, you must break the bone and lick out the substantial marrow—that is to say the meaning which I intend to convey by these Pythagorean symbols—in the hope of assurance of becoming both wiser and more courageous by such reading. For here you will find an individual savour and abstruse teaching which will initiate you into certain very high sacraments and dread mysteries, concerning not only our religion but also our public and private life.
—François Rabelais, "Prologue," *The Histories of Gargantua and Pantagruel*

From the art of antiquity to the satire of Dada, surrealism, and more recently, pop art, there is an extensive history of humor and wit in Western art. In the parodies of Greek pottery, the ingenious drolleries of medieval manuscript illuminations, the playful wit of Renaissance grotesques, the delightfully humorous sculpture of the baroque, the satirical paintings of Bruegel, Steen, and Hogarth, the mocking drawings of Thomas Rowlandson, the bizarre prints of Goya, the caricatures of Daumier, and the playful parodies of Picasso, we encounter a wide range of humorous or satirical commentaries on the human condition. This art is the visual counterpart to the vast tradition of comic literature from Homer, Aristophanes, and Ovid to Joyce, Giraudoux, and Ionesco. Relationships between humorous literature and art are frequently noted. The profound humor of Bruegel has frequently been compared to that of his contemporary, Rabelais, and sometimes direct relations exist, as in the case of Fielding's discussion of Hogarth.

It is a curious fact that while scores of books have been written about the history or criticism of humorous or comic literature, considerably less attention has been paid to wit or humor in art. An exceptional case is Wright's generally neglected, mid-nineteenth-century survey, *A History of Caricature and Grotesque in Literature and Art*.[1] More recently, Gombrich and Kris have surveyed the subject in their little volume, *Caricature*.[2] But students of art history have generally avoided discussing it. Gombrich and Kris have observed that comic art has always been ranked inferior. According to them, "Sometimes it was reproached for lack of content" and "sometimes it was considered incompatible with the 'grand manner.'" Moreover, the visual arts are not as easily relegated to specific genres of humor as is literature. While books such as Gilbert Highet's *The Anatomy of Satire* trace the evolution of written satire, there are no corresponding studies of satire in the visual arts, even though countless satirical paintings, prints, and drawings exist.

1. Thomas Wright, *A History of Caricature and Grotesque in Literature and Art.*

2. E. H. Gombrich and Ernst Kris, *Caricature.*

More than one hundred years ago Jacob Burckhardt in a discussion of satire, surveyed the general character of wit in the Italian Renaissance; a short time later, John Addington Symonds discussed the burlesque and satire in Italian Renaissance literature.[3] Since then there has been some discussion among art historians of the humor in Italian Renaissance art, but for the most part it has been unsystematic. Edgar Wind, following the lead of R. Foster, has stressed the influence of Ovid and Lucian on satirical art of the Renaissance, and more than other art historians he stressed the comedy and satire in Renaissance art.[4] Erwin Panofsky, who has referred to such humorous aspects of Renaissance culture as the joking of Sebastiano del Piombo, has discussed the humor of Piero di Cosimo and its relation to the classic tradition.[5] Recently Charles Dempsey has examined the playful satire in major works by Raphael and Carracci and the relation of this satire to classical literature, and Bert Meijer has discussed the comic works of some interesting but minor North Italian artists.[6] In more general terms, Dagobert Frey and Eugenio Battisti have treated the humorous art of the period, and Sydney Freedberg has discussed the wit and humor in sixteenth-century painting, citing examples of both visual satire and parody.[7] Similarly, scholars have recently discussed the satirical and comic aspects in the work of Northern artists, the most notable of whom is Bruegel.[8] They have followed the lead of Huizinga, whose *The Waning of the Middle Ages* is full of examples of comic or burlesque art.[9] Nevertheless, the aspect of humor has been at best a secondary consideration in discussions of Italian Renaissance art. As Gombrich has recently observed: "In my own field, the history of art, we have become intolerably earnest. A false prestige has come to be attached to the postulation of profound meanings or ulterior motives. The idea of fun is even more unpopular among us than the notion of beauty."[10] The art of the period is more often discussed in relation to the serious humanist, Neoplatonic, or theological literature. The texts of writers such as Pico della Mirandola, Ficino, and Alberti have been carefully glossed by art historians, but scarcely a word has been said of the delightful comedy of Pulci, the facetious poetry of Berni, and the mock-heroic writings of Folengo, who influenced Rabelais. The facetious aspects of Aretino's writings have been generally ignored by art historians; the comedies of Bibbiena, Ariosto, Cecchi, Caro, and others have been neglected; and the satires of Doni, Niccolò Franco, and Gelli, and the *novelle* of Il Lasca, Firenzuola, and countless other comic writers who were well known in the Renaissance have been overlooked. Yet to obtain a balanced view of Italian Renaissance art, we need to take into account the ways in which the visual arts of the period relate to this comic tradition.

This book will explore some of the witty and humorous trends in Italian Renaissance art and their relationship to literature of the period. It is not conceived as an exhaustive catalogue of extant works of humor in Italian Renais-

3. Jacob Burckhardt, *The Civilization of the Italian Renaissance*; John Addington Symonds, *Renaissance in Italy*.

4. Edgar Wind, *Bellini's Feast of the Gods*, which includes an excellent introductory bibliography of studies of humor in Renaissance art and literature. Wind's *Pagan Mysteries in the Renaissance* also deals with the humor and playfulness in Italian Renaissance art.

5. Erwin Panofsky, *Studies in Iconology: Humanistic Themes in the Art of the Renaissance*.

6. Charles Dempsey, " 'Et Nos Cedamus Amori': Observations on the Farnese Gallery"; and Bert Meijer, "Esempi del comico figurativo nel rinascimento lombardo."

7. Dagobert Frey, *Manierismus als Europäische Stilerscheinung*, p. 41; Eugenio Battisti, *Antirinascimento*; Sydney J. Freedberg, *Painting of the High Renaissance in Rome and Florence*, and *Painting in Italy: 1500–1600*. Frederick Hartt also brings out the playfulness of Renaissance art in his *History of Italian Renaissance Art*.

8. Georges Marlier, *Erasme et la peinture flamande de son temps*. Konrad Oberhuber, *Die Kunst der Graphik IV: Renaissance und Barock*, pp. 15–16; and Svetlana Alpers, "Breughel's Festive Peasants." The extent of the increasing interest in the comedy of Northern art is reflected in Svetlana Alpers, "Realism as a comic mode: low-life painting seen through Bredero's eyes."

9. Johan Huizinga, *The Waning of the Middle Ages*, pp. 303–5.

10. E. H. Gombrich, "Huizinga and 'Homo Ludens,' " p. 1089.

sance art. Such an enterprise would transform a potentially enjoyable study into an unnecessarily pedantic one, tedious for the reader and author alike. Rather, I will in this brief survey attempt to outline some of the major tendencies and traits of wit and humor in the visual arts in Italy during the fifteenth and sixteenth centuries. In the following pages, I shall discuss well over a hundred works of art, primarily major works by well-known artists. They are grouped in chapters arranged in approximate chronological and geographical order. The purpose of this format is not to trace the evolution of wit and humor in Renaissance society. Rather I hope to place, at least summarily, the artists of a particular time and place in their social and literary contexts. The nine chapters of this book should be regarded as introductory, dovetailing studies that point in the direction of more systematic and analytic future studies of this vast topic. It will also be apparent that certain topics, including the erotic comedy of nuptial art, satire of the gods, and parody, transcend particular chapters and contribute to the thematic unity of my essay. The humorous art under discussion will be related not only to the comic literature of Italy noted above, but will also be related to the writings of some of the greatest comic masters of the age outside of Italy such as Erasmus, Rabelais, and Shakespeare. At the same time, some of the themes and devices of comic art in Italy will be related to humorous works of art by the northern European artists Bosch, Mabuse, Bruegel, and Cranach, in order to show common iconographical interests throughout Europe during the Renaissance.

This study is rooted in Huizinga's brilliant characterizations of play and culture in *Homo Ludens*.[11] Huizinga observes that the comic is closely related to play.

11. Johan Huizinga, *Homo Ludens*.

> All the terms in this loosely connected group of ideas—play, folly, wit, jest, the comic, etc.—share the characteristic which we had to attribute to play, namely that of resisting any attempt to reduce it to other terms. Their rationale and their mutual relationships must lie in a very deep layer of our mental being.[12]

12. Ibid., p. 6.

Play frequently has a humorous or comic tone in Renaissance culture, and Huizinga relates the play element of the Italian Renaissance to *irony*, *jocosity*, and *laughter*. This playful humor pervades the witty conversations of the courts, which are preserved for us in the writings of Castiglione, Guazzo, and Romei. In their witty devices, Italian courtiers play also with mottos and images that were frequently meant to be laughable. Rabelais, who is invoked by Huizinga as a supreme example of the play spirit in Renaissance culture, humorously plays on the playfulness of Renaissance culture by mocking the ridiculous wit of courtly devices and the ludicrous color symbolism of courtly dress.

Mention of Rabelais reminds us of course that much Renaissance humor was neither witty nor refined, and we need only look to the playful antics of court buffoons, read the comedies performed at court, or examine the art of the period to find a strain of coarser humor. Playful humor is pervasive not only in courtly conversations and literature, but in the playful decorations painted or carved by notable artists in the *saloni*, staircases, loggias, and even bedrooms and baths of palaces and villas. The artifacts that fill these buildings—inkwells by Riccio, witty and grotesque utensils, and humorous majolica, to give but a few examples—are frequently playful in spirit. One need only glance at Giulio Romano's drawing for a platter, teeming with fish, to delight in the wit displayed at the Renaissance banqueting table (Figure 1–1). The gardens of villas contain humorous sculptures, playful hidden fountains that jokingly soaked unsuspecting visitors, and bizarre, witty grottos filled with sculpture and painting in a humorous vein. This playful spirit is epitomized in the villa of the rich Sienese banker, Agostino Chigi, which was decorated in the early cinquecento by Raphael, Peruzzi, Sodoma, and Sebastiano del Piombo. Chigi's playfulness was apparent when he had the silver and gold plates used at banquets in his villa tossed into the Tiber after each course in order to impress his guests. Chigi was a good friend of Pope Leo X, who enjoyed comedies, burlesque ceremonies, buffoons, and good jokes, and his entourage included Aretino, the brilliant and facetious writer. In the Rome of Pope Leo X, Chigi, Raphael, and Aretino, we encounter an ebullient playfulness.

Before we can begin our survey, we must acknowledge the difficulty of defining wit and humor. To begin with, there are no precise, universally accepted definitions of humor and wit. From Aristotle to Bergson and Freud, philosophers and psychologists have discussed humor and the related concepts of comedy, wit, and laughter. These thinkers have provided us with insights into the character of wit and humor, but not with strict definitions that can always be applied or agreed upon. Therefore, I shall use the term *humor* in a very general way; according to various usages, I shall include comedy, play, caricature, satire, parody, and irony. I shall use *wit* in referring to ingenious artistic devices that are largely cerebral, conforming to the definition of wit as knowledge or intelligence found in Renaissance authors such as Sidney or Shakespeare. It should not be forgotten, however, that many of the witty utterances Castiglione recounts in *The Book of the Courtier* are what we would today refer to as humorous, heavy-handed jokes. I am perfectly aware that various further distinctions are frequently made between the concepts of humor, wit, and variations upon them that are employed here, but it will be more useful in a preliminary survey of wit and humor in Renaissance art to take a broad perspective on what Huizinga referred to as "this loosely connected group of ideas."

A few words should be said about the terminology in this book, some of which relates directly to the language of the Renaissance. The vocabulary of wit and humor in Bibbiena's famous speech on the things that cause laughter ("le cose che movono il riso"), in Book 2 of Castiglione's *The Book of the*

Figure 1–1. Giulio Romano. *Study for a Platter*. Chatsworth Settlement.

Courtier, echoes the rhetoric of Cicero and Quintilian.[13] One might well adapt, and not inappropriately, this language of ancient rhetoric as a means of describing the humorous effects in Renaissance art. Following Quintilian's discussion of wit in the *Institutio Oratoria*, for example, one might single out the graceful and charming wit (*urbanitas*) in Botticelli's *Mars and Venus* (see Figure 2–12), a work that is polished (*facetus*) and playful (*iocus*). One might note the boisterous and hilarious humor in Piero di Cosimo's *Discovery of Honey* (see Figure 2–14), a work of free and lively humor (*lascivum et hilare*). And the jests in Michelangelo's art (see Figure 3–5) can be seen as

13. All of my translations, except in Chapter 7, are from Baldesar Castiglione, *The Book of the Courtier*.

Figure 2–12, p. 39

Figure 2–14, p. 46

Figure 3–5, p. 62

bitter (*asperum*) and abusive (*contumeliosum*). But while it is instructive to note the language of humor and wit used by ancient authors and assimilated by men like Castiglione and Giorgio Vasari in the Renaissance, one does not want to reduce the humor in Renaissance art simply to the terminological formulas of rhetoric.

The term *humor*, which we have been using in a general sense, is no longer associated with its original meaning. According to the tradition of ancient and medieval physiology, which persisted in the Renaissance, the four cardinal humors were blood, phlegm, choler, and melancholy (black bile), and the ideal man had a balanced mixture of the four. An imbalance of the humors was thought to create the comic vices of fools, and the theory of the humors became the basis for comedy, especially for Ben Jonson, who discussed the subject at the beginning of his *Every Man Out of His Humor*. It is debatable whether the humorous aspects of Renaissance works of art in the modern sense were generally intended to refer to the theory of the humors. But perhaps we can speak, for example, of Sebastiano del Piombo's humorously brooding *Polyphemus*, as having an excess of black bile (see Figure 4–3).

Figure 4–3, p. 81

In the Renaissance, the term *ridicolosa*, which has its roots in the Latin word, *ridere*, to laugh, intended what we usually mean by comic or humorous. Thus, Bibbiena's famous speech on humorous sayings concerned "le cose che

14. Antonio Manetti, *Novella del Grasso Legnaiuolo*, in Aldo Borlenghi, ed., *Novelle del Quattrocento*, ill. opposite p. 384.

Figure 8–5, p. 191

15. A great deal of information on *burle* or *beffe* in Italian Renaissance literature has been collected in two volumes edited by André Rochon, *Formes et Significations de la "Beffa" dans la Littérature Italienne de la Renaissance*.

16. *Murray's English Dictionary*, vol. 5, pt. 2 (Oxford, 1901), p. 599 (under "joke").

17. Many of these *facezie* are collected in Poggio Bracciolini, *The Facetiae of Poggio*.

Figure 6–3, p. 146

movono il riso." When the *Novella del Grasso Legnaiuolo* was introduced by the frontispiece of the 1576 edition as "Cosa molto piacevole et ridiculosa," this description suggested that the tale was both pleasing and humorous.[14] Humorous paintings were referred to in the same period, in a disparaging way, by Cardinal Paleotti as *pitture ridicole*. And indeed the subjects of many works of art in the Renaissance, for example the Hercules in Dosso Dossi's *Bambocciata*, are ridiculous or laughable (see Figure 8–5). *Ludicrous* is another term that we might apply to the subject of Renaissance works, and it should be recalled that this word has its roots in the Latin term, *ludere*, to play. The term *burlesque*, which can be used to describe much art of the Renaissance, is derived from *burla* (joke).[15] Bibbiena cites many examples in *The Book of the Courtier*, and we shall consider numerous instances of burlesque or joking in the courts of Italy and in the art and literature done in these courts. The modern term *joke* is derived from the Latin, *jocus*, which is the source of the Italian, *gioco*, defined in the sixteenth century by Florio as "game, play, sport, jest."[16] We find playful joking by the satyrs of Botticelli's *Mars and Venus*, who sport or *giocano* with the arms of Mars, just as the *amorini* in Poliziano's *Stanze per la giostra del magnifico Giuliano de' Medici* joked or jested (*scherzavan*) as they flew around Mars and Venus. Much of the art from the Renaissance is facetious, as Edgar Wind has shown, and this art can be compared to the *facetiae*, the humorous sayings and tales told by Poggio, Poliziano, Domenichi, and others, as well as Bibbiena's *facezie* in *The Book of the Courtier*.[17] The ironic (*ironico*), which is discussed by Bibbiena, also has its counterpart in the visual arts. It can be found in Bronzino's *Venus, Cupid, Folly, and Time* (see Figure 6–3) and in the architecture of Michelangelo. *Travesty* is another term which, like *humor*, no longer carries its original meaning. It is now used to suggest burlesque or caricature, but the term comes from *travestir*, to disguise or take another's dress. We will encounter this form of humor, with its original connotations, in the writings of Bibbiena and Benvenuto Cellini, as well as in Dossi's *Bambocciata* where Hercules is feminized. Finally we need to note that during the Renaissance the word comedy still referred specifically to the theater. And there are some specific references to the comic theater in art; for example, Raphael's lost *Fra Mariano*, done for a performance of Ariosto's *Suppositi* at the Vatican. In addition, *comedy* will frequently be used in the general sense.

Other terms, which will be used below to describe the humor in Renaissance art, need to be defined. *Satire* tends to ridicule its subject, evoking amusement or scorn, and various examples will be discussed below, including Dossi's *Bambocciata*, which satirizes a rather ridiculous Hercules. *Parody* is another form of derision that mocks a work or its style by adapting and deliberately distorting its features, and Pellegrino Tibaldi's frescoes in the Palazzo Poggi in Bologna, which playfully mock Michelangelo's style, are a superb example (see Figure 8–7). *Caricature* is the portrayal of a subject that makes that subject ludicrous by exaggerating or distorting its features. It is used, for example, as part of the satire of Hercules in Dossi's *Bambocciata* and as a means of parody in Tibaldi's Palazzo Poggi frescoes. *Playfulness* is a comic expression in which laughter is frequently evoked as an end in itself. We find innumerable examples in the humorous antics of *putti*, including Titian's delightful creatures in the *Festival of Venus* (see Figure 7–2). *Wit* is more cerebral than humor and usually is not funny. It reveals ingenuity (from *ingegno*) and is based on incongruity, ambiguity, and unexpected effects. Wit is apparent in some of the ingenious illusionistic decorations of the Renaissance by Mantegna and Peruzzi and in works that play on the ambiguities of illusionism, by artists like Giulio Romano. It is manifest in the ingenious *grotteschi* of Raphael and Michelangelo, and it is found in the strange and surprising *bizzarrie* of Parmigianino and Bronzino. These forms of wit and humor are not mutually exclusive. We have already noted that caricature can be used as part of satire or parody. Similarly, satires and parodies can be playful and witty. It should also be kept in mind that witty or humorous works of art are not necessarily laughable or funny. In fact wit and satire are frequently inseparable from seriousness, as can be seen in the work of Michelangelo. His wit can frequently be nasty and have a sharp bite, particularly in its satirical form.

Figure 8–7, p. 196

Just as there is no definitive meaning of the term *humor*, there is also no absolute way of determining what was thought to be humorous or witty in the Renaissance. We must be guided by our intuition and general knowledge of the period in our attempt to gain a sense of the humor in Renaissance art. There are clues to determining the intention of the artist who created this humor. Playfulness and caricature are usually recognizable because they often employ overt devices such as gestures and facial expressions. Parodies of style may be identified, at least tentatively, if we can determine the predominant stylistic conventions of the period. Similarly, satire can be discerned by referring to satirical traditions in literature. Analogies of attitude, tone, or subject seem to exist between art and literature, and the study of humorous or witty tendencies in literature sometimes helps to shed light on humorous aspects of art. Castiglione's *The Book of the Courtier* is especially valuable to our understanding of wit and humor in the Renaissance. In his extended discourse in Book 2, Bibbiena describes various forms of verbal wit, including puns and plays on words. A number of works of art from this period similarly rely on witty manipulations of form, including the work of Raphael, a friend of Castiglione and Bibbiena. Also notable is the extent to which the humor illustrated by Bibbiena mocks or ridicules its subject. There are many parallels to this mocking humor in Italian Renaissance art, for example in mythological works where the gods and goddesses are mocked or teased, especially in the work of Raphael. Love and sex are topics that, although not necessarily humorous, are

Figure 7–2, p. 162

frequently joked about by Bibbiena and other authors of Renaissance *novelle*, joke books, comedies, poetry, and satirical treatises. It is therefore not surprising to find that painters also joked about these topics, as Raphael did in the *stufetta* of Cardinal Bibbiena. Both the art and literature of the period mocked the voyeur, the frustrated lover, the cuckold, and the vanquished lover. These are but a few of the humorous topics of Renaissance art that I have pursued. But there are countless other humorous themes, such as the mockery of the fool or gull and the satire of the clergy that I have only briefly noted. The wit in grotesque decorations is another vast topic in Renaissance art that I have only touched upon.

The art and literature of the Renaissance can also inform us about possible differences between Renaissance and contemporary humor. The libidinous old man, for example, was frequently mocked in the Renaissance, while he is less often a subject of contemporary humor. Moreover, some of the humor in the Renaissance seems cruel to us today.

> "We laugh at deformed creatures," says Philip Sidney, but he does not speak for the twentieth century. . . . When Nashe tells of the trick Jack Wilton played on a Captain and how the best of the joke was, that the Captain was arrested as a spy, racked, and flogged, we stop laughing long before Nashe does.[18]

18. Northrop Frye, "The Nature of Satire."

We are not, as Northrop Frye observes, as amused by the cruel humor of the Renaissance picaresque (Thomas Nashe's *Unfortunate Traveller*) as the sixteenth-century reader was. Neither are we amused by the story of the monk who was flogged and tossed in a blanket when his comedy failed to please Leo X, even though the pope and his entourage laughed at the spectacle.[19] "We laugh at deformed creatures," says the Renaissance poet, following Cicero and Quintilian, and one suspects that the deformed characters in some of Leonardo's drawings were meant to be laughable. Similarly the exaggerated expressions of pain on the faces of Giulio Romano's giants in the Palazzo del Te were probably intended to amuse the beholder, although the humor in Giulio's creatures has been little discussed in the modern literature. The cruel pranks in the famous Spanish picaresque novel, *La vida de Lazarillo de Tormes*, were also meant to be laughable, as was an ugly Milanese whose injury was graphically described by another picaresque author, Benvenuto Cellini.

19. Ludwig Pastor, *The History of the Popes*, 8: 155–56.

> He was very ugly, and his mouth, which nature had made large, had been expanded at least three inches by his wound; so that what with his ludicrous Milanese jargon and his silly way of talking, he gave us so much matter for mirth that, instead of bemoaning our ill-luck, we could not hold from laughing at every word he uttered.[20]

20. Benvenuto, Cellini, *The Life of Benvenuto Cellini*, p. 320.

In *The Waning of the Middle Ages*, Huizinga describes the cruel humor of an *esbatement* held in Paris in the early fifteenth century. Four blind men were armed with sticks which they used to hit each other in trying to kill a pig, the prize of their combat. No doubt they were laughed at as they paraded before the combat, "all armed with a great banner in front, on which was pictured a pig, and preceded by a man beating a drum." This mockery of the blind immediately brings to mind the ridicule in Bruegel's parable, *The Blind Leading the Blind* (Naples). Perhaps the grimmest example of this kind of humor comes to us from the pages of the chronicler, Pierre de Fenin. In describing the death of a gang of brigands, he concludes, "and people laughed a good deal, because they were all poor men."[21]

The humorous art of the Italian Renaissance was made by men who were known to be witty and jest loving. In the late Middle Ages, Giovanni Boccaccio and Sacchetti recount tales that illustrate the wit of Giotto. While these and other tales told later by Vasari are presumably fictional, they may in part be based in fact, and the general indications that they give us of the artist's sense of humor are supported by his actual works.[22] At the right of his *Marriage at Cana* in the Scrovegni Chapel, for example, Giotto portrayed an amusingly paunchy steward tasting the wine that Christ had miraculously created from water. He also depicted a humorously hideous, buck-toothed St. Luke in a decorative medallion of the chapel's vault, and he exploited the comic possibilities of ugliness in his allegories of the Vices. For example, his grotesque *Invidia* or *Envy* is portrayed as a monstrous hag with a poisonous serpent emerging from her mouth and with a gigantic, deformed left ear, and his *Stultitia* or *Folly* is a bloated, comical oaf with a club in his hand (Figure 1–2). Students of literature have frequently noted that the deformities of Vices were intended to provoke laughter or ridicule. The same intentions are apparent in the visual arts of the late Middle Ages and Renaissance, as in Giotto's moralizing Vices of the Scrovegni Chapel.[23]

Many artists were fond of playing jokes. For example, Boccaccio tells us how Buffalmacco and Bruno, two followers of Giotto, deceived the famous simpleton Calandrino (also a painter) into believing he was invisible.[24] Buffalmacco, a "uomo burevole," was especially noted for his jokes. He made beetles into "devils" that terrified his master, Tafi; he painted a St. Ercolano solemnly crowned with fishes; and he overpainted a Christ Child as a bear.[25] In the well-known fifteenth-century *novella, Il Grasso Legnaiuolo*, Brunelleschi and his friend, Donatello, deceived the simple, Calandrino-like carpenter into believing he was someone other than himself.[26] Donatello's sense of humor is also well known from the *Facezie* ascribed to Poliziano, and according to Vasari, Donatello poked fun at the extremes of Uccello's perspective studies.[27] Vasari tells us of the humor of numerous artists. Uccello joked with the friars of San Miniato; Piero di Cosimo's sayings made his listeners burst with laughter; and Botticelli played pranks on pupils and friends.[28]

21. Huizinga, *The Waning of the Middle Ages*, p. 26.

22. Giorgio Vasari, *Le vite dè più eccellenti pittori scultori et architettori*, 1: 406.

23. Giotto's sense of humor has recently been noted by Laurie Schneider, *Giotto in Perspective*, p. 4. On religious humor, see D. W. Robertson, *Preface to Chaucer*, and V. A. Kolve, *The Play Called Corpus Christi*.

24. Giovanni Boccaccio, *The Decamerone*, 8th day, 3d novella.

25. Vasari, *Le vite*, 1:499ff.

26. Manetti, *Novella del Grasso Legnaiuolo*, pp. 337ff.

27. Vasari, *Le vite*, 1:216.

28. Ibid., 2:207, 216; 4:142.

Figure 1–2. Giotto. *Folly*. Scrovegni Chapel, Padua.

We might dwell for a moment on Botticelli's sense of humor as we will pay special attention below to the playfulness, facetiousness, and satire of his charming *Mars and Venus*. Vasari recounts the tale of how Botticelli playfully deceived his disciple, Biagio.

> Sandro was a man of very pleasant humor, often playing tricks on his disciples and his friends; wherefore it is related that once, when a pupil of his who was called Biagio had made a round picture exactly like the one mentioned above, in order to sell it, Sandro sold it for six florins of gold to a citizen; then, finding Biagio, he said to him, "At last I have sold this thy picture; so this evening it must be hung on high, where it will be seen better, and in the morning thou must go to the house of the citizen who has bought it, and bring him here, that he may see it in a good light in its proper place; and then he will pay thee the money." "O, my master," said Biagio, "how well you have done." Then going off into the shop, he hung the picture at a good height and went off. Meanwhile Sandro and Iacopo, who was another of his disciples, made eight caps of paper, like those of the eight citizens, and fixed them with white wax on the heads of the eight angels that surrounded the Madonna in the said picture. Now, in the morning, up comes Biagio with his citizen, who had bought the picture and was in the secret. They entered the shop, and Biagio, looking up, saw his Madonna seated, not among his angels, but among the Signoria of Florence, with all those caps. Thereupon he was just about to begin to make an outcry and to excuse himself to the man who had bought it, when, seeing that the other, instead of complaining, was actually praising the picture, he kept silent himself. Finally, going with the citizen to his house, Biagio received his payment of six florins, the price for which his master had sold the picture; and then, returning to the shop just as Sandro and Iacopo had removed the paper caps, he saw his angels as true angels, and not as citizens in their caps. All in a maze, and not knowing what to say, he turned at last to Sandro and said: "Master, I know not whether I am dreaming, or whether this is true. When I came here before, these angels had red caps on their heads, and now they have not; what does it mean?" "Thou are out of thy wits, Biagio," said Sandro; "this money has turned thy head. If it were so, thinkest thou that the citizen would have bought this picture?" "It is true," replied Biagio, "that he said nothing to me about it, but for all that it seemed to me strange." Finally, all the other lads gathered round him and wrought on him to believe it had been a fit of giddiness.[29]

Vasari's delightful and entertaining tale may not be true. Indeed, the very way in which Biagio is deceived reminds one of Boccaccio's Calandrino and Manetti's fat carpenter, suggesting Vasari's adaptation of a *topos*. But as the Italian proverb goes, "Se non è vero, è ben trovato." If Vasari's tale is not true, it could be, for the spirited playfulness of Botticelli's joke can be associated with the facetious character of his personality as seen in his *Mars and Venus*. Vasari's tale brings out an aspect of Botticelli's personality that we also sense from his humorous art. The tale may not be objective art history, but it is a type of criticism that helps us to understand the artist.

Vasari's words are probably closer to the truth when he writes about artists of his own century. He tells us that Leonardo, who indulged in various

29. Giorgio Vasari, *The Lives of the Most Eminent Painters, Sculptors, and Architects*, trans. Gaston Du Vere, 3:251.

30. Vasari, *Le vite*, 4:46.

31. Ibid., 6:382.

32. Ibid., 6:609ff.

pazzie, fastened scales to a lizard, dipped it in quicksilver so that it trembled as it moved, added eyes, a horn, and a beard, and after taming it, showed it to his friends to terrify them.[30] Leonardo's humor and taste for the grotesque are also apparent in numerous drawings such as the well-known Windsor study of grotesque heads (Figure 1–3). Vasari also describes the eccentricities and playful antics of Sodoma, who worked for the fun-loving Chigi. Sodoma frequently played the fool, and he was in fact called *Il Mattaccio* by the monks of Monte Oliveto.[31] Vasari gives us an especially interesting insight into the humorous and playful spirit of Renaissance artists in his account of the life of the Florentine sculptor, Rustici.[32] Here we learn of the amusing activities of artists in Florence who belonged to the Company of the Cauldron in the early sixteenth century. Each artist in the company (which included Rustici, Puligo, and Andrea del Sarto) made elaborate and witty culinary inventions for their banquets. One of the most extraordinary of these was made by Andrea del Sarto, who confected an octagonal structure like the Baptistery of Florence. The pavement was made out of jelly, its columns, which looked like porphyry, were large sausages, the bases and capitals were of parmesan cheese and the tribune of marzipane. Sarto's playful tour de force in what might be called gastroaesthetics (a neglected field) is reminiscent of the witty and elaborate culinary creations described by Petronius in the *Satyricon*, and it seems possible that the Company of the Cauldron was playfully cooking and eating *all'antica*. Rustici also belonged to the Company of the Trowel, which indulged in banquets and for years performed comedies such as Bibbiena's *La Calandria*, Ariosto's *I Suppositi*, and Machiavelli's *La Mandragola*. The ingenious gastronomic inventions of Sarto and his companions also bring to mind the witty portraits of Arcimboldo, who worked at the imperial court in Prague. Arcimboldo's painting in Vienna of a man as various fish, including lobsters, and crabs, is one of the artist's most ingenious and amusing works (Figure 1–4). A related example of Arcimboldo's humorous work is discussed by Gregorio Comanini in his late cinquento treatise, *Il Figino*, in which the artist's witty gastronomic metaphors and their satirical intent are revealed.

> On the command of the Emperor Maximilian he painted a most ridiculous likeness of a certain doctor whose entire face was ravaged by the pox with the exception of a bit of beard on his chin. He composed the whole of animals and divers grilled fish, and with this ruse he succeeded so well that everybody recognized it as a true likeness of the great jurist. Of the amusement this caused to the Emperor and the laughter it raised at court I need not talk; you can imagine it yourself.[33]

33. Rudolph Wittkower and Margot Wittkower, *Born Under Saturn*, pp. 283ff. The allegorical significance of Arcimboldo's portraits has recently been discussed by Thomas Da Costa Kaufmann, "Arcimboldo's Imperial Allegories."

34. Vasari, *Le vite*, 1:408.

Even if Vasari's tales about artists, especially of the fifteenth century, were not accurate, we nevertheless find in them valuable clues to the humorous or witty intentions in actual works of art. Vasari tells us, for example, that Giotto played a joke on Cimabue by painting a fly on the nose of a Christ figure and that Cimabue, who was fooled, tried to chase the fly away.[34] It seems rather

Figure 1–3. Leonardo da Vinci. *Study of Five Heads*. Royal Library, Windsor Castle.

Figure 1–4.
Arcimboldo. *Water*.
Kunsthistorisches
Museum, Vienna.

Figure 1–5. Carlo Crivelli.
Madonna and Child.
Metropolitan Museum of Art,
New York.

35. I have to confess that upon seeing Crivelli's painting for the first time, I tried to brush the fly away.

36. Huizinga, *Homo Ludens*, p. 11.

likely that Carlo Crivelli, as part of his attempt to demonstrate his artfulness, similarly meant to fool the beholder when he painted a fly on the ledge in front of his *Madonna and Child* (Figure 1–5).[35] The illusionistic flies of Giotto and Crivelli, and countless other artists of the Renaissance, bring to mind the illusionistic devices of the ancients described by Pliny, and frequently alluded to by Renaissance writers. They are a manifestation of witty play, and it is worth recalling here, as Huizinga tells us, that illusion means literally "in-play" (from *inlusio, illudere, inludere*).[36]

A final word should be said about the limits of this book. Most of the works of art discussed have various allegorical implications that are political, theological, philosophical, or moral in nature, and most of these works are in various respects serious. The humor in art needs to be seen in these serious contexts, but because these issues have already been discussed in considerable detail by art historians, and in order not to obscure the basic theme of my work, I have devoted little attention to these aspects. It has been observed that the seriousness of Renaissance thought was frequently expressed in a playful way, and I wish merely to stress the humorous and witty character of play that has so often been casually dismissed or ignored. On the whole it would seem that, although the playfulness of Renaissance art has been touched on by art historians on various occasions, the theme of *serio-ludere* has not been as fully explored by them as by students of Renaissance literature. This book is admittedly very speculative and is intended to a large extent to provoke discussion. The analogies made here between art and literature are meant as suggestions rather than as definitive interpretations. I hope that my own sense of humor is not so eccentric as to prevent the reader from finding some ground of agreement with me about the humorous and witty intentions of Italian Renaissance art.

II. *Quattrocento Mirth*

He's laughing still and will laugh for eternity.—Luigi Pulci, *Morgante Maggiore*
(on Margutte, who died laughing)

A comprehensive iconology of humor in the Renaissance, and specifically of the quattrocento, has yet to be written. In part this is because the rich and varied comic literature of this period has yet to be given extensive treatment by historians of Italian Renaissance art. This literary context demands a judicious and detailed analysis of the sort that cannot be readily presented here. A complete survey of humorous literature in the Renaissance would take into account works written in both Latin and the *volgare* in the various courts of Italy such as Ferrara, Mantua, Urbino. Yet we can briefly survey some notable expressions of humor by limiting ourselves to Florence.

The novelistic tradition of Boccaccio flourished in quattrocento Florence and was sustained in such tales as Antonio Manetti's *Il Grasso Legnaiuolo* in which both Donatello and Brunelleschi playfully deceived the comic fat carpenter. In the same vein, we find witty vulgarity in the realistic poetry of the barber-poet, Burchiello, and this tradition persisted later in the century in the work of Matteo Franco, Pulci, and Bellincioni, and in the cinquecento in the work of Berni, Michelangelo, and Firenzuola. This poetry has its analogue, as we shall see, in the coarse humor of Cellini's autobiography. Popular humor related to the *novella* tradition can also be found in the appealing and sympathetic sermons of the Sienese preacher, San Bernardino, who preached to the Florentines. A more caustic and ironic humor was employed later in the century by the Ferrarese Dominican, Savonarola, who harangued the Florentines.[1]

Although the humor of *novelle*, satirical poetry, and sermons has a certain popular base, we should bear in mind that this kind of coarse humor was cultivated by wealthy, class-conscious patricians. Much of it is collected in various joke books, histories, and letters of the period. Vespasiano da Bisticci, the Florentine bookseller, tells us of Cosimo de' Medici's dry and cutting wit.[2] An example of the humor of Cosimo's son, Piero, is noted by Poliziano in his *Bel Libretto*.[3] The humor of Piero's son, Lorenzo de' Medici, can be found not only in the poetry that he wrote and read but also in the tales told later about him by Ludovico Domenichi in his book of *Facetiae*.[4] There are also the *Motti e Facetiae* of Piovano Arlotto and the *Facetiae* of Poggio Bracciolini,

1. Much of this background is treated in vol. 2 of John Addington Symonds, *Renaissance in Italy*.

2. Vespasiano da Bisticci, *The Vespasiano Memoirs*, p. 226.

3. Quoted by André Rochon, *La Jeunesse de Laurent de Medicis*, p. 49, n. 38.

4. Poggio Bracciolini, *The Facetiae of Poggio*, pp. 48, 50.

5. Piovano Arlotto, *Motti e Facetiae*, pp. 739ff; and *Facezie e Motti del secc. XV e XVI ined.*

6. Antonio Beccadelli, *Hermaphroditus*, pp. 6ff.

7. Paul Oskar Kristeller, *The Philosophy of Marsilio Ficino*, pp. 281–83.

8. Lorenzo de' Medici, *Opere*, ed. Attilio Simoni, 2:157ff. A full explication of the poem is given in Chapter 11 of Rochon, *La Jeunesse*.

which further document the range and character of Florentine humor.[5] If this humor is frequently vulgar in the joking of Lorenzo de' Medici and Pulci, it is more subtle and delicate in the odes of Politian. Humor and wit are frequently part of a larger erotic context. A delicate, and sometimes not so delicate, humor is found in much of the playful, erotic poetry of the period as in Beccadelli's *Hermaphroditus*, which was dedicated to Cosimo de' Medici.[6] One also finds an ironic humor in the most unexpected places, including the letters of Marsilio Ficino, who makes jokes on his own deeply serious Neoplatonic thought.[7]

Much of this quattrocento humor cannot be appreciated or enjoyed when quoted out of context. It becomes tedious like Bibbiena's list of jokes in *The Book of the Courtier*. Yet let us pause for a moment and consider just an aspect of the sense of humor of Lorenzo de' Medici, who seems to have inherited the wit of both Cosimo and Piero. Lorenzo, who at one moment is receiving a playful letter from Ficino on Platonic love, at another is laughing at Pulci's *Morgante Maggiore*, and at another is teasing Michelangelo, wrote some of the most spirited comic poetry of the Renaissance—poetry that ranges from a gentle playfulness to gross satire. His *I Beoni: ovvero il Simposio*, for example, is written in a coarse Tuscan dialect.[8] It has much in common with the tradition of Burchiello and the poets in Lorenzo's *brigata*, including Pulci, Matteo Franco, Pulci's facetious enemy, as well as Bernardo Bellincioni. Lorenzo, as we might expect, had all of these poets' works in his library. Lorenzo's poem satirically describes the gluttonous appetites and prolific drinking of his many Florentine friends, including Carlo Pandolfini, one of the judges at the joust of 1469; Antonio Vettori, a *priore* in Florence; and possibly the jocose painter, Botticelli, who was employed by Lorenzo to decorate his villa near Volterra. In his facetious portrayal of Botticelli, Lorenzo seems to play on the corpulence of the artist who returns from dinner "a botte pieno" (a full barrel). Botticelli eats so much, according to Lorenzo, that he has a "corpo omnipotente." Scholars have questioned whether the Botticelli in Lorenzo's poem is the artist Sandro Filipepi, who was called Botticelli. However, Rochon presents evidence to support that conclusion, noting Botticelli's presumed self-portrait in the *Adoration of the Magi* in the Uffizi, where Botticelli appears with considerable corpulence. Lorenzo's poem is written in *terza rima* and is clearly a parody of the *Divine Comedy*. Lorenzo's teacher, Landino, wrote a commentary on Dante's poem, and Botticelli illustrated it for Lorenzo's cousin, Lorenzo di Pierfrancesco. Much of the language in Lorenzo's poem also makes light of Petrarch, reminding one of the pervasive anti-Petrarchan literature in the period, frequently written by Petrarchan poets. And finally the title, *Simposio*, is a play on the Platonic dialogue of the same name, which was so important in Lorenzo's circle. Lorenzo's teacher, Ficino, had translated and written a commentary on it. Lorenzo's poem, which still needs to be rendered into English, is a highly self-conscious and artful work of satire and parody, uniting the vulgarity and wit that blend so frequently in quattrocento Florence.

We find humor and wit in varying degrees and quality in the most mundane situations. We find it, for example, in the belt buckle made for Filippo Strozzi in the middle of the fifteenth century. The merchant Marco Parenti, writing to Filippo in Naples, noted that the figures symbolize Parenti, Strozzi, and Naples "per figura e per similitudine di qualche segno." Parenti expected that Filippo would be amused and laugh at this invention ("et ai inteso mia fantasia, che forse te ne riderai").[9] This kind of playfulness is made visible in the lovely art of Ghirlandaio who reveals to us a Florentine bedroom in his *Birth of the Virgin* done for the Tornabuoni in Santa Maria Novella.[10] The scene takes place in a matter-of-fact way; Zacharias appears in the background, Anna is abed, and lovely young girls attend her. Behind Anna's bed, however, we see a playful, Donatellesque relief of smiling *putti*, who dance and make music in celebration of the Virgin's birth. Ghirlandaio also adds a charming detail in the capital of one of the pilasters framing the composition. Here we see a *putto* emerging from the capital, extending his arms which metaphorically join the scrolls swirling outward to form an ionic capital.

Laughing and smiling characters abound in the painting and sculpture created for the Florentines in the quattrocento. In his ornate and exquisite *Adoration of the Magi*, painted for the chapel of Pala Strozzi in Santa Trinita, Gentile da Fabriano depicted some joking among the entourage of the Magi, as is apparent in the smiling face of the figure above the white horse to the right.[11] We also find smiling protagonists on Donatello's *Cantoria* for the cathedral where joyful angels dance, and again in Antonio Pollaiuolo's Torre del Gallo frescoes where two of the rhythmical nudes smile broadly as they dance.[12] In a landscape painted as part of a fresco decoration originally in Santa Maria del Carmine, we find that a close follower of Fra Filippo Lippi painted a delightful beaming monk seated with other Carmelites.[13] Even though this fresco is not by Lippi himself, it is very close to the style and spirit of Lippi, whose humor was especially appreciated by Vasari. Lippi painted himself with an engagingly curious, almost melancholic "humor" in the Barabadori altar piece now in the Louvre.[14] There is an almost impish quality in this delightful self-portrait. There is also a strange humor in one of his best-known works, the Tarquinia *Madonna*, where a monstrous Christ Child seems to lunge at the Virgin's throat.[15] We need to recall that what twentieth-century society considers ugly or monstrous was frequently regarded as laughable in the Renaissance, and although we might further suspect that a monstrous Christ Child is inappropriate, we need only recall the exploits of the

9. Roger Sale, "An Iconographic Program by Marco Parenti."

10. Frederick Hartt, *History of Italian Renaissance Art*, pl. 369.

11. Ibid., p. 151 and pl. 179.

12. Giovanni Colacicchi, *Antonio del Pollaiuolo*, pl. 24.

13. Mary Pittaluga, *Filippo Lippi*, pl. 1.

14. Hartt, *History of Italian Renaissance Art*, pl. 203.

15. Ibid., pl. 202.

16. Ibid., pl. 204.

17. Giorgio Vasari, *Le vite dè più eccellenti pittori scultori et architettori*, ed. Gaetano Milanesi, 2:207.

18. Federico Zeri, "Major and Minor Artists in Dublin," p. 72; and Michael Baxandall, *Painting and Experience in Fifteenth Century Italy*, p. 89.

Christ Child in the medieval infancy Gospels, which were intended to be laughable. Moreover, in a painting that is aggressively naturalistic in its sculptural style, and in its references to contemporary architecture and fashion, the humorous activity of a seemingly real baby seems perfectly plausible. Babies will lunge at their mothers in various humorous ways, and Lippi's exploitation of this detail heightens the naturalism of his painting. Lippi's humor is tempered and restrained in his *Madonna and Child* (Uffizi), in which a smiling angel points to the Christ Child as it joyfully gazes out at the beholder.[16] This particular angel's smile would more accurately be described as joyous than humorous. The gesture of the angel, who seems to be lifting the Christ Child, may be a naturalistic allusion to the elevation of the Host, and the angel's smile conveys the joy of those in the presence of the Lord.

Paolo Uccello, whose joking with the friars of San Miniato was noted above, is among the most playful artists of the quattrocento.[17] Recently Federico Zeri has spoken of Uccello's "perspective humor," and Michael Baxandall has discussed a possible "geometrical joke" in Uccello's London *Battle of San Romano*—an aspect that would have been appreciated by Lorenzo de' Medici, in whose bedroom the painting originally hung.[18] Uccello's perspective humor or wit is especially manifest in the San Romano paintings (Figure 2–1). Here we behold horses and armed knights, fallen upon the ground like toy soldiers. They are projected into space by the most disarmingly witty foreshortening, reminding us again of the etymological connection between illusion and play (from *ludere*). It is as if these fallen knights have not been vanquished by their foes within the paintings but by a playful *artista ex-macchina* from without. In short, Uccello's San Romano paintings, for all of their political and military allusions, have something of the charm of a puppet show.

At the beginning of the quattrocento, humor in major works of art is generally not pronounced. As interest in both the form and content of ancient art increased, the comic aspect was emphasized in Italian art. Initially, this comedy is not specific but is of a generally playful sort. The principal actors are *putti*, or angels, who are revivals of Hellenistic *amorini*. We frequently find them in the sculpture of Donatello, whose joyful *Cantoria* we have already noted. In one instance, Donatello represented *amorini* who participate in Bacchic revelry on the pedestal of the moralizing statue of *Judith*, which was created for the Medici (Figure 2–2). Even if they allude to the sensuality of the evil Holofernes, who was subdued by Judith, their humor is obvious as they make music, carry glasses, and dance around humorously plump reclining figures who have grotesque faces in the manner of ancient masks. One of Donatello's most charming works is the bronze statue in the Bargello. It has frequently been misidentified as Eros or a satyr but actually represents the

Figure 2-1. Paolo Uccello. *Battle of San Romano*. Uffizi, Florence.

Figure 2–2. Donatello. *Bacchic Revel* (base of *Judith* statue). Piazza della Signoria, Florence.

ancient household deity, Genius, who was associated with Bacchus in the Renaissance (Figure 2–3).[19] This benevolent and delightful satyrlike creature, who at one time may have held grapes in his extended hand, smiles broadly as his leggings sag below his exposed genitals and bottom in a manner that charms the beholder. It has been supposed that Donatello's statue may have been made for a hearth, alluding to the ancient *Lares* or genius of the hearth. Yet we should recall that Genius presided over the nuptial couch or *lectus genialis*, as Horace called it, and his fertile role was invoked in Renaissance epithalamia by Edmund Spenser and Ben Jonson. Thus, we might entertain the possibility that Donatello's little creature was done on the occasion of a marriage, possibly for a bedroom. Donatello's figure conforms to various accounts of Genius in Roman literature, but he is more youthful than the figures of Genius in Roman sculpture. Perhaps by making a youthful Genius, Donatello did intend an allusion to Eros or Cupid.

Playful humor, conveyed largely through gestures and facial expressions, can also be found in the north of Italy in the work of Andrea Mantegna, who was influenced by Donatello's work at Padua.[20] In his well-known decorations for the Ovetari Chapel, Mantegna introduces a variety of humorous effects.[21] Despite the somber subject of these frescoes, which depict the life of St. James, *putti* frolic among illusionistic garlands of fruit that hang in front of the narrative scenes. In the fresco of St. James brought before the Roman Council, a little boy wearing a helmet and holding a shield stares out intensely with a bizarre expression on his face that is clearly out of character with the grave event enacted behind him (Figure 2–4). He even seems to convey an awareness that he is out of place, like a child who continues to play near adults having a serious discussion, even after they have requested that he play elsewhere. In the depiction of the martyrdom of St. James, the severed head of the martyred saint seems on the verge of falling down into the chapel. This kind of intense illusionism has a quality of wit about it, however macabre it may be.

Mantegna also exhibited playfulness in an incidental way, in his grand San Zeno altarpiece in Verona (Figure 2–5). After we initially observe the Virgin upon her throne, surrounded by music-making angels and saints, we eventually discern the legs of two angels supporting the throne below. While they are revealed as the support of her throne, their heads are covered by a magnificent carpet, creating a somewhat bizarre but charming effect. These angels are not depicted as flesh-and-blood creatures, as are the others, but are painted gray to stress their role as caryatids supporting the throne. Mantegna has created a delightful ambiguity between the lifelike forms of these little creatures and their inanimate stonelike appearance. Ambiguity, as Cardinal Bibbiena points out in *The Book of the Courtier*, is an important basis of wit: "Now, of the ready pleasantries that consist of brief sayings, those are the keenest which

19. Donatello's statue was identified by Maurice L. Schapiro, "Donatello's *Genius*."

20. For Mantegna's playful outing on the Lago di Garda, described by Feliciano, see Giuseppe Fiocco, *L'arte di Andrea Mantegna*, pp. 119–20; and Paul Kristeller, *Andrea Mantegna*, pp. 523ff.

21. The Ovetari Chapel decorations are illustrated in Renata Cipriani, *All the Paintings of Mantegna*, 1: pls. 4ff.

Figure 2–3. Donatello. *Genius*. Bargello, Florence.

25

Figure 2-4. Andrea Mantegna. *St. James Before Herod Agrippa*. Chiesa degli Eremitani, Padua.

Figure 2-5. Andrea Mantegna. *San Zeno Triptych* (detail). Chiesa di San Zeno, Verona.

arise from ambiguity (although they do not always cause laughter because they are oftener praised for being ingenious rather than comical)."[22]

Perhaps the most widely known example of Mantegna's wit appears in his decoration of the Camera degli Sposi, painted for Ludovico Gonzaga in Mantua. This virtuoso performance of illusionism, based on the perspective systems of Central Italian art, presents scenes from the court of Gonzaga. In it is a kind of "perspective wit" that is reminiscent of Uccello. With extraordinary visual wit, Mantegna paints architecture and curtains that seem to be extensions of the room itself. In one scene Mantegna represents Ludovico Gonzaga seated and surrounded by various members of his court, including a court dwarf. His presence should make us aware that, like the playful antics and joking of dwarfs, fools, and buffoons, the art of a court painter like Mantegna was often solicited to amuse the court.[23] For example, we find a delightful and charming pictorial joke in the brilliant illusionistic dome that Mantegna painted in the ceiling (Figure 2–6). Here he painted a potted plant that precariously hovers over the spectator. The playful tone of the dome fresco is sustained by a smiling woman who peers down at us and by *putti*, who are younger relatives of Donatello's creatures. Some of these *putti* stand in the dome and look out, but one of them seems to have caught his head in the architecture, and the expression of frustration on this *poverino* is disarmingly laughable.

The side walls of the *camera* are decorated with scenes from life at the court, reminding us that the room served for ceremonial audiences. A recently discussed document from 1462 indicates that the room had also served as a bedroom, and another document from 1474, when Mantegna's frescoes were finished, indicates the presence of a *lectera* or bed in the room.[24] We should recall that during the Renaissance bedrooms were not private in the modern sense and were used for ceremonial purposes. Whether or not the bed served only for a ceremonial purpose in 1474, it seems possible that the bed had symbolic importance (as it later did at Versailles), denoting a specific place where the family line was perpetuated. Indeed the principal scenes of the *camera* represent the marquis with his progeny. It also seems that the playful imagery of the dome above is appropriate in a room that was or had been a bedroom. The *amorini* above recall the countless little cupids who sport above the nuptial couch in epithalamia by Catullus, Spenser, Jonson, and others, and they can also be compared to the *amorini* disporting above the nuptial couch in Sodoma's fresco for Agostino Chigi of the marriage of Alexander and Roxanne, which was probably a pictorial epithalamium. The smiling lady above who holds a comb is also appropriate in the boudoir. Finally, what are we to make of the peacock in the dome? This bird is symbolic of many things, but given the possible function of the room as a bedroom, we might ask whether it is not depicted as the symbol of Juno "whose great powers protect the

22. Baldesar Castiglione, *The Book of the Courtier*, trans. Charles Singleton, p. 157.

23. Court fools in the Renaissance are discussed by Enid Welsford, *The Fool*, esp. Chapter 6; and Erica Tietze-Conrat, *Dwarfs and Jesters in Art*.

24. Clifford M. Brown, "New Documents of Andrea Mantegna's Camera degli Sposi," p. 862.

Figure 2–6. Andrea Mantegna. Ceiling decoration (detail). Camera degli Sposi, Palazzo Ducale, Mantua.

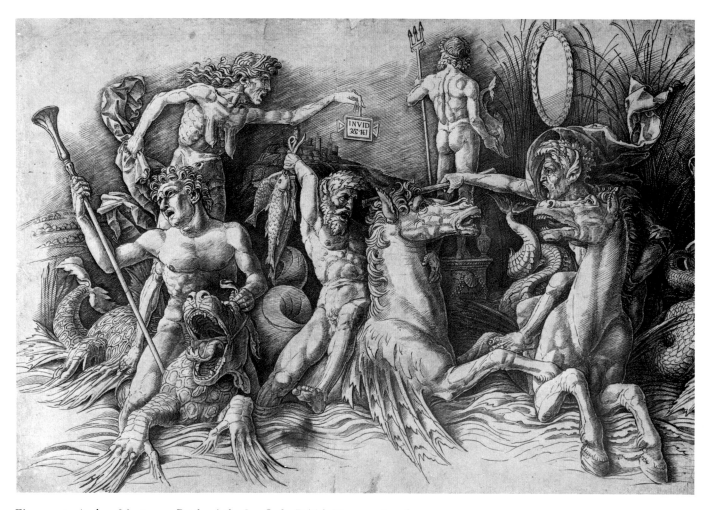

Figure 2–7. Andrea Mantegna. *Battle of the Sea Gods*. British Museum, London.

marriage-bed, with great effect," according to Jonson. The scene in Mantegna's dome evokes the staged effects of masques, in particular, Jonson's *Hymenaei*, where Juno was seen in the "upper part of the scene" surrounded by "spirits of the air" and ladies "attired richly."[25]

    I do not think we can overestimate Mantegna's comic genius, which abounds in his wonderful engraving. In his famous prints of sea battles, we observe a mock-heroic fury as figures upon grotesque sea beasts battle amidst the swirling, tumultuous waters (Figure 2–7). It is only after a moment that we recognize that some of these marine gladiators are fending off their foes with bunches of dead fish—ludicrous, if appropriate, weapons. This kind of mock-heroic playfulness recalls the mock-fury that exists not only in Uccello's Battle of San Romano paintings but also in so much of the romantic literature of the period, especially in Ariosto and Rabelais. In his Bacchic prints, Man-

25. Ben Jonson, *Selected Masques*, ed. Stephen Orgel (New Haven and London, 1975), pp. 47ff. I am grateful to Norman Land, who stimulated my thinking about the significance of the ceiling fresco.

Figure 2–8. Andrea Mantegna. *Triumph of Silenus*. British Museum, London.

tegna exhibits a delightful and playful exuberance, especially in the *Bacchus with a Wine Vat*, where satyrs with bells on their legs dance loudly as Bacchus is crowned. Mantegna's humor is in a more fully blown Rabelaisian key in his *Triumph of Silenus* (Figure 2–8). Here we are less concerned with the crowning of Silenus than with the ridiculous fact that three bacchantes are barely able to support this huge comic figure. The humor of the print is amplified by the figure on the left, who tries to lift a magnificently huge "Lady Silenus" off a tree stump. We cannot help but anticipate what will happen when this Gargantuan lady lifts her foot from the stump.[26]

Returning to Florence of the late quattrocento, we discover an exceptional wit in the work of Botticelli. The witty devices in his art relate in their evocative charm and preciosity to the similarly ingenious poetical conceits in the poetry of Politian and Lorenzo de' Medici. Botticelli's wit is evident in the

26. A full account of these prints is given in Jay Levenson et al., *Early Italian Engravings from the National Gallery of Art*, pp. 182ff.

Figure 2–9. Sandro Botticelli. *Primavera*. Uffizi, Florence.

27. Aby Warburg, *Gesammelte Schriften*, pp. 32ff.

Primavera done for Lorenzo di Pierfrancesco de' Medici, cousin of Lorenzo il Magnifico (Figure 2–9). It is apparent in the wonderful invention—surely one of the most extraordinary in the entire Renaissance—of Zephyr raping Chloris, who is transformed into Flora. This image, as Warburg persuasively demonstrated, was inspired by Ovid's *Fasti*, a rich source for Italian artists and writers alike.[27] As Zephyr caresses Chloris, the metamorphosis begins. We only dimly perceive the contours of flowers between her legs, but then flowers begin to issue from her mouth, leading us to Flora, symbolizing spring, who both scatters flowers and spills them in abundance from her lap. These flowers blend so subtly with those on Flora's dress that it becomes almost impossible to distinguish the real ones from the ones that are part of the pattern on her dress. A similarly witty transformation is seen in Botticelli's *Mars and Venus*. As the beholder admires the intricate coiffure of Venus, his gaze follows the braided hair that descends Venus's shoulders, culminating it would seem at the broach above her breasts, yet continuing as gold bordering in her dress below. Botticelli effects the metamorphosis or transformation of hair to cloth with such subtle and almost magical wit that it almost goes unnoticed.[28]

28. This detail was kindly pointed out to me by Barbara Mustain.

A similar preciosity of wit can be found in the work of Botticelli's younger colleague, Filippino Lippi. Filippino painted various works that abound in grotesque effects, some of which were probably inspired by the recently rediscovered grotesques in Rome. In his Strozzi Chapel frescoes in Santa Maria Novella, for example, he added to his somber narrative scenes decorative effects inspired by the decorations of ancient Rome. In the scene of St. Philip exorcising the demon from the temple of Mars, Filippino filled the temple with strange objects *all'antica*. Like Mantegna, Filippino plays here on the ambiguity between the actual sculptural nature and the lifelike quality of the figures. The strange statue of Mars, like Mantegna's San Zeno caryatids, seems to be alive. At the left of the fresco stands a soldier whose armor is made of a series of animal heads; marine creatures also wiggle across his breastplate (Figure 2–10). The soldier's armor gives a strangely incongruous effect as it seems to pulsate with life. Filippino seems to delight in this witty ambiguity. The effect is highly contrived, and like other elements of sophistication in this fresco, it anticipates the taste of mannerism.

In the late quattrocento, when artists began to paint large-scale mythological works, the story of Mars and Venus became a major theme for playful, as well as erotic, treatment. Mantegna's *Parnassus*, painted for the *studiolo* of Isabella d'Este in Mantua, represents Mars and Venus united in front of a couch atop Parnassus (Figure 2–11).[29] Cupid, who is near them, aims a blow pipe or trumpet at Vulcan below. In the foreground the Muses dance to the music of Apollo's lyre, and Mercury leans gracefully against his steed. Mantegna's painting has elicited a great deal of scholarly commentary. Perhaps

29. A detailed discussion of the *Parnassus* is in Phyllis Lehmann, *Samothracian Reflections*, pp. 59ff. The allegorical interpretation of the painting is discussed by E. H. Gombrich, "An interpretation of Mantegna's 'Parnassus,'" *Journal of the Warburg and Courtauld Institutes* 16 (1953): 196ff; reprinted in *Symbolic Images*, pp. 82–84.

Figure 2-10. Filippino Lippi. *St. Philip Exorcising the Demon from the Temple of Mars* (detail).
Strozzi Chapel, S. M. Novella, Florence.

Figure 2-11. Andrea Mantegna. *Parnassus*. Louvre, Paris.

the most persuasive interpretation of the painting was put forward by Gombrich, who suggested that the union of Mars and Venus is an allegory of Harmony. This theme is found in ancient literature, and Gombrich also finds it exemplified during the Renaissance in Pontano's *Urania*. Certainly the graceful, rhythmical dance of the Muses and the performance of Apollo, as well as the intertwining of Mars and Venus, give emphatic visual expression to this theme of harmony. Edgar Wind has added to this basic iconographical analysis a delightful interpretation of the erotic and comic innuendoes in the painting. However, a recent scholar, Egon Verheyen, has sought to deny the erotic and comic overtones of the work.[30] Verheyen observes, "There is no allusion to the adulterous relation of the two gods," and he insists that there is an "absence of any stress on erotic elements" in this work "where there is no place for sensuality." For Verheyen the erotic tone of the painting is incompatible with his reading of its serious meaning as the "triumph of reason." One cannot but wonder whether Verheyen is really talking about Mantegna's painting. Even Gombrich, who concedes but a footnote to the painting's sexual meaning, acknowledges the "naughty" character of the scene. It should be observed that Mantegna has painted his gods in front of a couch! Venus and Mars stand together, their arms entwined, and Mars suggestively places his foot over that of Venus! The goddess of love is naked and a ribbon of drapery billows around her voluptuous body, passing caressingly between her legs. The Muse at the lower right places her thumb and index finger around the thumb of the adjacent Muse, a conspicuously sexual gesture, as Wind has pointed out. The general mood of this work is both playful and mocking. Venus and Mars gaze into each other's eyes with coy expressions on their faces. The drapery that swirls around Venus moves in a capricious way, reenforcing this playful effect. Below, a little rabbit charmingly peers out at us, and Pegasus seems to smile.

Meanwhile, Mantegna's clumsy and lame Vulcan, who gazes in the direction of Mars and Venus, seemingly in despair, is mocked by Cupid. Anyone looking at the painting in the Renaissance would no doubt have been amused by the cuckolded spouse of Venus, reminding us that cuckoldry was a pervasive subject of humor in Renaissance culture whether in the tales of Bandello or the plays of Shakespeare. If the spoof of Vulcan is relatively restrained in the *Parnassus*, it could be more explicit and erotic in the art of the period, as for example in the familiar print by Aenea Vico, which shows Vulcan, that "gig of a cuckold's horn" as Shakespeare might say, working at his forge, while unbeknownst to him Venus and Mars engage in amorous battle.[31]

Once again Mantegna's work may have nuptial significance, as Phyllis Lehmann noted.[32] The red, blue, gold, and white colors of Venus, Mars, and their couch beautifully harmonize, in accord with the picture's allegory, the colors of the d'Este and Gonzaga houses. Thus, Mantegna's painting seem-

30. The humor of the painting is brought out by Edgar Wind, *Bellini's Feast of the Gods*, pp. 9ff, while the picture is taken too seriously by Egon Verheyen, *The Painting in the Studiolo of Isabella d'Este at Mantua*, pp. 37ff.

31. Vico's print is listed in Adam Bartsch, *Le Peintre Graveur*, 15:294. The quotation is from *Love's Labor's Lost*, act V, scene i, l. 73.

32. Lehmann, *Samothracian Reflections*, pp. 165–66.

ingly alludes to the union of Isabella d'Este and Gianfrancesco Gonzaga in 1490. Mars and Venus were of course appropriate symbols of the bridegroom and bride as we know from Renaissance portraits which actually depict the bridal couple in the guise of these gods. We should not be surprised by the prominent mocking of the cuckold, Vulcan, in a picture with nuptial significance. This kind of banter is common in nuptial art. In the final song from Shakespeare's *Love's Labor's Lost*, for example, which ends harmoniously in marriage, we hear the refrain: "Cuckoo, cuckoo. O word of fear/ Unpleasing to a married ear!"[33]

The allegory, pantomime, and dancing of Mantegna's painting are evocative of courtly masques, performed on the occasion of marriages and other important events, and we might ask to what extent the *Parnassus* is related to the masques performed at the court of Mantua and elsewhere in Italy. We have only a limited knowledge of these performances at court in the quattrocento and early cinquecento (we know more about the work of Jonson and Jones for the Stuart court), yet paintings like this one by Mantegna or Botticelli's *Primavera* might help us to visualize them. Might we think of each of Mantegna's protagonists as delivering an imagined recitation as we listen to the painting's music and witness its graceful dance? There are various close associations between paintings and court fêtes in the Renaissance that might be cited. For example, Raphael's *Parnassus*, which includes Apollo, the Muses, and the great ancient and modern poets, was painted in the Stanza della Segnatura, and its position on the wall facing the theater of the Belvedere begun by Bramante was presumably intentional. Thus one gazed through the window of the Parnassus wall to the theater which was in the realm inspired by Apollo and the Muses. In 1512, there was, according to Paris de Grassis, a coronation of a poet in the garden of the Belvedere, with Orpheus and the Muses presiding, and one wonders whether this event took place in the theater below the *Parnassus*.[34] Not only is this iconography of the courtly celebration related to that of Raphael's fresco, but one might well suppose that the performers in this fête looked something like the protagonists in Raphael's fresco. Returning to the central theme of Mantegna's painting, we should note that, according to Thomas Elyot in his *The Boke Named The Governour*, the "adultery" of Mars and Venus was actually danced.[35] Anton Francesco Doni tells us in his *I Marmi* that the story of Mars and Venus was performed as an *intermezzo* at the court of Duke Cosimo de' Medici.[36] We unfortunately can only imagine the continued dance of Mars and Venus in Mantega's painting, the moment after Mars gently and erotically places his foot on that of Venus, just as we can only imagine the performance of the *intermezzo* at the Medici court.

The painting of Mars and Venus by Botticelli is certainly one of the finest and most charming versions of this subject that were created during the Re-

33. *Love's Labor's Lost*, act VIII, scene ii, ll. 891–92.

34. Herbert von Einem, *Das Program der Stanza della Segnatura im Vatikan*, p. 35.

35. Thomas Elyot, *The Boke Named The Governour*, pp. 91–92.

36. Anton Francesco Doni, *I Marmi*, 1:20.

naissance (Figure 2–12). Its playfulness and humor are especially notable, but before considering these qualities, let us briefly note the visual and literary traditions to which Botticelli's work belongs. Botticelli presents the goddess of love and the god of war reclining out of doors, surrounded by playful satyrs. This general setting *al fresco* has a literary tradition behind it that can be traced back to Lucretius's *De rerum natura*.[37] This iconographical tradition, which associated the union of Mars and Venus with the harmony or fecundity of nature, persisted later in antiquity in Reposianus's *De concubitu Marte et Veneris* and could still be found in the late quattrocento in Pontano's *Eridanus*.[38] Both of these poems, like Botticelli's painting, have their roots in Lucretius. The visual sources for Botticelli's painting have received only scant attention. The reclining figures in his painting can be related to those of an artist whose work is generally acknowledged to have influenced him. Botticelli's Venus is strikingly close in posture, dress, linear rhythm, and even in small details (such as the positioning of the legs) to Verrocchio's drawing of Venus with Cupid.[39] An antecedent of Botticelli's Mars, but not necessarily an influence, is the extraordinary terracotta of a nude, sleeping man, attributed to Verrocchio (Berlin).[40] In more general terms, Botticelli's figure, like Verrocchio's, seems to stem from that classical tradition that is found in the ancient relief sculpture, the so-called *Bed of Polyclitus*, a highly influential work in the Renaissance that was owned by Ghiberti. In sum, just as Botticelli's image was inspired by classical literature, its form is derived from the visual arts of antiquity. This is not to say, however, that a courtly medieval tone has entirely vanished from his work.

Scholars have emphasized the various moral and astrological implications of the painting.[41] Frequently, there is much to support these interpretations. It seems reasonable, as art historians have suggested, that the painting symbolizes the triumph of love over war, and it may be that Botticelli's figures allude to the planets Venus and Mars. But in these extensive scholarly exegeses, the satire and playful sexuality of the work are ignored or scarcely noted. A balanced interpretation of the painting requires somewhat more extensive consideration of the playful means by which the serious allegory is conveyed. Botticelli's painting is an excellent example of *serio-ludere*, and its ludic or playful character, which is so charming, deserves more attention. It is perhaps symptomatic of much recent iconographical work that J. A. Symonds's tongue-in-cheek appreciation of the painting is usually ignored, even though Symonds fully grasped the facetiousness of Botticelli's painting.[42] But let us now turn to a more detailed account of Botticelli's painting and some recent interpretations of his masterpiece.

In his classic essay on Botticelli's mythologies, Gombrich provides a "Ficinian" interpretation of Botticelli's *Mars and Venus*.[43] He relates the figures

37. Charles Dempsey, "*Mercurius Ver*: The Sources of Botticelli's *Primavera*," p. 263, n. 50.

38. The possible relationship of Botticelli's painting to Reposianus was suggested by Frans Wickhoff, "Die Hochzeitsbilder Sandro Botticelli," p. 206.

39. Günter Passavant, *Verrocchio*, pl. 95.

40. Ibid., pl. 60.

41. The vast literature on the *Mars and Venus* is summarized by Martin Davies, *National Gallery Catalogues: The Earlier Italian Schools*, pp. 100–101. For an excellent review of the literary traditions of Mars and Venus, see Janet Adelman, *The Common Liar: An Essay on Antony and Cleopatra*, pp. 83–101.

42. Symonds, *Renaissance in Italy*, 1:702–3.

43. E. H. Gombrich, "Botticelli's Mythologies: A Study in the Neoplatonic Symbolism of His Circle," *Journal of the Warburg and Courtauld Institutes* 8 (1945): 46ff; reprinted in *Symbolic Images*, pp. 31–81.

Figure 2–12. Sandro Botticelli. *Mars and Venus*. The National Gallery, London.

in it to an astrological passage in Ficino's commentary on the *Symposium*:

> Mars is outstanding in strength among the planets because he makes men stronger, but Venus masters him . . . Venus, when in conjunction with Mars, in opposition to him, or watching him from sextile or trine aspect, as we say, often checks his malignance. . . . she seems to master and appease Mars, but Mars never masters Venus.

Gombrich goes on to discuss the moral aspect of the myth of Mars and Venus, quoting Chaucer's *Complaint of Mars* where an astrological interpretation of the myth has a moral application. He then suggests that this moral overtone, the lordship of gentle Venus over ferocious Mars, is compatible with Ficino's astrological passage and then intimates that Botticelli may have intended this meaning in his painting.

Wind takes issue with Gombrich's astrological interpretation of Botticelli's painting by observing that "with all due allowance for the wide influence of horoscopy," Botticelli's picture is "emphatically *not* an astrological image." He then suggests that to interpret the painting in relation to the astrological sextile and trine would spoil its "peculiar poetry."[44] We may not be certain that Botticelli's painting refers to the passage cited by Gombrich, but the astrological implications of Venus are so very common in Renaissance literature that the possible existence of this type of overtone cannot be entirely dismissed. The powers of the planet are discussed not only by Ficino but also by Pico della Mirandola. Lorenzo de' Medici, in his *Canzona de' sette pianeti*, describes the planet Venus in terms that might well be applied

44. Edgar Wind, *Pagan Mysteries in the Renaissance*, pp. 85–91.

to Botticelli's Venus: "Graceful, luminous and beautiful Venus/ inspires love and kindness in the heart."[45] While Wind rejects the astrological reading of Botticelli's painting, he too accepts the idea that it does have a moral overtone. He suggests that the painting relates to the docrine of contraries in the writing of Pico della Mirandola, whom he believes was influenced by Plutarch. After quoting from Plutarch, he discusses the text from Pico's *Commento*, part of which is quoted below:

45. De' Medici, *Opere*, 2:251.

> And since in the constitution of created things it is necessary that the union overcomes strife . . . for this reason it is said by the poets that Venus loves Mars, because Beauty, which we call Venus, cannot subsist without contrariety; and that Venus tames and mitigates Mars, because the tempering power restrains and overcomes the strife and hate which persist between the contrary elements. Similarly, according to the ancient astrologers, whose opinion Plato and Aristotle follow, and according to the writings of Abenazra the Spaniard and also of Moses, Venus was placed in the center of heaven next to Mars, because she must tame his impulse which is by nature destructive and corrupting, just as Jupiter offsets the malice of Saturn. And if Mars were always subordinated to Venus, that is the contrariety of component elements to their due proportion, nothing would ever perish.

Thus, an allegory of Harmony may have been intended in Botticelli's painting, just as it more surely was in Mantegna's *Parnassus*.

Wind also suggests a more general approach to the painting by observing that its subject alludes to the familiar notion that "Love is more powerful than Strife." He finds this notion in both Plato's *Symposium* and in Lucretius's *De rerum natura*. Indeed, when we look back over the various texts cited by both Wind and Gombrich, we find that they all basically refer to this idea. Plato observes that Venus "masters him [Mars]"; Lucretius describes Mars in the lap of Venus, "wholly vanquished by the ever-living wound of love"; Chaucer tells us that "she [Venus] hath take him [Mars] in subjeccioun"; Ficino observes that Venus "seems to master and appease Mars"; and Pico notes that "Venus tames and mitigates" Mars. The idea of love vanquishing strife is clearly a literary commonplace, and it is likely that Botticelli intended to portray this notion with its moral implications. But there is neither internal evidence in Botticelli's painting nor documentary evidence to establish its specific connection to Pico's doctrine of contraries, just as there is no conclusive evidence to support the "Ficinian" astrological interpretation of the painting.

The writings of Ficino and the poetry of Poliziano have also been used recently by Ferruolo as the bases for the interpretation of Botticelli's painting.[46] This author argues that *Mars and Venus*, along with *Primavera* and *Birth of Venus*, relates to the "circle of love" in Poliziano's *Stanze*, which is influenced by the major themes of Ficino, light and love. Ferruolo links Botticelli's painting, in particular, with Poliziano's description of Mars and Venus in the *Stanze per la giostra* (a passage also related to Lucretius), but in doing

46. Arnolfo B. Ferruolo, "Botticelli's Mythologies, Fincino's *De Amore*, Poliziano's *Giostra*: Their Circle of Love."

so he inaccurately describes both the text and the painting. He tells us that in the poem "Mars is utterly overcome by the beauty of the goddess, feeds on the light of her eyes, worships her." But this is not quite what Poliziano says. Rather the poet writes:

> He found her seated on the edge of the bed/ just out of the arms of Mars,/ who, facing the opposite direction from her, reclined in her lap/ feeding his eyes on her face;/ A nimbus of roses rained down upon them/ to renew their amorous passion:/ Venus willingly gave to him/ one thousand kisses on his forehead and eyes.[47]

47. Angelo Poliziano, *Tutte le poesie italiane*, ed. G. R. Ceriello, p. 43.

Politian describes the eyes of Mars feasting on the face of Venus, but there is no mention of "worship" or of "the light of her eyes." Ferruolo also conveniently avoids discussing the erotic character of the scene, which is not compatibile with a "Ficinian" interpretation. He fails to observe that, as roses fall upon the lovers, Venus is eagerly implanting one thousand kisses upon the face of Mars. There is nothing "Ficinian" about this lovemaking. Ferruolo's description of the painting is equally inaccurate. According to him, Mars is "vanquished by the power of her beauty . . . lying back with dazed eyes." Yet a look at the painting makes it clear that Mars is not lying back with dazed eyes; his eyes are shut, for he is sound asleep.

It is remarkable that Wind, Gombrich, and Ferruolo all generally ignore the delicate humor and erotic innuendo of Botticelli's painting. Gombrich invokes "The Lordship of gentle Venus over ferocious Mars" without considering the manner of Venus's triumph. Wind, who does note the "bucolic raillery" of the satyrs, intimates that Venus has triumphed over Mars by "putting Mars to sleep." And according to Ferruolo, Mars "is . . . vanquished by the power of her beauty." Vanquished by the power of her beauty, indeed! The nudity and deep slumber of Mars clearly indicate to the beholder that he has been vanquished by something more tangible than the splendor of divine beauty. Botticelli has surrounded his lovers with bushes to isolate them. And he has surrounded Mars with satyrs—known for their licentiousness and sexual appetites—unsubtle clues to Venus's means of vanquishing Mars. The relaxed attitude of Mars's sensuous body evokes the muscular relaxation not only of sleep but the pleasurable lassitude that follows the act of sex. A satyr trumpets in his ear, another satyr places a piece of armor on his finger, and wasps buzz around his head. But lovemaking has so exhausted Mars that his sleep is undisturbed. The piece of armor on Mars's finger, the position of his right index finger across his thigh, and his extending lance take on a sexual overtone in this context. The playful satyr below Mars and the middle satyr holding the lance open their mouths and stick out their tongues lasciviously, heightening the erotic tone of the painting. Venus appears demure and detached, and at first it seems that she remains aloof from this erotic play. Yet her gaze is one of conquest, and her physical appearance suggests some of the weapons she employed in her amorous "battle" with Mars. Venus's left hand directs the observer's attention to the diaphanous drapery seductively revealing her left leg to the knee. Although fully dressed, her softly draped gown suggests her long limbs and full thighs, hips, and abdomen, while the gold around her breasts and shoulders emphasizes her sensual womanly figure. In short, Botticelli has depicted a delightful satire of Mars, the mightly god of war who has been subdued in lovemaking by Venus. The satyrs, who are principal actors in the painting, are intended quite literally to satirize the vanquished god.

It would further seem that the significance of these satyrs has generally been underestimated. Gombrich has stressed that some of these creatures are based on a passage from Lucian who described *amorini* sporting with the armor of Alexander in an ancient painting illustrating the latter's marriage.

> On the other side of the picture, more Loves play among Alexander's armour; two are carrying his spear, as porters do a heavy beam; two more grasp the handles of the shield, tugging it along with another reclining on it; playing king, I suppose; and then another has got into the breast plate, which lies hollow part upwards; he is in ambush, and will give the royal equipage a good fright when it comes within reach.[48]

48. Gombrich, *Symbolic Images*, p. 68.

But emphasis should be placed on the fact that Botticelli chose to transform Lucian's *amorini* into little satyrs, not only heightening the sexual tone of the painting, but as we have already noted, its satirical intention. Moreover, Botticelli's satirical satyrs not only allude to Lucian's text but convey the general spirit of Lucian's satirical writing. Botticelli's painting, for all its allegorical implications, needs also to be seen in the satirical tradition of Lucian, who influenced major Renaissance writers, including Erasmus, More, Aretino, and Rabelais, and other artists whose work will be discussed later.

Botticelli's painting is not only a satire but may also be a parody. Mars and Venus are traditionally represented in both ancient and Renaissance art as fully mature, heroic types. In the fresco of Mars and Venus at Pompeii, for example, or in Veronese's painting of the lovers in the Metropolitan Museum in New York, we find a muscular, heroic Mars, and a mature, full-bodied Venus.[49] Botticelli's delicate and slender-limbed Venus is no older than the teenage girls who appear in Ghirlandaio's Tornabuoni Chapel decorations, and Mars is also conspicuously an adolescent. Venus is not simply a Botticellian type, for Botticelli painted her as more mature in the *Birth of Venus* (Uffizi). The seeming parody here, like the satire, is gentle and charming. Botticelli's delicate humor brings to mind the tone in Alberti's light-hearted little treatise on love, *Ecatonfilea*.[50] There is a tone of innocence in this little-read work which stresses the sweetness of love, although there is also a sensual overtone in it. Alberti's motto in the treatise is "Love and you will be loved." His playful advice is given to the "nobile donzelle fiorentine," who are like

49. For Veronese's painting, see Wind, *Pagan Mysteries*, pl. 76.

50. Leon Battista Alberti, *Opere volgari*, ed. Cecil Grayson, 3:199ff.

the elegant young Florentine girl playing Venus in Botticelli's painting.

Although Botticelli's painting seems to have moral and astrological overtones, its playfulness and eroticism stand apart from the serious passages in the philosophical writings of Ficino and Pico quoted by Gombrich, Wind, and Ferruolo. The erotic character of Botticelli's painting can be compared to Poliziano's description of Mars and Venus in the *Stanze per la giostra*, as we noted above. Botticelli's humorous and frolicsome little satyrs have also been compared to the playful *amorini*, who fly around Mars and Venus in Poliziano's poem: "Above and around the little naked Loves/ played, flying now here and now there."[51] Botticelli's painting is clearly not an illustration of Poliziano's text, but the playful and sensuous tone of the painting is similar to that in Poliziano's description of Mars and Venus.

Botticelli's painting can also be related in its basic comic and erotic character to Lorenzo de' Medici's poem, *Amori di Marte e Venere*.[52] Lorenzo's Venus playfully invites Mars to bed after the departure of Vulcan:

51. Poliziano, *Tutte le poesie italiane*, p. 43.

52. De' Medici, *Opere*, 2:15–18. Lorenzo's poem has only occasionally been discussed in relation to Botticelli's painting; see Enrico Barfucci, *Lorenzo dei Medici e la società artistica del suo tempo*, p. 107.

> Come, for nude and in bed I invite you:/ don't dally for time passes and flies by:/ I have covered my breasts with purple flowers./ Come, Mars, come, come, I am all alone./ Turn out the lights; only mine never goes out./ There is no longer anyone here who speaks to me.

Mars replies with a light-hearted reference to the cliché about the victory of love over war:

> I do not come to your chamber as an enemy,/ My beautiful Venus, but without arms;/ because against your arms blows are useless.

Mars goes to Venus, and the poet continues, not by describing their love-making, but by having Mars imagine what it will be like:

> To kiss her mouth and serene forehead,/ the two celestial lights and her white breasts/ her long hand full of every beauty;/ Yet another matter it is to lie in the golden bed/ with my sweet friend, and to sing songs,/ rather than to fatigue the body in warfare;/ to taste that fruit which can make me happy,/ the ultimate climax of a trembling pleasure./ It is time for love, time for swords and arms.

Like Botticelli's painting, the passage from Lorenzo de' Medici's poem above is a playfully erotic suggestion of the pleasure Mars experiences with Venus. If Lorenzo suggests that Mars will "taste the fruit" that is the culmination of a "trembling pleasure," Botticelli's depiction of Mars suggests, perhaps somewhat more delicately, that he has already enjoyed this pleasure. In Lorenzo's poem, the Sun discovers Mars and Venus in bed and then calls all the gods to witness the "adulterous Venus" with her lover. The Sun moralizes about their "sin" but in a light tone of satire rather than in one of serious moralizing. The poem concludes with the appearance of the silly, cuckolded Vulcan, who (not to be taken seriously) grumbles: "Venus my Venus, foam of the sea,/ you adulterous Mars, will pay the penalty,/ because a grave crime deserves serious punishment." The poet, like the painter, not only alludes to the triumph of love over war, but he also humorously dwells on how this formidable victory was achieved.

Botticelli's *Mars and Venus* is among the first comic-erotic mythological paintings of the Italian Renaissance and anticipates the even more erotic comedy in sixteenth-century works by Giulio Romano, Parmigianino, Titian, and others. Yet, in their zeal to analyze the astrological, moral, and philosophical overtones of the painting, scholars have neglected this interesting fact. The erotic tone and humor of the painting relate in spirit to the poetry of Botticelli's contemporary, Lorenzo de' Medici, which is steeped in the tradition of ancient love poetry. Indeed, in its very voluptuousness of form and conceit and in its ebullient and mocking tone, Botticelli's painting captures much of that ancient poetical tradition that permeated Florentine culture in the late quattrocento.

Finally, we should recall that Gombrich, who identified the wasps or *vespae* in the painting as an emblem of the Vespucci, further suggested that Botticelli's work may have in fact been made for a Vespucci wedding. It should be remembered that other notable humorous works of art such as Sodoma's *Marriage of Alexander and Roxanne* (see Figure 4–10), Rosso's *Mars and Venus* (see Figure 5–6), and Carracci's Farnese ceiling decorations (all discussed below) have been associated with marriages. We may eventually be able to define more sharply the playful and satirical trends in art works done for wedding festivities, which would include masques and plays. It is not unreasonable to suggest, however, that Botticelli's painting might have been commissioned as an object of bedroom furniture in honor of a marriage. If we bear in mind the patterns of iconography and tone frequently found in bedroom art, including most notably Sodoma's *Marriage of Alexander and Roxanne* done in the bedroom of Agostino Chigi and the Camera degli Sposi decorated by Mantegna for the Gonzaga, Botticelli's little satyrs might be seen along with Mantegna's and Sodoma's *amorini* as part of pictorial epithalamia appropriate to the boudoir.[53]

Botticelli's painting probably influenced the similar painting of Mars and Venus by Piero di Cosimo in which the playfulness has also been neglected (Figure 2–13). Piero has depicted the two gods stretched out in front of a landscape that is more open and expansive than Botticelli's. If Piero's image of Mars and Venus is derived from Lucretius *De rerum natura*, as Panofsky suggests, it is not inconceivable that Piero's landscape, with its field, hills, flowers, and water, alludes to the similar aspects of nature that are celebrated in some detail as the realization of Venus's fecundity in Lucretius's poem.[54] Piero's Venus, who is joined by Cupid and a rabbit, is essentially naked. Only scant draperies cover her arms and pudenda, making the sexual character of the

Figure 4–10, p. 93

Figure 5–6, p. 114

53. Although there is a vast literature on nuptial art, including numerous recent articles, this subject has never been systematically studied. I am grateful to James Ackerman for first calling my attention to the importance of this subject.

54. Erwin Panofsky, *Studies in Iconology: Humanistic Themes of the Renaissance*, p. 63, n. 77. The possible relationship of Piero's landscape to Lucretius's text was suggested to me by Candace Gorham.

Figure 2–13. Piero di Cosimo. *Mars and Venus*. Gemäldegalerie, Berlin.

scene even more explicit than in Botticelli's painting. Mars is again asleep, presumably alluding to the moment after lovemaking. Their amorous activities are also suggested by the kiss of the two doves between Mars and Venus. Like the little satyrs in Botticelli's painting, the *amorini* playing with the arms of Mars suggest a satire of the subdued god of war. The spirit of this passage is similar to that in Giovanni Pontano's *Eridanus*, where Cupid plays with Mars's armor after Venus has subdued him: "Tell me, Mars, tell me oh powerful Gradior, where is your spear, where is your pike?/ Venus knows; your arms are abandoned on the river bank, handled by the laughing son of Venus."[55] The presence of Cupid in Piero's painting also brings to mind Pontano's remark that it was Cupid who revealed to his mother the many ways of making love.

Although the comedy in Piero's painting is scarcely remarked upon, it is obviously less subtle than the humor in Botticelli's painting. Not only is Mars sound asleep after lovemaking, but Venus, even in her wakeful state, seems stunned. She gazes out as if in a daze. By painting two figures in these postures, Piero has given us a humorous evocation of the energies spent in this monumental "amorous battle" between the goddess of love and the god of war. The rabbit in Piero's painting seems not to be just a symbol of the fertility of Venus (appropriate to a Lucretian interpretation of the painting) but also appears to be a *scherzo* on the sexual character of the scene. The animal peers out over the hip of Venus and nuzzles the hand of Cupid, which holds the transparent drapery covering Venus's pudenda. The Latin word for rabbit, *cuniculus*, was frequently used in the Renaissance as a pun on

55. Giovanni Pontano, *Eridanus*, p. 692.

Figure 2–14. Piero di Cosimo. *Discovery of Honey*. Worcester Art Museum, Worcester, Massachusetts.

the female pudenda, *cunnus*. For example, in the first lines of his *In Puellam Suam*, Poliziano, echoing Catullus, compares his lover to a rabbit: "Puella delicatior lepuscolo et cunicolo" (My mistress, softer than a little hare and rabbit).[56] The very proximity of the rabbit to the pudenda of Venus in Piero's painting suggests that the artist is making a similar reference. The explicit sexual reference in Piero's painting also brings to mind the kind of humor that appears even more bluntly in the opening lines of Antonio Alamanni's contemporary sonnet: "Mars had the arrow from his pants to a point/ To wound Venus between her thighs."[57]

Piero di Cosimo is of course well known for the comic types that appear in his paintings. His strong sense of humor is especially present in the *Discovery of Honey* and related mythological works (Figure 2–14).[58] In Piero's painting, based on Ovid's *Fasti*, a group of satyrs who make noise by banging pots and pans follow bees to their hive in a grotesque, comically shaped tree—the trunk of which evokes a human face—where honey is discovered. In the background we see astride his ass, Silenus, an amusingly puffed and ugly

56. Ibid., p. 1050.

57. Il Burchiello, *Sonnetti del Burchiello del Bellincioni e d'altri poeti fiorentini alla burchiellesca*, Alamanni, VII.

58. Piero's mythologies are fully discussed in Chapter 2 of Panofsky, *Studies in Iconology*.

Figure 2–15. Piero di Cosimo. *Discovery of Honey* (detail). Worcester Art Museum, Worcester, Massachusetts.

59. Langton Douglas, *Piero di Cosimo*, pp. 62–63.

60. This detail was pointed out to me by Elizabeth Wilson.

figure who jocularly waves at us. Langton Douglas referred to Piero's Silenus "as a kind of classical Sir Toby Belch."[59] He also associated Piero's Silenus with Lucian's Silenus in the dialogue *Dionysius*. Even if there is no firm evidence that Piero was specifically referring to Lucian here, Piero's Silenus is certainly related in his coarse and playful tone to Lucian's character: "short, thickset, old man, with a big belly, a flat nose, and large upright ears, who trembled perpetually, and who, when walking, leaned upon his staff—though for the most part he rode upon an ass." When we look with care at Silenus, who is waving at us as he is crowned, we also see that this jovial man with a big belly is like Mantegna's unsupportable Silenus; for the hind legs of the ass supporting him have buckled (Figure 2–15)![60] Next to Silenus we encounter a ludicrous lady satyr who is improbably and elegantly posed with her hand upon her waist, like a lady of the court. Yet as we contemplate this foolish courtly rustic, perhaps thinking of Shakespeare's romances, we observe that her pudenda are covered by a ridiculous seashell. This object is not only bizarre in its own right, like the seashell penis of Mabuse's famous Neptune, but may well have been intended as a kind of sexual pun.

Like his *Mars and Venus* and the version by Botticelli, Piero's *Discovery of Honey* is imbued with the playful literary humor of Ovid and Lucian. Piero's Silenus might almost be a visualization of a character in Pulci's burlesque *Morgante*, and he can also be compared to his comic counterpart, so graphically presented, in Lorenzo de' Medici's famous carnival song, *Trionfo di Bacco ed Arianna*: "This Ass's burden coming up behind is old Silenus, drunk and happy, full of flesh and years. He cannot stand upright, yet he laughs and ever rejoices."[61] Piero's pictorial carnival song pulsates with vibrant rhythms that can also be compared to the dynamic dance beat of Lorenzo's poem. In the foreground of Piero's painting, Bacchus and Ariadne appear, not as noble and idealized figures, but with grotesque features. Bacchus, especially, has a humorously ugly expression on his face, and his slightly unstable posture and empty wine cup suggest the probable influence of wine. In front of Bacchus and his consort an ugly satyr is seated, holding an onion and leering out at us. Onions were traditionally regarded as an aphrodisiac, and in this context, the onion is probably an unsubtle allusion to the relationship of Bacchus and Ariadne.[62] The leering smile of the satyr is mocking and is intended, one might suppose, to be satirical.

If Botticelli's satyrs are charming, Piero's are coarse and gross. This coarseness and the mockery in Piero's painting are very close in spirit to the vulgar comedy in the contemporary poetry of Lorenzo de' Medici. In Lorenzo's delightful *I Beoni*, the poet laughs at vulgar, guzzling Rabelaisian Florentines. He mocks their ugly and coarse acts ("atti rozzi e brutti") like those we see in the *Discovery of Honey*. Bertoldo Corsini drinks so much that he pisses like a mule, and Checco Spinelli and Giuliano Ginori eat Gargantuan quantities of food. The fat Steccuto, "the true master" of the art of drinking

> . . . drinks so much wine,
> that to talk or think of it frightens me;
> by himself he drinks for all of us of Dragoncino.
>   When he has already drunk and falls asleep,
> he snores so loudly in his sleep,
> that one has to listen twice to hear above the noise;
> and he always sweats, and rather heavily, you know.[63]

Piero's coarse satyrs, bloated Silenus, and tipsy Bacchus, like Lorenzo's gross and gluttonous Florentines, reflect polite Renaissance society's taste for vulgar comedy.

61. Lorenzo de' Medici, *Carnival Song*, p. 225.

62. Panofsky, *Studies in Iconology*, p. 63, n. 78.

63. Lorenzo de' Medici, *Opere*, 2:157ff.

Figure 2–16. Piero di Cosimo. *Misfortunes of Silenus*. Fogg Museum, Harvard University, Cambridge, Massachusetts.

Piero's *Discovery of Honey* was part of a series of "storie baccanarie" done for Giovanni Vespucci, which included the *Misfortunes of Silenus* (Figure 2–16). The Bacchic iconography (which has its counterpart in the *camerino* of Alfonso d'Este) must have been extensive in the late quattrocento. Recently published Medicean inventories reveal that in one room of Lorenzo di Pierfrancesco de' Medici's palace the walls contained a "storia di Bacho," and according to Vasari, Botticelli painted a Bacchus lifting a barrel (*botte*) of wine.[64] There is the same kind of carnival spirit in the *Misfortunes of Silenus* as in the *Discovery of Honey* and in Lorenzo's *poesia baccanaria*. Silenus topples from his ass and is lifted by tipsy, frolicsome satyrs, including one who comically uses a large branch under Silenus's buttocks as a lever to pry him off the ground. At the left, satyrs attend his wasp stings, applying mud to his face. But Silenus also seems to be the subject of derision, a kind of scapegoat, as some satyrs appear to be slinging mud at him in a moment of cruel humor; figures identified as Bacchus and Ariadne look on.

64. Webster Smith, "On the Original Location of the *Primavera*," p. 39, appendix 3; and Vasari, *Le vite*, 3:322.

Two other pictures by Piero, one in Hartford, the other in Ottawa, illustrate the myth of Vulcan.[65] These works, of similar dimensions, which were possibly done as part of the same commission, reveal Piero's humor in a more restrained key. Once again, these paintings, like those by Piero discussed above, have been interpreted by Panofsky as illustrations of the early civilization of man. In the Hartford painting, smiling Botticellean nymphs who have been picking flowers discover the young Vulcan after his fall on Lemnos. Piero has depicted Vulcan in a rather awkward posture, no doubt alluding to his lameness, that was the result of his fall and that was the subject of mockery in ancient and Renaissance literature, as for example, in Lorenzo's *Amori di Marte e Venere*. In the Ottawa painting, the mature Vulcan, rendered in caricature, is seen working on (and as Panofsky has suggested, perhaps inventing) the horseshoe. He is surrounded by other primitive types and animals. His lameness is again alluded to, for he is working while seated. Vasari mentions that Piero painted another Vulcan painting, now lost, which also included Mars and Venus, and it is tempting to consider Panofsky's hypothesis that this lost picture belonged with the two paintings we have been discussing. At any rate, one can well imagine the humorous aspects of the lost painting in light of the Mars and Venus paintings already discussed. Furthermore, the Vulcan pictures of Piero share with Mantegna's *Parnassus* the derision of the lame god. This theme persists in the cinquecento in Tintoretto's *Mars and Venus* and in a fresco by the Lombard painter, Morazzone, for his own house (hung over his fireplace), showing Vulcan in his smithy, leaning on a crutch.[66] According to Virgil (*Aeneid*, VIII), Vulcan's assistants were Cyclopes. As we shall see, these monstrous freaks, who were derided in antiquity and the Renaissance, became the subject for considerable comic art in the Renaissance.

65. Panofsky, *Studies in Iconology*, p. 33.

66. Marianna Haraszti-Takács, *The Masters of Mannerism*, no. 23.

III. *Michelangelo's Sense of Humor*

> If Petrarch loved the laurel so much it was because it is good with sausages and thrushes.—Leonardo da Vinci, *Notebooks*

Traditionally, the literature on Michelangelo has emphasized the serious character of his art and given inadequate attention to his extraordinary wit and comic bent. Throughout his career, Michelangelo exhibited an especially keen wit in his painting, sculpture, and architecture, as well as in his poetry and letters. Vasari tells us tales about young Michelangelo's sense of humor that may not be true but nevertheless seem indicative of Michelangelo's temperament. As a young man, Michelangelo was encouraged by Lorenzo de' Medici, and he sought to impress his patron by counterfeiting in marble "an antique head of a Faun that was there, old and unwrinkled, which had the nose injured and the mouth laughing." When Lorenzo saw Michelangelo's work, he was astonished by it, but he added, teasing Michelangelo, "Surely you should have known that old folks never have all their teeth." According to Vasari, Michelangelo, in his simplicity, proceeded to break one of the teeth of the satyr and hollow out the gum, as if the tooth had dropped out. When Lorenzo saw the result he laughed some more but then arranged to take young Buonarroti into his household. In Vasari's tale, the youthful Michelangelo is a bit simple and the butt of a joke, but he also exhibits a typical quickness of wit.[1]

Another, less plausible tale by Vasari about Michelangelo is related to the traditional type of story told about how an artist deceives a patron, and it is probably thus a *topos* imposed by Vasari on the life of Michelangelo. Since the butt of Michelangelo's joke, according to Vasari's tale, was the Republican Gonfaloniere, and since Vasari dedicated his *Lives* to the anti-Republican Duke Cosimo de' Medici, there may have been an underlying political motive for the telling of this tale. The tone is nevertheless characteristic of Michelangelo's sense of humor:

> It happened at this time that Piero Soderini, having seen it (Michelangelo's *David*) in place, was well pleased with it, but said to Michelangelo, at a moment when he was retouching it in certain parts, that it seemed to him that the nose of the figure was too thick. Michelangelo noticed that the Gonfalonier was beneath the Giant, and that his point of view prevented him from seeing it properly; but in order to satisfy him he climbed upon the staging, which was against the shoulders, and quickly took up a chisel in his left hand, with a little of the marble dust

1. Giorgio Vasari, *Le vite dè più eccellenti pittori scultori et architettori*, ed. Gaetano Milanesi, 7:142.

that lay upon the planks of the staging, and then, beginning to strike lightly with the chisel, let fall the dust little by little, nor changed the nose a whit from what it was before. Then, looking down at the Gonfalonier, who stood watching him, he said, "Look at it now." "I like it better," said the Gonfalonier, "you have given it life." And so Michelangelo came down laughing to himself at having satisfied that lord, for he had compassion on those who, in order to appear full of knowledge, talk about things of which they know nothing.[2]

Among Michelangelo's earliest works are his attempts to rival the style of the ancients. In addition to the *Faun* for Lorenzo de' Medici, while he was in Rome, Michelangelo made a *Sleeping Cupid* that appeared to be antique and that was apparently sold as an ancient work. While in Rome he also made a *Bacchus* for Iacopo Galli, which captures much of the sensuality in ancient Roman sculpture (Figure 3–1).[3] Although it was at first known to be a work by Michelangelo, after the Sack of Rome, Martin van Heemskerck sketched it in its damaged state as if it had been an ancient work. The statue has been characterized in terms of its possible Christian connotations, and it has been interpreted as an allusion to the familiar dictum, *In vino veritas*.[4] It has sometimes been noted that Michelangelo presents the god of wine in a state of intoxication. Whatever allusive allegory Michelangelo intended, its tone is humorous. Thus, any allusion the statue makes to *In vino veritas* is made playfully. Michelangelo's sensuous and fleshy god of wine seems to stagger forward as he raises his cup of wine. His unstable posture, his open mouth, and his blank eyes all convey the effect that he is potted.[5] The humorous character of the work is underscored by the presence of Bacchus's smiling companion, the satyr who is eating grapes. Like the satyrs of Botticelli and Piero di Cosimo, Michelangelo's satyr seems to suggest a satirical intention. The satire in Michelangelo's work is reminiscent of the mocking of Bacchus in Renaissance literature, as for example, in Erasmus's contemporary *The Praise of Folly*: "Why is it that Bacchus is always a stripling and bushy-haired? but because he is mad and drunk and spends his life in drinking, dancing, revels, and May games, not having so much as the least society with Pallas."[6] Like Erasmus's verbal representation of Bacchus, Michelangelo's playful satire of the drunken god of wine brings to mind the prevalent mock-heroic paintings and prints of the gods in Northern European art during this period. One might point, for example, to Jan Mabuse's *Neptune and Amphitrite* (Staatliche Museen, Berlin) in which Neptune, endowed with an improbable seashell penis, is made to appear slightly ridiculous. Or again we are made to think of a rather comical Hercules in a print by Albrecht Dürer or of Hendrik Goltzius's mock-heroic print of Hercules, who is preposterous in his muscular grandeur.[7]

Bacchus's intoxication is central to Michelangelo's humorous presentation of him, a reminder of how often drunkenness is the subject of humor in art

2. Giorgio Vasari, *The Lives of the Most Eminent Painters, Sculptors, and Architects*, trans. Gaston Du Vere, 9:16–17.

3. Vasari, *Le vite*, 7:150.

4. For the Christian implications of the *Bacchus*, see Sydney J. Freedberg, *Painting of the High Renaissance in Rome and Florence*, 1:31. For the possible allusion to *In vino veritas*, see Frederick Hartt, *Michelangelo: The Complete Sculpture*, p. 70.

5. In a lecture given in 1964, Sydney Freedberg alluded to the humor in Michelangelo's statue, noting that the *Bacchus* "is ever so slightly boiled." This humor was reluctantly acknowledged by Heinrich Woefflin, *The Art of the Italian Renaissance*, p. 54.

6. Erasmus, *The Praise of Folly*, trans. John Wilson, p. 23.

7. The comic *Great Hercules* of Goltzius is discussed by Christopher White, *Recent Acquisitions and Personal Gifts, National Gallery of Art*, p. 159 and pl. 108.

Figure 3–1. Michelangelo. *Bacchus*. Bargello, Florence.

Figure 2–3, p. 25   *Figure 2–2, p. 23*   *Figure 2–14, p. 46*   *Figure 7–1, p. 159*

Figure 7–3, p. 163

and literature from antiquity through the Renaissance. We have already encountered Donatello's possibly Bacchic *Genius* (see Figure 2–3) and *amorini* on the *Judith* (see Figure 2–2), Piero di Cosimo's potted Bacchus and Silenus in the *Discovery of Honey* (see Figure 2–14), and Lorenzo de' Medici's ridiculous, guzzling *Beoni* or big drinkers. There are countless other humorous drinkers in Renaissance art and literature, including the gods in Bellini's *Feast of the Gods* (see Figure 7–1) and the allegorical characters in Titian's *Andrians* (see Figure 7–3). In the North, the supreme comic drinkers of the Renaissance are Rabelais's giants and Bruegel's peasants. Sometimes holy personages also participate in this Bacchic revelry, as for example, the jovial and tipsy St. Peter in Aertsen's *Christ in the House of Martha and Mary* (Rotterdam).[8]

Michelangelo returned to Bacchic subject matter later in his presentation drawing for Tomaso Cavalieri, the *Bacchanal of Children* (Figure 3–2). The specific meaning of this drawing is obscure, although it has been suggested that it is an allegory on base sensuality.[9] In it we see a group of *putti* carrying a dead animal, some *putti* cooking animals; others are drinking, some are with a sleeping and presumably drunken man, and two are with a satyress. The tone of the drawing is somber if not macabre, yet we find playful details in it: the *putto* who is drinking and pouring wine into his cup at the same time; the *putto* pissing into a cup that is simultaneously filled with wine from a barrel (seemingly a play on the spout of the wine barrel); and the various *putti* around the bubbling cauldron, especially the one who wears a comic mask. Attention has been recently called to the grotesque in Michelangelo's theory of art, and we should note here that the concept of one *putto* pissing into a cup being drunk from by another is similar to passages in early cinquecento grotesque decorations.[10] Some of the figures in the drawing echo earlier inventions of Michelangelo, and as Panofsky observed they "might be termed self-parodies."[11] For example, the figure holding the bundle of logs to be used for the

8. K. P. F. Moxey, "Erasmus and the Iconography of Pieter Aertsen's *Christ in the House of Martha and Mary* in the Boyman van Beuningen Museum," pl. 56a.

9. Michelangelo's drawing is discussed in Erwin Panofsky, *Studies in Iconology: Humanistic Themes in the Art of the Renaissance*, pp. 221ff.

10. David Summers, "Michelangelo's Architecture." For the detail of the *putto pisciatore* similar to Michelangelo's in a grotesque, see Jay Levenson, et al., *Early Italian Engravings from the National Gallery of Art*, pl. 110.

11. Panofsky, *Studies in Iconology*, p. 222.

Figure 3–2. Michelangelo. *Bacchanal of Children*. Royal Library, Windsor Castle.

cauldron is a reworking of the similar figure in the Sistine *Sacrifice of Noah*. Both the intermingling of seriousness and play and the self-parody of this drawing are salient features of Michelangelo's art.

Michelangelo also exhibits his sense of humor in the Sistine ceiling, although it is clearly subordinated to the heroic depictions of the major scenes in the ceiling. The grandeur and sheer force of Michelangelo's scenes from the Old Testament and of his prophets, sibyls, and *Ignudi*, as well as their complex allegorical meaning, have frequently been discussed in exalted terms. Yet Michelangelo's playfulness exists even within this setting of magnificence and spiritual grandeur. While the principal scenes of the ceiling symbolize the coming of Christ, Michelangelo painted Jesus' ancestors in the lunettes of the chapel. Attempts have been made to explain their symbolic meaning, but scant

Figure 3–3. Michelangelo. *Boaz*, Sistine Ceiling. Vatican Palace, Rome.

attention has been paid to what they are doing. Michelangelo has expressed in them an immediate sense of their humanity, which is contrasted to the more idealized figures in the ceiling, who are closer to grace. Christ's ancestors, who exist before redemption, are seated, waiting. Some peer out suspiciously; others seem lost in thought. Some are impatient, while others are bored. Their facial expressions are frequently done in caricature, and the postures of their bodies are sometimes bizzare.[12] The grotesque Boaz is especially appealing (Figure 3–3). He gazes intently at the head on his staff, which is almost the mirror image of his own. Boaz's staff brings to mind a fool's marot or bauble, and we might ask whether Michelangelo was suggesting a connection between Boaz's pre-Christian condition of ignorance and folly. It would seem that play has a greater impact when it is expressed not just in itself but in a larger and fundamentally serious context. This seems to be the case in the Sistine ceiling. Michelangelo's ancestors of Christ participate in the universal history of man: his creation, his fall, and finally his redemption. The fusion of playful elements and tragic grandeur in the Sistine ceiling can perhaps be compared to the similar assimilation of comic devices to the Passion in the medieval play written anonymously, *The Second Sheperds' Pageant*, or to the tragedy of Shakespeare's plays.

From what we know about Michelangelo, this humor is not surprising. For example, in a note to Luigi del Riccio that accompanied epitaphs for the tomb of Cecchino Bracci, he joked: "I don't want to send this one, because it is very awkward, but the trout and truffles would force Heaven itself," or "For the salted mushrooms, since you have nothing else," or "This the trout say, not I; so, if you don't like the verses, don't marinate them again without pepper."[13] And despite the exalted subject of the Sistine ceiling decorations and Michelangelo's frequent references in his letters to the great difficulties of painting it, Michelangelo was capable of mocking his own work on it. Next to a sonnet to Giovanni da Pistoia, Michelangelo drew himself painting a seated figure in the ceiling; he represents himself as a cartoonlike caricature with spikey hair and big circle eyes. The sonnet itself is filled with self-mockery. The descriptions of his difficulty in painting the ceiling are filled with tortuous imagery that brings to mind the bizarre strain of the bronze nudes in the ceiling. It also reads as a parody of his more heroic image of himself at work on the ceiling:

> I've got myself a goiter from this strain.
> As water gives the cats in Lombardy
> Or maybe it is in some other country;
> My belly's pushed by force beneath my chin.
>
> My beard toward Heaven, I feel the back of my brain
> Upon my neck, I grow the breast of a Harpy;
> My brush, above face continually,
> Makes it a splendid floor by dripping down.

12. The caricature of Michelangelo's figures is discussed by Sydney J. Freedberg, *Painting of the High Renaissance*, 1:111.

13. Michelangelo Buonarroti, *Complete Poems and Selected Letters of Michelangelo*, trans. Creighton Gilbert and Robert N. Linscott, p. xviii.

My loins have penetrated to my paunch,
My rump's a crupper, as a counterweight,
And pointless the unseeing steps I go.

In front of me my skin is being stretched
While it folds up behind and forms a knot,
And I am bending like a Syrian bow.

    And judgment, hence must grow,
Borne in the mind, peculiar and untrue;
You cannot shoot well when the gun's askew.

    John, come to the rescue
Of my dead painting now, and of my honor;
I'm not in a good place, and I'm no painter.[14]

Michelangelo's best-known poetry was Neoplatonic and in the Petrarchan form; but there is a facetious strain in his poetic work that in part seems to reflect the influence of the satirical poet, Francesco Berni.[15] Elements of grotesque caricature, analogous to those in his art, are found in such works as "I' sto rinchiuso come la midolla," in which Michelangelo describes himself as surrounded by spiders and dung heaps.[16] In the cinquecento it was of course the fashion to write in the manner of Petrarch. This interest in Petrarch is illustrated, for example, in Andrea del Sarto's portrait of a young girl holding her *Petrarchino* and in Bronzino's portrait of Lucrezia Buti, poetess and wife of Ammanato Ammanati, also holding a volume of Petrarch.[17] (We will not consider here Cellini's aside that Madama Lucrezia was less pure than Petrarch's Laura.)[18] At the same time that *Petrarchismo* was the fashion, poets began to parody both Petrarch and the ridiculous absurdities of the Petrarchan poets. When Michelangelo's former patron, Lorenzo de' Medici, described the imagined orgasm of Mars in his lovemaking with Venus in the *Amori di Marte e Venere* ("gusta quel frutto che può lieto farmi/ ultimo fin d'un tremante diletto"), he just might have been playing on the submerged sensuality in the similar but more idealized words of Petrarch's *Canzoniere*, 72 ("certo il fino dei miei pianti . . . ven da begli occhi al fin dolce tremanti,/ ultima speme de cortesi amanti").[19] Michelangelo himself, perhaps influenced by Berni's parody of a Petrarchan sonnet that was probably written by Bembo, wrote a delightful and amusing parody of Petrarch, "Tu ha 'l viso più dolce che la sapa."

You have a face more beautiful than a turnip,
Sweeter than mustard; it appears the snail
Has walked on it, it shines so; like a parsnip
The whiteness of your teeth is, and like treacle
The color of your eyes; surely the Pope
To such as this must be susceptible,
Whiter and blonder than a leek your hair;
So I shall die if I don't get your favor.

14. Ibid., pp. 5–6.

15. Michelangelo's comic poetry and its relation to Berni's work are discussed by Robert J. Clements, *The Poetry of Michelangelo*, pp. 259ff.

16. Michelangelo, *Complete Poems*, pp. 149–51.

17. Sydney J. Freedberg, *Andrea del Sarto*, 1: pl. 214; and Edi Baccheschi, *L'opera completa del Bronzino*, pl. 61.

18. Benvenuto Cellini, *The Life of Benvenuto Cellini*, trans. John Addington Symonds, p. 482.

19. Lorenzo de' Medici, *Opere*, ed. Attilio Simoni, 2:17.

I think your beauty much more beautiful
Than ever in a church a painted man,
And your mouth is just like a pocketful
Of beans, it seems to me, and so is mine.
Your eyebrows seem dyed in a crucible,
And more than a Syrian bow they twine.
Your cheeks are red and white when you sift flour,
Like fresh cheese and poppies mixed together.

And when I look upon you and each breast,
I think they're like two melons in a satchel,
And then I am like straw, and start to flash,
Although I'm bent and broken by the shovel.
Think, if my lovely cup I still possessed,
I'd follow you past others like a beagle,
And if I thought that getting it was possible,
Here and today I'd do something incredible.[20]

20. Michelangelo, *Complete Poems*, pp. 11–12.

Michelangelo's poem, which evokes the mocking tone of Lorenzo de' Medici's *Nencia da Barberino* as well as the facetious poetry of Berni, would no doubt have been enjoyed by Shakespeare, who conceived of a similar, if more subtle, Petrarchan travesty, "My mistress' eyes are nothing like the sun."[21] Michelangelo's comic hag, with breasts like melons, also evokes the various hideous women in Renaissance art. She might be compared to the caricatured women in Leonardo da Vinci's drawings and to the monstrous *Ugly Woman* of Quentin Metsys (Figure 3–4), who is closely related to the vain old women mocked by Erasmus in *The Praise of Folly* for wanting still "to play the goat."[22]

21. The Petrarchan and anti-Petrarchan traditions in the Renaissance were studied in an exemplary essay ("Petrarchismo ed Antipetrarchismo") by Arturo Graf, *Attraverso il Cinquecento*, pp. 3ff. The relationship of Renaissance art to *Petrarchismo*, a subject in need of further research, has recently been discussed in a suggestive essay by Elizabeth Cropper, "On Beautiful Women, Parmigianino, *Petrarchismo*, and the Vernacular Style," pp. 374–94.

22. Erwin Panofsky, "Erasmus and the Visual Arts," p. 214.

Like Shakespeare, Michelangelo parodies not only the conventions of the Petrarchan tradition but also his own Petrarchism. Both poets shared the self-consciousness so typical of the sixteenth century, which frequently resulted in the ironic parody of one's most serious ambitions. It might be objected that it is our own modern taste for irony that causes us to see this element in works by Michelangelo. Nevertheless, the more we learn about Michelangelo, the more it becomes evident that, like that of the greatest writers of his age, including Ariosto, Aretino, Montaigne, and Shakespeare, he had a highly developed sense of irony.

If Michelangelo could joke about physical torment in his poetry (the sonnet to Giovanni da Pistoia) he could also play on the physical anguish in his art, as he did in the Medici Chapel. This great structure, a mausoleum for the Magnifici Lorenzo and Giuliano and for the recently deceased Medici dukes of the same names, celebrates the dynastic ambitions of the Medici, and to borrow a phrase of Vasari, it symbolically celebrated their "regnare perpetuo."[23] The highly idealized dukes, represented almost as Caesars, seem to transcend the ravishes of time, although the strain of temporal existence is still felt in the allegorical figures and the architecture in the lower part of the

23. Vasari's phrase is from a discussion of his portrait of Duke Alexander de' Medici (*Le vite*, 8:241–42). The political significance of the Medici Chapel was stressed by Frederick Hartt, "The Meaning of Michelangelo's Medici Chapel," in *Essays in Honor of Georg Swarzenski*.

Figure 3-4. Quentin Metsys. *The Ugly Woman*. The National Gallery, London.

chapel. The space of the chapel is oppressive and creates a disquieting effect in the beholder, as do the taut, almost muscular forms that articulate the chapel walls. There is only a release from this oppressiveness in the upper or heavenly realm of the chapel toward which the vertical members of the architecture lead the beholder's eye. This physical tension in the chapel is also the basis of Michelangelo's neglected wit. Behind the tombs of the dukes Lorenzo and Giuliano is a cornice that incorporates the traditional classical motif of the egg and dart (Figure 3–5). In the lower sequence of eggs and darts, Michelangelo has transformed the eggs into grotesque faces based on classical masks, making a parody of the egg-and-dart convention. The grimaces of these faces convey tension and pain, alluding to the unbearable weight of the architecture upon them. The play between eggs and masks and the agonized expressions of the masks add a touch of wit to what is a profoundly serious and intensely expressive work.

This curious wit is also apparent in one of Michelangelo's drawings for the chapel, a chalk study in the Casa Buonarroti for the profile of a pilaster base (Figure 3–6).[24] Michelangelo's humor here depends in part on the anthropomorphic character of his architecture, which has been eloquently discussed by Ackerman. He observes that it causes "an immediate identification of our physical functions with those of the building."[25] This emphatic connection is delineated literally in the profile study where Michelangelo has metaphorically converted the architectural profile into a human one by indicating the eye of a human face. Once again the effect is grotesque and can be likened to Renaissance grotesque decorations like the surprising and delightful detail in a grotesque engraving by Giovanni da Birago.[26] For all of its grotesqueness, Michelangelo's profile has an intensity and fierceness in it which is also expressive, like the witty egg-and-dart frieze, of the tensions in the architecture.

There are other delightful grotesque elements in the Medici Chapel, including the heads in the capitals above the tombs of the dukes. The word *capital* (*capitello*) is of course derived from *caput*, the Latin word for head. And it seems that Michelangelo, like others before him, was probably playing on this relationship when he designed these "little heads." One of these is a satyr head with two front teeth, reminiscent of the faun he had done years before for Lorenzo de' Medici. Michelangelo's grotesque heads, which are also found in many of his drawings, are not unrelated to the monstrous self-image that he presents in his *terza rima*: "My face has the shape that causes fright;/ In wind when there's no rain my clothes would scare/ Crows from the seed, without another dart."[27] In the same stanzas, Michelangelo presents aspects of physical existence with a macabre humor that would no doubt have been appreciated by Montaigne or Shakespeare:

24. Frederick Hartt, *Michelangelo Drawings*, no. 209.

25. James S. Ackerman, *The Architecture of Michelangelo*, pp. 37ff.

26. Levenson et al., *Early Italian Engravings*, pl. 110.

27. Michelangelo, *Complete Poems*, p. 151.

Figure 3–5. Michelangelo. Medici Chapel, detail of frieze. S. Lorenzo, Florence.

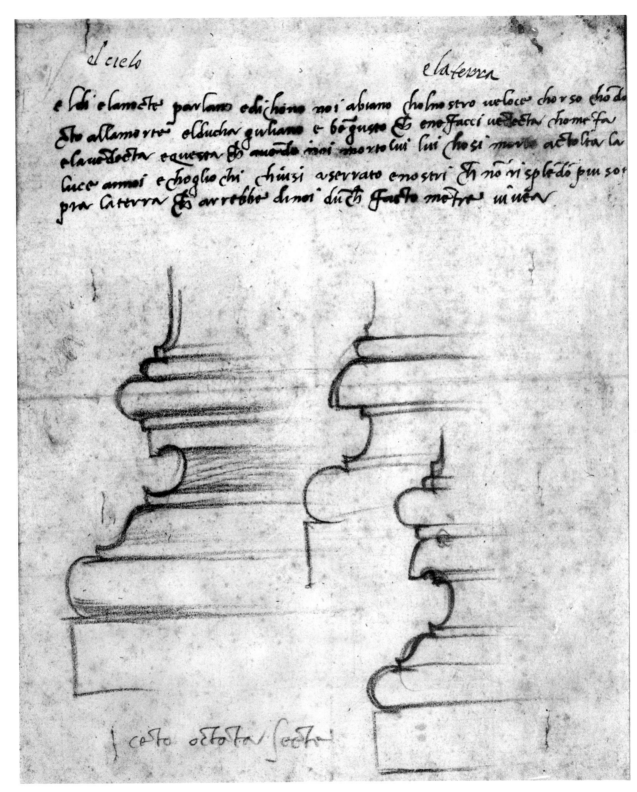

Figure 3–6. Michelangelo. *Architectural Studies*. Casa Buonarroti, Florence.

There is the dung of giants at my door;
Those who eat grapes or take some medicine
Go nowhere else to empty in great numbers.

Then I have made acquaintance too with urine
And the tube it comes out of, through the slit
That summons me before it's day each morning.[28]

28. Ibid., p. 150.

Although the imagery is grotesque, it has nevertheless much of the same expressive urgency as in Michelangelo's more noble painting, sculpture, and architecture. Sometimes Michelangelo expressed his grotesque notions casually and with more whimsy in his drawings. There are drawings of various grotesque or humorous subjects that have not traditionally been attributed to Michelangelo, perhaps because of their seemingly crude or base subject matter. One sheet (Figure 3–7), which was accepted by Wilde, and then by Hartt, includes a phallus, that "tube" Michelangelo writes about, a strange giraffelike

Figure 3–7. Michelangelo. *Miscellaneous Studies*. Ashmolean Museum, Oxford.

29. Hartt, *Michelangelo Drawings*, no. 312.

30. Ackerman, *The Architecture of Michelangelo*, pp. 112–13; and John Shearman, *Mannerism*, pp. 74–75.

31. D. C. Muecke, *Irony*, p. 4.

32. For a more general discussion of the subject, see Rosalie Colie, *Paradoxica Epidemica: The Renaissance Tradition of Paradox*.

creature, and a curious ladder, which all together convey what Hartt has referred to as a Miroesque fantasy.[29]

Returning to the Medicean works at San Lorenzo, we find that there is an element of wit in the vestibule which Michelangelo designed for the Medici Library (Figure 3–8). The expressive intensity of the vestibule, especially its dramatic staircase, is deeply moving and can be seen as the architectural counterpart to Michelangelo's emotionally charged sculpture and painting. This *terribilità* may also have been intended to evoke the grandeur and might of Michelangelo's Medici patrons. There is nevertheless a rather subtle irony underlying the grave and intense surface of the vestibule. Although columns usually support a load, Michelangelo sets his columns into the walls of the vestibule as seemingly nonstructural sculptures. Yet paradoxically and ironically, they do help to support the load. Beneath these columns Michelangelo projects powerfully expressive but unorthodox brackets that emerge from the wall as if they were sculptures. Michelangelo inverts conventional forms by making the shafts of his niches narrow at the base, and he deliberately uses fluted brackets at the bottom of the niches, although they suggest triglyphs that should be used at the top of an order.[30] Michelangelo's expressive manipulation of form is based on his sophisticated knowledge of classical forms, which the sixteenth-century beholder would have recognized and appreciated. Michelangelo's inversions of classical conventions may also be interpreted as a form of architectural parody, and his manipulations of columns and other forms is a rather unusual instance of irony in architecture. This architectural irony is interesting to reflect upon in light of D. C. Muecke's recent observations.

> It is difficult, though not impossible, for some arts to be ironical. There is, I suppose, hardly any ironical architecture or landscape gardening. One reason is not far to seek; to be ironical is to be ironical about something. Their object is not to represent things which would be to make appearances, but to make things, to construct "reality" in the shape of designs in spaces, lines, colors, stone, gold, musical sounds.[31]

Michelangelo's architecture is ironical about architecture. In the highly self-conscious cinquecento, art is frequently about art. In other words, artistic conventions are one of the subjects of art, and Michelangelo, like his contemporaries, was constantly dealing with or commenting on these conventions.

The seemingly paradoxical effects in Michelangelo's architecture, especially in his expressive use of columns in the vestibule of the Laurentian Library, is related to the appreciation of paradox during the cinquecento.[32] It can be found in the writings of Michelangelo's illustrious compatriot, Machiavelli, who writing to Guicciardini in the period when Michelangelo began the Medici Chapel, observes: "For a long time I have not said what I believed, nor do I ever believe what I say, and if sometimes I happen to tell the truth,

Figure 3–8. Michelangelo. Vestibule of the Laurentian Library. S. Lorenzo, Florence.

33. Niccolò Machiavelli, *The Chief Works and Others*, trans. Allan Gilbert, 2:973.

I hide it among so many lies that it is hard to find."[33] The question of course is whether Machiavelli is telling the truth here. Like Michelangelo, he could be profoundly serious and at the same time was capable of extraordinary irony, wit, and humor.

Machiavelli's ambiguous utterance is based on the ironic tendency of his thought, which is central to his great, influential, and ultimately mysterious book, *The Prince*. It may be in large measure the irony in this book that makes it so difficult to interpret. From the Elizabethans to Leo Strauss, critics have regarded it as an evil work, while many scholars have viewed Machiavelli's book sympathetically. Ernst Cassirer saw the book as a scientific work in political theory, analogous in its method to the work of Galileo, while Chabod, at the opposite extreme, considered it as collected political memoranda to the Medici. These and other discrepancies of interpretation are, I believe, based on the fact that the thought of the book, like much of the art and literature of the period, is deliberately ambiguous or equivocal. Perhaps Garrett Mattingly wrote with tongue in cheek when he interpreted the book as an ironic, political satire of the Medici, but if so, his observations may not have been too extreme:

> I suppose it is possible to imagine that a man who has seen his country enslaved, his life's work wrecked, and his career with it, and has, for good measure, been tortured within an inch of his life should thereupon go home and write a book intended to teach his enemies the proper way to maintain themselves, writing all the time, remember, with the passionless objectivity of a scientist in a laboratory. It must be possible to imagine such behavior, because Machiavelli scholars do imagine it and accept it without a visible tremor. But it is a little difficult for the ordinary mind to compass.[34]

34. See the brilliant but often neglected essay by Garrett Mattingly, "Machievelli's Prince: Political Science or Political Satire."

These and other questions raised by Mattingly have not been answered by Machiavelli scholars, who in fact seem to have ignored his interpretation and the question of irony in *The Prince*. Machiavelli's ironic view, especially apparent in his discussion of *fortuna*, emerges in his discussion of Cesare Borgia. Machiavelli carefully recites in detail all of Valentino's accomplishments and extols the *virtù* that made Borgia a seemingly perfect example of the ideal prince. He then undercuts his conclusion by pointing out, in a beautifully understated way, so understated in fact that the irony is usually lost on Machiavelli's readers, that Borgia forgot to take into account just one thing: that he would die just as he was on the verge of dominating Italy.

In discussing the "novelty" of the Medici Chapel architecture, Vasari remarked that Michelangelo "departed not a little from the work regulated by measure, order, and rule, which other men did according to a common use and after Vitruvius and the antiquities, to which he would not conform."[35] While the gravity of Michelangelo's irony can be compared to the irony of Machiavelli, the freedom of his architecture might also be likened to the

35. Vasari, *The Lives of the Most Eminent Painters*, 9:44.

spirit of Rabelais's writing, which is so eloquently described by Auerbach:

> But Rabelais' entire effort is directed towards playing with things and with the multiplicity of their possible aspects; upon tempting the reader out of his contemporary and definite way of regarding things, by showing him phenomena in utter confusion; upon tempting him out into the great ocean of the world in which he can swim freely, though it be at his own peril.[36]

36. Erich Auerbach, *Mimesis*, p. 242.

In the vestibule of the Medici Library, Michelangelo exhibits a freedom from the architectural conventions that limited his academic contemporaries, including his followers. Michelangelo's play with the multiplicity of meanings "in a twilight between jest and earnest"[37] connects his art to that of the greatest minds of the period including not only Rabelais but also Shakespeare and Cervantes. If Michelangelo's architecture in its playful fantasy can be called Rabelaisian, Rabelais's architecture can be called Michelangelesque. Of course Rabelais did not design buildings, but he did describe delightful architectural fantasies. They are not as emotionally expressive as Michelangelo's works, but, like a good deal of Michelangelo's architecture, they are playful and witty. Perhaps Rabelais's architecture, which is worthy of the attention of art historians, would be more appropriately called architecture *alla maniera*. We will consider Rabelais's architectural *bizzarrie* in a discussion of the painter Rosso.

37. Ibid., p. 246.

Michelangelo's conceptions of humorous works of art were not always realized in tangible forms. Like Rabelais, he sometimes simply imagined them. Thus, in the period when he was working for the Medici in Florence, he imagined a delightful burlesque of the scheme for an eighty-foot colossus to be erected by the loggia of the Medici garden. Writing to his friend, Giovan Francesco Fattucci, he noted:

> As to the colossus eighty feet high that you inform me of, which has to go or, rather, is to be put on the corner of the loggia of the Medici garden opposite Master Luigi della Stufa's corner, I have thought about it, and not a little, as you tell me; and it seems to me it doesn't go well on the aforesaid corner, because it would take up too much of the street; but on the other, where the barber shop is, it would turn out much better in my opinion, because it has the square in front and wouldn't disturb the street so much. And since maybe removing the aforesaid shop will not be tolerated, for the sake of income, I thought the aforesaid figure might be made seated, and the seat might be made high enough so the barber shop would go underneath, by making the aforesaid work hollow inside, since it is most appropriate to make it in pieces, and the rent would not be lost. And also since the aforesaid shop ought to have a way to expel the smoke, as it does not, I feel the aforesaid statue should have a horn of plenty in its hand, hollow inside, which would serve it for a chimney. Then, since I would have the head of the figure hollow inside like the other members, I think some use ought to be got out of that too, since there is a shopkeeper here on the square, a great friend of mine, who has told me in secret he would make a fine dovecote inside. Then too another notion occurs to me that would be much better, but the figure would have to be made

38. Michelangelo, *Complete Poems*, pp. 246–47. I have been told that James Beck discussed this letter in a recent College Art Association meeting.

39. Isabel Hyman, "Notes and Speculations on S. Lorenzo, Palazzo Medici, and an Urban Project by Brunelleschi."

40. Michelangelo, *Complete Poems*, p. 247.

41. Auerbach, *Mimesis*, pp. 233ff.

42. Edward Lucie-Smith and Aline Jacquiot, *The Waking Dream: Fantasy and the Surreal in Graphic Art: 1450–1900*, pl. 82.

much bigger, and it could be done, since a tower is made up of pieces, and this is that the head could serve as a bell tower for San Lorenzo, which badly needs one, and if the bells were stowed inside and the sound came out of the mouth, the aforesaid colossus would seem to be crying mercy, and especially on feast days when the ringing is more frequent and with bigger bells.[38]

As Isabel Hyman has recently suggested, there was probably an elaborate project, dating back to the time when Cosimo de' Medici returned from exile, to establish a direct relationship between the Medici palace and San Lorenzo as part of a magnificent urban setting. Vestiges of this scheme seem still to have been alive in the early cinquecento when Luca Landucci, the Florentine pharmacist, discussed his idea for the piazza San Lorenzo, and the early scheme may have been revived when Leonardo was called in after the election of Pope Leo X to provide a new magnificent design for the Medici palace. Leonardo's never-realized project, along with Michelangelo's plans for the facade of San Lorenzo, the Medici Chapel, and the Laurentian Library, was part of an elaborate attempt on the part of the Medici to celebrate their power through great works of art.[39] By facetiously proposing that the statue behind the garden of the Palazzo Medici serve as the bell tower of San Lorenzo, Michelangelo seems to make wonderful fun of Medici pretensions. But he also more specifically may have been making a farce of the recently revived scheme of magnificently linking the Medici palace and San Lorenzo. Michelangelo's delightful travesty of the pompous gigantic colossus, which is worthy of Rabelais, did not, however, amuse the papal functionary, who replied to his letter: "About the statue to be made, his Holiness would have you to understand it is the truth and not a joke, and he wishes it to be made."[40] Michelangelo's mock-colossus was of course never made, but it is an important, if ridiculous, part of a little-considered iconographic tradition in the cinquecento, the inner landscape and chambers of giants. One of the greatest scenes of Renaissance comedy, inspired by Lucian, took place inside of the mouth of Pantagruel.[41] (One can well imagine that, had they met later in papal circles in Rome, Rabelais and Michelangelo would have had much to talk about.) The cinquecento visitor to the Ariostian gardens at Bomarzo would have gaped into the forbidding mouths of gigantic, mock-heroic beasts. One also thinks of the cutting humor in the Bruegelian print of the seated giant, *Flattery*, who is approached by flatterers who enter the giant through an orifice other than his mouth.[42] Later we will return to this iconography when we consider the comical activities inside of Cellini's colossus for Francis I and note Giovanni da Bologna's delightful giant, *Appenine*, which was made for Francesco de' Medici at Pratolino, and whose interior charmed Montaigne.

Giants are also humorous in their outer aspect, and we should remember the galaxy of comic giants in the Renaissance such as Giulio Romano's giant clods at Mantua. The various versions of the ridiculous Cyclops painted in the

Renaissance are humorous, including those done by Sebastiano del Piombo (Villa Farnesina), Giulio Romano (Palazzo del Te), and Pellegrino Tibaldi (Palazzo Poggi). They all belong to the tradition of humorous giants that we encounter in the literature of the period, notably the creatures of Rabelais, and the romantic fantasies of Don Quixote, who tilted with windmills that were giants. A Hercules covered by pygmies (Graf), a comical subject based on Philostratus, was painted by Battista Dossi, brother of the more distinguished Dosso, at the court of Ferrara.[43] In short, the cinquecento was a period of gigantism in which gigantic statues and decorations and inflated hyperbole and rhetoric (be it at the court of Leo X, Francis I, or Henry VIII) celebrated great rulers as giants among men. Sometimes this kind of rhetoric was parodied, as in the ironic writing of Aretino and, perhaps in an unself-conscious way, in the autobiography of Cellini.[44] Some of the humorous giants in the panels, frescoes, and sculpture of the Italian Renaissance had a similar function, for they reveal the way in which the cinquecento, for all its inflated rhetoric and gigantism and celebration of heroic ideals, could ironically tease the grandeur of its own aspirations. The imagined giant of Michelangelo, like those of other writers and artists of the period, belongs to the extensive story of the mock-heroic in the Renaissance.

During his years in Rome, Michelangelo was friendly with and assisted the witty painter, Sebastiano del Piombo. Sebastiano, who stopped painting toward the end of his life and who lived a life of leisure (on his papal stipend) in his abode near the Porta del Popolo, is especially known for his humor and, in particular, for the joke in his letter to Michelangelo in which he suggested that a Ganymede might look nice in the cupola of the Medici Chapel. Sebastiano suggested that Michelangelo "could give him a halo so that he would appear as St. John of the Apocalypse carried to Heaven." Michelangelo's friend may have been aware of the allegorical tradition associating Ganymede and St. John, as Panofsky has suggested, but it is highly questionable whether Sebastiano took this allegory, at least in his joke to Michelangelo, as seriously as Panofsky has.[45] In earlier years, Michelangelo joked about himself in characteristic fashion when, after the death of Raphael, he tried to obtain work in the Vatican for his friend Sebastiano. Writing to Cardinal Bibbiena, the papal secretary whose sense of humor we have already noted, Michelangelo implored:

Monsignore: I beg your most reverend lordship, not as a friend or servant, since I do not deserve to be either the one or the other, but as a base, poor, crazy man, that you permit Bastiano the Venetian painter to have some part of the work in the Palace, since Raphael is dead; and if your reverend lordship feels you would be throwing away your favors on somebody like me, I think one can on rare occasions find some enjoyment even in doing a service to mad men, just as one does with onions as a change of diet when one is bored with capons.[46]

43. Felton Gibbons, *Dosso and Battista Dossi,* pl. 139.

44. I appreciate that the concept of unwitting parody is a contradiction of terms, yet I know of no better way at present to approach the psychological complexity and ambiguity of Cellini's *Life,* which need further elucidation.

45. Panofsky, *Studies in Iconology,* pp. 212ff. E. H. Gombrich has also observed that Panofsky "possibly projects too much" into Sebastiano's joke; see *Symbolic Images,* p. 200, n. 30.

46. Michelangelo, *Complete Poems,* p. 230.

47. Ibid., p. 243.

48. Ibid., pp. 58–61.

49. Cellini, *Life*, p. 145.

50. John Addington Symonds, *Renaissance in Italy*, 2:238.

51. Annibale Caro, *Gli Straccioni*, in *Commedie del Cinquecento*, Nino Borsellino, ed., 2:202–5.

52. Charles De Tolnay, *Michelangelo*, 5:19ff.

53. Vasari, *Le vite*, 7:211.

54. Jacob Bean and Felice Stempfle, *Drawings from New York Collections 1: The Italian Renaissance*, p. 78.

For all of his humor, however, Michelangelo was frequently depressed, as for example when he wrote to Sebastiano from Florence, "I came out of my melancholy a bit, or rather out of my madness."[47]

In Rome, Michelangelo was also a friend of humorous writers such as Berni and Caro. Berni, whose work we have noted probably influenced Michelangelo, wrote a long poem to Sebastiano that received an equally good-humored reply from Michelangelo, although the latter's poem was written as if Sebastiano was actually replying himself.[48] Michelangelo was also on familiar terms with the rising young *letterato*, Annibale Caro, who worked for the Farnese and who belonged to the literary circle that assembled at the home of Giovanni Gaddi, clerk of the Papal Camera. Cellini brags that both he and Sebastiano del Piombo "were admitted to their society."[49] Caro was well known for his translation of *Daphnis and Chloe*, among other works, but he also scribbled some humorous pieces:

> A "Diceria di Nasi," or discourse on noses, and a dissertation called "Ficheide," commenting on Molza's "Fichi," prove that Caro lent himself with pleasure to the academical follies of his contemporaries. It seems incredible that a learned man, who had spent the best years of his maturity in diplomatic missions to the Courts of princes, should have employed the leisure of his age in polishing these trifles. Yet such was the temper of the times that frivolity passed for commendable exercise of ingenuity.[50]

Caro also wrote a comedy, *Gli Straccioni*, which was dedicated to his Farnese patrons. It would seem from the prologue of this play that the stage set showed the Palazzo Farnese.[51] Begun by Antonio da San Gallo, this palace was of course completed by Caro's friend and fellow employee of the Farnese, Michelangelo.

Michelangelo's satirical bent is revealed in his great apocalyptic fresco, the *Last Judgment*, begun for Pope Clement VII in the Sistine Chapel.[52] Here amidst heroic grandeur and human tragedy, Michelangelo painted the papal secretary Biagio da Cesena, who, according to Vasari, so infuriated the artist that Michelangelo represented him coiled by serpents and in the pit of hell.[53] It is as if Michelangelo had painted the visual equivalent to the familiar Italian expression, "va al diavolo." In a sense, this satirical passage in Michelangelo's fresco is a kind of pictorial pasquinade, like the literary attacks on various important personages, including the popes, that were attached to the famous Pasquino statue to the south of the Piazza Navona. Michelangelo's satire brings to mind other visual pasquinades, including Federico Zuccaro's subsequent *Porta Virtutis* composition of 1580 which attacked the artist's critics in the papal household, who were likened to asses (Figure 3-9).[54] We should also remember that artists, like writers, put their pasquinades in words. In his autobiography, Benvenuto Cellini did a marvelously funny descriptive parody of the bulging muscular *Hercules* statue by his enemy, Baccio Ban-

Figure 3–9.
Federico Zuccaro.
*Study for the Porta
Virtutis.* Städelsches
Kunstinstitut, Frankfurt.

Figure 3–10.
Michelangelo. *Last Judgment* (detail), Sistine Chapel. Vatican Palace, Rome.

dinelli, to which he likened, among other things, a great sack full of melons. If we return for just another moment to the hell fires of Michelangelo's *Last Judgment*, we find that Michelangelo's devils and condemned souls are especially grotesque; for example, the skeletons that stare out of darkness or the devil at the lower right, who with his tongue stuck out, pulls down a terrified soul. His diabolical characters remind us that devils are frequently meant to be humorous, if not horrifying, in the art and literature of the Middle Ages and Renaissance. Some of his demons not only recall the grotesque devils in Signorelli's Orvieto frescoes, but can also be compared in their ridicule to the macabre humor of the witches and figures of death in the work of Baldung Grien. It is also not surprising, as we shall see, that the demonic passages of the fresco were readily transposed into caricature and parody by the brilliant mannerist, Pellegrino Tibaldi.

In the upper register of the fresco, below Christ, there appears St. Bartholomew, holding up his flayed skin (Figure 3–10). In Nicolaus Béatrizet's print after the *Last Judgment*, Michelangelo's name appears below this skin, and it has frequently been supposed that this flayed hide is a self-portrait.[55] Less certain or probable is the hypothesis that St. Bartholomew, holding the skin, portrays the brilliant Pietro Aretino, who exchanged ironical letters with Michelangelo concerning the fresco and who eventually condemned the painting. There is of course nothing humorous about Michelangelo's identifying so intensely with a martyred saint. Yet perhaps one might speak without exaggeration of this image as grotesque, for it reminds us of the similarly grotesque self-images in some of Michelangelo's poetry, where he in fact compares himself to a scarecrow. Michelangelo, as we have repeatedly seen, could play on the deepest and most serious matters, and in the end, his sense of humor brings to mind Nietzsche's insight that a joke is an "epigram on the death of a feeling."[56]

55. De Tolnay, *Michelangelo*, 5:118, n. 62.

56. From Friedrich Nietzsche, *Mixed Opinions and Maxims* in *The Portable Nietzsche*, ed. Walter Kaufmann, p. 66.

IV. *Facetiae by Raphael and His Friends*

No one should ever be ridiculed, however great an enemy he may be.
—Giovanni della Casa, *Galateo*

1. The various interpretations are given in Luitpold Dussler, *Raphael: A Critical Catalogue of His Pictures, Wall-Paintings, and Tapestries*, pp. 73ff.

2. Redig De Campos, *The "Stanze" of Raphael*, p. 20.

Whereas Michelangelo's humor is usually based on tension and pain, the comedy in the art of his contemporary, Raphael, is frequently delicate and charming, and his wit has a lighter touch. One of Raphael's greatest achievements, the *School of Athens*, belongs to the cycle of decorations done for Pope Julius II in the Stanza della Segnatura of the Vatican. The iconographical and formal complexity of these decorations has been the subject of considerable discussion.[1] The four walls of the chamber illustrate, in a subtle, complex, yet ultimately lucid way, the four faculties of learning: theology, law, poetry, and philosophy. Philosophy is visualized in the *School of Athens*. By sophisticated formal means, Raphael is able to reveal the depth of meaning in groups of figures and in single figures as is apparent in his subtle and deeply moving pair, Plato and Aristotle, who are the formal and iconographical focal point of the fresco. Here we find the reconciliation through gestures, glances, colors, and linear configurations of related yet divergent philosophies; cosmology and ethics, heaven and earth, and spirit and matter are harmonized. There is also an element of wit in Raphael's manipulation of form, and content, especially in his invention of Heraclitus (added after the Ambrosiana cartoon), who is seated on the steps toward the center of the fresco (Figure 4–1). It has been observed that not only does the figure reflect the influence of Michelangelo but also that Raphael's Heraclitus may actually be a portrait of Michelangelo.[2] Raphael's Heraclitus-Michelangelo is a variation on Michelangelo's Jeremiah in the Sistine ceiling. The brooding attitude of the prophet was not only an appropriate form for the melancholic philosopher but was also an appropriate form for Michelangelo himself. Raphael's ingenuity in manipulating both the form and content of the Heraclitus transcends mere cleverness, yet there is an analogy between his wit and the double meanings in the word play of courtiers described by his courtier friend, Castiglione. One suspects that the topical, double reference to Michelangelo by Raphael in his great fresco would have elicited at least a knowing smile from the courtiers of Julius II.

If Raphael's sense of humor was frequently delicate, it could also be less than subtle. According to Castiglione in *The Book of the Courtier*, Bibbiena recounted a blunt joke on the part of their mutual friend, Raphael.

Figure 4–1. Raphael. *School of Athens* (detail of Heraclitus). Stanza della Segnatura, Vatican Palace, Rome.

3. Baldesar Castiglione, *The Book of the Courtier*, trans. Charles Singleton, p. 173.

... the painter Raphael replied to two cardinals with whom he was on familiar terms and who in his presence (in order to make him talk) were finding fault with a picture he had painted—in which St. Peter and St. Paul were shown—saying that the two figures were too red in the face. Then Raphael replied at once: "Gentlemen, you must not wonder at this, for I have made them so quite on purpose, since we believe that St. Peter and St. Paul are as red in heaven as you see them here, out of the shame that their church should be governed by men such as you.[3]

According to Vasari, Raphael received assistance in the design of the noble architecture for the *School of Athens* from the papal architect, Bramante, who along with Raphael and Michelangelo was employed by Pope Julius II to create works celebrating the grandeur and power of his reign as a second Caesar. Bramante, who began the vast and splendid papal villa "Belvedere," as well as the new St. Peter's, planned also to adorn the former in hieroglyphs, including both his name and the pope's. Bramante's hieroglyph, which may have been influenced by an inscription in Colonna's *Hypnerotomachia Poliphili*, as Gombrich suggests, was rejected and burlesqued by the pope, who laughed at the architect's scheme:

> The fancy took Bramante to make, in a frieze in the outer facade of the Belvedere, some letters after the manner of ancient hieroglyphs, representing the name of the Pope and his own, in order to show his ingenuity; and he had begun thus: 'Julius II, Pont. Max.', having caused a head in profile of Julius Caesar to be made, and a bridge with two arches, which signified, 'Julius II, Pont.', and an obelisk from the Circus Maximus to represent 'Max'. At which the Pope laughed, and caused him to make letters in the ancient manner, one braccio in height, which are still there to this day, saying that he had copied this folly from a door at Viterbo. There one Maestro Francesco, an architect, had placed his name, carved in the architrave, and represented by a St. Francis (Francesco), an arch (*arco*), a roof (*tetto*), and a tower (*torre*), which interpreted in his own way, denoted 'Maestro Francesco Architettore'.[4]

4. E. H. Gombrich, "Hypnerotomachiana," *Journal of the Warburg and Courtauld Institutes* 14 (1951): 120ff; reprinted in *Symbolic Images*, pp. 102ff.

The papal patron no doubt appreciated the wit and humor of the artists who worked for him and could also joke himself.

Pope Julius not only did not approve of Bramante's hieroglyphs, he also rejected the scheme to align the papal villa along the same axis as the new church of St. Peter's, a project that would have been too bold. Nevertheless, just the idea of building a new St. Peter's in place of the venerable Early Christian church was in itself so audacious that this project and other vices of the pope were ridiculed in a dialogue attributed to Erasmus, *Julius exclusus*.[5] The great Dutch humanist was in Rome in the early cinquecento, and he was a friend there of Johan Goritz, the patron of Raphael, and of Tommaso Inghirami, who may have furnished Raphael with the literary scheme for the Stanza della Segnatura frescoes and who sat for a portrait by Raphael.[6] Even

5. Erasmus, *The Julius exclusus of Erasmus*, trans. P. Pascal, pp. 88–89.

6. Paul Künzle, "Raffaels Denkmal für Fedro Inghirami auf dem Letzten Arazzo," *Mélanges Eugène Tesserant*.

if the dialogue is not by Erasmus, it certainly has a sharp Erasmian tone. In it we find the mighty and *terribile* Julius II at the gate of Paradise not allowed entry by St. Peter, who reminds the militant and imperial pontiff of his sinful acts, which include the erection of a new St. Peter's in place of the original church.

During his years in Rome, Raphael painted a portrait of his friend, Cardinal Bibbiena, which is now in the Palazzo Pitti in Florence.[7] Bibbiena, who was a secretary to Leo X, was also the author of the comedy, *La Calandria*, which was performed in the Vatican for Pope Leo in 1514. As we have already seen, Bibbiena also discussed wit and humor at great length in *The Book of the Courtier*, and according to Castiglione, "several times he promised us he would write on this subject."[8] Bibbiena's portrayal as an elegant and noble figure is reminiscent of Raphael's portrait of Castiglione. Each embodies the ideal of the perfect courtier. However, in the portrait of Bibbiena, Raphael incorporated a slight smile into Bibbiena's expression as an indication of his sense of humor. Raphael's subtle allusion to Bibbiena's humor might be compared to the similar effect in various portraits of the great ironist, Erasmus, that were painted during the same period.[9]

Raphael decorated the bath of his friend, Bibbiena, in the Vatican. These decorations consist of grotesques and scenes depicting the powers of love.[10] *Amorini* play capriciously in the scene of Vulcan forging Cupid's arrows, and there are various comic masks and other bizarre passages, the meanings of which are still obscure. For example, a bearded figure, who is perhaps Diogenes the cynic, is holding up a lantern. And an *amorino* rides a chariot led by a snail. Then there is a stork that stabs the snout of a boar with its long bill. These images, which recall the marginalia of medieval illuminated manuscripts, are witty in their visual form and suggest implicit wit in their verbal meaning that remains to be discovered.[11] They may also allude to private jokes between the erudite Bibbiena, Leo X, and his circle, in a manner similar to those between the lines of *The Book of the Courtier*. The playful and erotic tone of these frescoes also conforms to the similar taste underlying Bibbiena's *La Calandria*, which abounds in comic erotica. Bibbiena's Plautine comedy plays on mistaken identities and sexual ambiguities (between *Lidio maschio* and *Lidio femina*), which are alluded to in the speech of the exasperated necromancer, Ruffo, at the end of Act IV, scene ii:

> Rest in peace. With much reason is Love painted blind because he who loves never sees the truth. She [Fulvia] is blinded by love so that she thinks a spirit can make a person both female and male: as if there were nothing more to do than cut off the "root" of a man and make it into a cleft and so make a woman; and to resew the "mouth" from below and add a prick (*bischero*) and make a man. Oh, oh, oh! the credulity of love! Here are Lidio and Fannio already undressed.[12]

7. Dussler, *Raphael*, pl. 92.

8. Castiglione, *The Book of the Courtier*, p. 143.

9. For example, Charles Cuttler, *Northern Painting*, pl. 547.

10. Hans Dollmayr, "Lo Stanzino del Cardinal Bibbiena."

11. Various examples are given in Lillian Randall, *Images in the Margins of Gothic Manuscripts*.

12. Bernardo Dovizi da Bibbiena, *La Calandria*, in *Commedie del Cinquecento*, ed. Nino Borsellino, 2:79.

As improbable as it might seem, some of the grotesques by Raphael in the Vatican, especially in the Loggia for Leo X, might be compared to the fantastic and grotesque details in paintings of the same period by Hieronymus Bosch such as *The Garden of Delights* in the Prado. Raphael's grotesques are cheerful and sensual in their wit, while Bosch's forms are part of a more grim and macabre humor. Raphael's grotesques are a playful decorative background to a celebration of love, whereas Bosch's are part of a condemnation, if ambiguous, of love. Nevertheless, one suspects that Bosch, whose work was enjoyed by Philip II, was popular in the sixteenth century because of the grotesque wit underlying his bizarre and fantastic creatures. The fact that Fra José Siqüenza later referred to the maccheronic character of Bosch's work is suggestive of this taste.[13] In Raphael's frescoes we find strange plants ingeniously interwoven with exotic beasts such as sphinxes and griffins, which are strikingly like some of the beasts in Bosch's work. However terrifying Bosch's imagery may have been, it was humorous, and this grotesque humor was surely appreciated in the sixteenth century.[14] The various fruits and animals of Bosch may have had meanings that now elude art historians, but like Raphael's grotesques they remain ridiculous or laughable.

Raphael also painted humorous works in the villa of Agostino Chigi, the wealthy banker who was a friend of Pope Leo X. It has been observed that these works, as well as the decorations in the villa by the Sienese painters, Sodoma and Peruzzi, are largely about love.[15] Less attention is paid to the fact that they are also generally playful.[16] The rooms of Chigi's magnificent villa are filled with a laughter-provoking playfulness, just as are the pages of Castiglione's *The Book of the Courtier*. In the Sala di Galatea, Raphael painted Galatea fleeing from the Polyphemus done by Sebastiano del Piombo, Michelangelo's witty friend (Figure 4–2, 4–3). A moral allegory in Raphael's fresco seems to be emblematically stated in the detail of the dolphin beneath Galatea which is devouring an octopus.[17] According to Oppian's third-century *Halieutica*, the probable source for this detail, the benevolent dolphin was associated with love and the octopus with bestiality. Thus, this detail could allude to the triumph of Love (Galatea) over Lust (Polyphemus). Since Raphael seems to acknowledge Castiglione's influence on the fresco, we might consider the possibility that Raphael's learned friend furnished him with this emblematic conceit.[18] The familiar tale of Galatea and Polyphemus was told in antiquity by Theocritus and Ovid and in the Renaissance by Poliziano, and frequently the ugly giant was mocked. Raphael's Galatea appears to be fleeing from Sebastiano's brutish, Michelangelesque Cyclops, who sits dolefully upon the shore. There is something incongruous, if not grotesque, about the "humorous sadness" (to borrow a phrase from Shakespeare)[19] of this one-eyed monster pining over the beautiful Galatea. One suspects that Sebastiano's cloddish

13. Fra José Siqüenza, "History of the Order of St. Jerome," in *Bosch in Perspective*, pp. 34–41.

14. Ludwig Baldass, *Hieronymous Bosch*.

15. John Shearman, "Die Loggia der Psyche in der Villa Farnesina und die Probleme der letzten Phase von Raffaels graphischem Stil."

16. Oskar Fischel, *Raphael*, pp. 166, 186; and Philipp Fehl, "Raphael as Archeologist."

17. Duncan Kinkead, "An iconographic note on Raphael's *Galatea*."

18. Raffaello Sanzio, "Letter to Count Baldassare Castiglione," in *Italian Art: 1500–1600*, pp. 32–33.

19. *As You Like It*, act IV, scene i, l. 19.

Figure 4–2. Raphael. *Galatea*. Villa Farnesina, Rome.

Figure 4–3. Sebastiano del Piombo. *Polyphemus*. Villa Farnesina, Rome.

giant would also have evoked in the beholder's mind Ovid's well-known image of the Cyclops:

> There on a green plateau the burning Cyclops
> Sat at his restless ease, his sheep neglected;
> And though they followed him, they seemed to drift astray.
> He dropped his walking stick, a huge pine tree
> That should have been a mast for some fair ship,
> Then in an absent-minded mood he raised
> His home-made pipes, plucked from a hundred reeds.
> As he made music, all the mountains trembled;
> So did the waves.[20]

20. Ovid, *Metamorphoses*, trans. Horace Gregory, p. 374.

As the love-sick giant pines for his love, Galatea sails away from him. Her flight is aided, as Meiss noted, by technology, for her dolphin-powered barque also has a paddle wheel.[21] The *amorini* in Raphael's fresco contribute a playful tone to the image, relating to the tone of the poets who told the same tale.

21. Millard Meiss, *The Painter's Choice*, pp. 203ff.

That Polyphemus was the subject of ridicule can also be seen from a satire written in Rome at about the same time that Raphael painted the *Galatea*. Shortly after the famous Capitoline festivities of 1513, celebrating Pope Leo X's brother, Giuliano de' Medici, Giulio Simone Siculo composed four hundred supposedly uninspired hexameters on this celebration. Although the poet was given a well-paid professorship by Leo X, a number of *letterati* composed a satirical, scholarly commentary on Siculo's poem. In their accompanying biography they pointed out not only that Siculo was the child of a priest and a nun but also that he was ultimately descended from a goat and Polyphemus.[22] Polyphemus was also ridiculed in the same period by Erasmus. When the Northern humanist mocked the excessive number of saints, he called St. Christopher the Polyphemus of Christians, and both in his *Adages* and *Colloquies* he invoked Polyphemus in the proverb about something outlandish or very inappropriate: "What a sight! Bacchus in a lion's skin—Polyphemus with a book—a cat in a saffron gown."[23]

22. Bonner Mitchell, *Rome in the High Renaissance*, p. 91.

23. Erasmus, *The Colloquies*, trans. C. R. Thompson , p. 416.

Raphael also decorated a loggia in Chigi's villa with frescoes representing the myth of Cupid and Psyche. Although Panofsky has suggested a Neoplatonic interpretation of these frescoes, they do not appear to relate to the Neoplatonic interpretation of the myth that can be traced back to Fulgentius.[24] Raphael's frescoes are sensuous and convey a sense of the *voluptas* found both in ancient art and in Apuleius's tale of Cupid and Psyche in his *Metamorphoses*. The beautiful nude figures, the sumptuous festoons of fruits, and the elaborate painted tapestries convey this effect. The predominantly spirited and playful tone in this work can be seen in the various *amorini* who fly across the painted sky. There is also a decisive element of satire in the narrative scenes, as Charles Dempsey has recently stressed.[25] Raphael depicts Jupiter implanting a grisly kiss on the cheek of Cupid, while putting too much weight

24. Erwin Panofsky, *Renaissance and Renascences in Western Art*, p. 191, n. 3.

25. Charles Dempsey, " 'Et Nos Cedamus Amori': Observations on the Farnese Gallery," pp. 363–74.

Figure 4–4. Raphael. *Jupiter and Cupid*, Loggia di Psiche. Villa Farnesina, Rome.

on his bedraggled eagle (Figure 4–4). Raphael mocks the frustration of Venus who throws her arms up in amazement when Psyche returns successfully with the urn of Stygian water (Figure 4–5). Venus's attempts to thwart the affair between her son, Cupid, and Psyche fail, and Raphael humorously dwells on her frustration and defeat. Raphael's mockery of Venus, which is in the tradition of satires of the gods by Botticelli, Piero di Cosimo, and Michelangelo, can also be compared in its general tone to the mockery of the goddess of love in Erasmus's *The Praise of Folly*: "Why Venus ever in her prime, but because of her affinity with me. Witness that color of her hair, so resembling my father, from whence she is called the golden Venus; and lastly, her laughing, if you give any credit to the poets, or their followers the statuaries."[26]

26. Erasmus, *The Praise of Folly*, trans. John Wilson, p. 24.

In the end, Cupid is triumphant and is united with Psyche as shown in scenes within simulated tapestries depicted by Raphael's students in the vault. The theme of triumphant Love is sustained by flying cupids in the lunettes, who bear the spoils that Love has won from the other gods. Their playful tone reflects the spirit of classical epigrams such as the following one by Philippus:

> Look how the Loves, having plundered Olympus, deck themselves in the arms of the immortals, exulting their spoils. They bear the bow of Phoebus, the thunderbolt of Zeus, the shield and helmet of Ares, the club of Hercules, the three-pronged spear of the sea-god, the thryse of Bacchus, Hermes' winged sandals, and Artemis' torches. Mortals need not grieve that they must yield to the arrows of the Loves, if the gods have given them their arms wherewith to busk themselves.[27]

27. Dempsey, " 'Et Nos Cedamus Amori,' " p. 367.

Even in the smallest details of the vault there are hints of humor. Both Middeldorf and Oberhuber have suggested that in the sumptuously painted festoons the figs and cucumbers, traditional sexual symbols, may have been intended as playful sexual allusions, appropriate to the iconography.[28] Fruits and vegetables do not necessarily have to have sexual implications; they seem not to, for example, in the witty metamorphic portraits by Arcimboldo. But they frequently do in the sixteenth-century poetry of Berni and others, including the Florentine painter-poet, Bronzino, who makes phallic jokes in his poems on the radish and the onion.[29] The sexual jokes in Raphael's decorations, which are appropriate in tone to the sensuousness of Apuleius's tale, also bring to mind an actual joke about the Farnesina frescoes supposedly told by Raphael, according to the sixteenth-century author of a joke book, Ludovico Domenichi. The joke presupposes the error that Raphael, not Sebastiano del Piombo, painted the Polyphemus for Chigi. According to this *barzelletta*, a lady praised Raphael's frescoes but complained that for the sake of his reputation the artist should have painted a nice rose or figleaf over the shame of Mercury. The smiling Raphael then said, "Pardon me, madam, that I did not think of this . . . . But why did you not suggest that I should do the same

28. These observations were made in conversations by Middeldorf and Oberhuber. Middeldorf has further noted a work potentially valuable for the study of sexual symbolism in Renaissance art and literature, Nora Galli dè Paratesi, *Semantica dell'Eufemismo*, Turin, 1964.

29. Agnolo Allori detto il Bronzino, *Li Capitoli Faceti*, pp. 399–402, 319–46.

Figure 4–5. Raphael. *Venus and Psyche*, Loggia di Psiche. Villa Farnesina, Rome.

thing for Polyphemus, whom you praised so much, and whose shame is so much larger?"[30]

The very subject of Raphael's frescoes might have had a particular meaning or made specific allusions. Konrad Oberhuber has put forward the enticing hypothesis that Raphael's decorations may allude to or celebrate Chigi's wedding to his mistress, Francesca Oderaschi.[31] Although the frescoes cannot be precisely dated, it is generally believed that Raphael and his assistants worked on them through 1518, months before the actual marriage in 1519.[32] Since Chigi thought of himself as a modern Cupid and may well have conceived of his villa as like the magnificent palace of Cupid described by Apuleius,[33] it does not seem unreasonable to suppose that the union of Cupid and Psyche and their wedding feast, which are prominent in Raphael's decorations, refer to Chigi's own nuptials. Various aspects of the decorations can be related to the conventions of nuptial festivities. The story of Cupid and Psyche was appropriate to marriage celebrations and was enacted as *intermezzi* on the occasion of Francesco de' Medici's wedding to Joanna d'Austria.[34] The *amorini* in the vault are related to the Loves who were depicted in the Medici palace on the occasion of Duke Cosimo's wedding to Elenora da Toledo.[35]

Raphael's playful cupids, who celebrate the triumph of love, are also reminiscent of the festive *amorini* in epithalamia. The sexual allusions in Raphael's frescoes are also not out of place in a nuptial celebration. This playful and priapean eroticism informs the very customs of Renaissance marriage celebrations as witnessed in Jonson's *The New Inn* where the bridegroom, Beaufort, playfully tosses off his codpiece points.[36] According to the mythological tale depicted by Raphael, Cupid and Psyche were united by Jupiter, reminding us, if coincidentally, that Chigi and his bride were wed by a very jovial individual, Pope Leo X. The playful teasing and joking of Raphael's frescoes would no doubt have delighted the pope.

Agostino Chigi also commissioned witty and humorous frescoes for his villa from the two Sienese artists, Peruzzi and Sodoma, who worked in Rome in the shadow of Michelangelo and Raphael. On the ground floor of the villa, Peruzzi did a frieze with scenes from Ovid, including a scene of excited satyrs gazing down upon a sleeping nymph, who is scantily draped.[37] The subject is akin to one depicted by Raphael in the Stufetta of Cardinal Bibbiena and to countless other works, including those by Giovanni da Bologna and Annibale Carracci discussed below. But this passage in Peruzzi's frieze is more than simply an erotic detail. Peruzzi mocks the lecherous expression of the one satyr and the not very subtle excitation of the other. As Otto Brendel pointed out in a discussion of Greek art, which alludes to the erotic in general, "The illustration of sexual actions may imply an element of ridicule, satire, or caricature. What satyrs do is funny by Greek standards. The not-quite-humans ape the humans—or is it vice versa?"[38]

30. Poggio Bracciolini, *The Facetiae of Poggio*, trans. Edward Storer, pp. 159–60.

31. This hypothesis was first put forward by Konrad Oberhuber. Oberhuber has further observed the possibility that the labors of Psyche may also have alluded to the trials of Chigi's mistress.

32. Dussler, *Raphael*, p. 99.

33. Shearman, "Die Loggia der Psyche," p. 60.

34. Giorgio Vasari, *Le vite dè più eccellenti pittori scultori et architettori*, ed. Gaetano Milanesi, 8:572. Cupid and Psyche stood for Francesco de' Medici and his bride, Joanna; A. M. Nagler, *Theatre Festivals of the Medici, 1539–1637*, p. 64.

35. Andrew C. Minor and Bonner Mitchell, *A Renaissance Entertainment*, p. 224.

36. Ben Jonson, *The Works of Ben Jonson*, p. 542.

37. Sydney J. Freedberg, *Painting of the High Renaissance in Rome and Florence*, 2: pls. 478ff.

38. Otto Brendel, "The Scope and Temperament of Erotic Art in the Greco-Roman World," in *Studies in Erotic Art*, p. 17.

39. Fritz Saxl, *Lectures*, 1:189ff.

40. Freedberg, *Painting of the High Renaissance*, 2: pl. 185.

41. Ibid., pl. 88.

42. Lorenzo de' Medici, *Opere*, ed. Attilio Simoni, 2:16.

43. Christolph Frommel, *Baldassare Peruzzi als Maler und Zeichner*, cat. no. 125.

In the ceiling of the room that takes its name from Raphael's *Galatea*, the Sala di Galatea, Peruzzi also painted an elaborate astrological configuration that Saxl suggested celebrates the birthdate of Chigi.[39] Peruzzi's depictions of mythological figures here are done with considerable charm. In the center of the ceiling, figures who have already been turned to stone by the Gorgon gaze up as if still alive, while Perseus slays the wicked culprit.[40] This kind of play between stone and lifelike figures recalls the similarly ambiguous wit in the work of Mantegna and Filippino Lippi. The faces of Peruzzi's stone people, especially of the older ones, are delightful caricatures. In his illustration of Venus in Capricorn, Peruzzi presents a coy and languid Venus who seductively stares out at the beholder as she tilts her head to comb her hair.[41] Not only the languid rhythms of her body but the slow rhythmical flight of the doves beside her contribute to this effect. She is the seductive Venus whom we have already encountered in Lorenzo de' Medici's *Amori di Marte e Venere* propositioning Mars: "Come, for nude and in bed I invite you;/ don't dally for the time passes by."[42] Once again Venus is the subject of gentle satire. If in Raphael's loggia the goddess's jealousy was mocked, here in Peruzzi's decoration her coy seductiveness is playfully teased.

In the *salone* of the *piano nobile*, Peruzzi produced a brilliant and witty piece of illusionism in the tradition of Mantegna, but more specifically of Raphael (Figure 4–6). He painted the architecture of an open loggia like the loggias of the villa itself and a view beyond the loggia of Rome as it might have been seen from Chigi's villa. These frescoes, which may convey something of the kind of illusionism that Peruzzi used in his stage sets for Bibbiena's *La Calandria*, performed in the Vatican in 1514, play on the very nature of illusionism. They project an intensely plausible illusion of reality but ultimately leave the beholder with the knowledge that this illusion is merely a fiction. Like subsequent mannerist art, which expressed the sophisticated courtly taste of Rome, Peruzzi's frescoes imply a self-conscious attitude toward reality and the relationship between art and reality. Peruzzi's frescoes, like those of Mantegna before and the mannerists later, would have been regarded as a tour de force of wit by his contemporaries. They might well have been thought of in terms of the ingenious illusionistic paintings of the ancients described by Pliny that were frequently discussed by the Renaissance writers, including the playful Rabelais.[43] In speaking of the theatrical character of Peruzzi's illusionistic frescoes, we should note that theatrical performances were actually put on in Chigi's villa; for example, the correspondent in Rome of Isabella d'Este observed that in July 1512 there was in Chigi's villa a "rapresentatione pastorale" performed by "putti e putte senesi." The spectators were probably seated in the gardens and looked toward the villa with its open loggia and painted facade with mythological subjects. As Chastel has suggested, the villa itself may have functioned as a kind of *frons scaenae*, and as he

Figure 4–6. Baldassare Peruzzi. Sala delle Prospettive. Villa Farnesina, Rome.

Figure 4–7. Baldassare Peruzzi. *The Purge of Mercury*. Cabinet des Dessins, Louvre, Paris.

44. André Chastel, "Cortile et Théatre," *Le Lieu Théâtral à la Renaissance*, pp. 41–42.

45. Vasari, *Le vite*, 3:610.

further suggests, one might well suppose that Peruzzi, who built Chigi's villa and helped to decorate it, was responsible for the idea of its "theatrical architecture."[44]

Although we can only imagine the character of Peruzzi's stage set designs from the illusionism of his Sala delle Prospettive frescoes, there is a drawing by Peruzzi, *The Purge of Mercury*, which seems to be related to the comic stage in two respects (Figure 4–7). First, the architectural background of classical buildings is like the architectural settings of stage design (seen in other drawings by Peruzzi), and second, the delightfully grotesque characters in the foreground, who give an enema to a statue of Mercury, have caricatural features that are closely related to the types of the *commedia dell'arte*. It may not be too much to suppose that Peruzzi's drawing allows us to perceive something of the Italian comic theater in the cinquecento, in the vein of Ruzzante and his contemporaries. Although Vasari suggested that the drawing is a satire on alchemists, its meaning is obscure and warrants further study.[45] A number of figures in it administer a purge to Mercury by blowing through a tube that is aimed at Mercury's bottom. The subject of the drawing is generally related to a pervasive phenomenon in the art of the sixteenth century (which has remained outside the compass of traditional iconographical considerations)— the special attention given to buttocks, which Detlef Heikamp has aptly characterized as *buchismo*.[46] It is found, for example, in Parmigianino's *Cupid Carving His Bow* (see Figure 5-14) and his drawing of Ganymede, Bronzino's *Venus, Cupid, Folly, and Time* (see Figure 6-3), Rabelais's *Gargantua*, and in Bosch's *Garden of Delights*, as it was earlier in medieval art such as Giovannino dei Grassi's Bergamo sketchbook, or later in the work of Callot and Hogarth.[47]

In the Villa Farnesina, we find that Peruzzi also painted scenes from Ovid in a frieze around the upper walls of the *salone*.[48] A number of painted caryatids punctuate the intense, sometimes capricious rhythms of these decorations. These creatures gesture humorously, as if alive, although they are supposedly of stone. Peruzzi uses a comic approach in the scene of Deucalion and Pyrrha, who turn stones into humans after the flood (Figure 4-8). These figures are bizarre in their coarse features and awkward shapes, and their transformation of stones into humans is made to appear somewhat ridiculous. In another scene we see a puffed and drunken Silenus, like the characterizations of Piero di Cosimo and Lorenzo de' Medici, following Bacchus and Ariadne (Figure 4-9). Both of these scenes are typical of the spirit that pervades the entire frieze.

In the bedroom of Agostino Chigi, adjacent to the *salone* decorated by Peruzzi, Sodoma depicted the wedding of Alexander and Roxanne, adapting a composition of Raphael that was based on Lucian's description of a painting of the *Marriage of Alexander and Roxanne* (Figure 4-10).[49] The playful humor of Sodoma's personality was recognized by his contemporaries. We have already noted that the monks of Monte Oliveto referred to him as Mattaccio (The Little Fool). Moreover, Vasari tells us that Sodoma's mocking personality delighted his patron, Chigi.

> ...he always made a mock of everything and worked as his fancy took him, caring for nothing so much as for dressing pompously, wearing brocaded coats, capes adorned with gold cloth, the richest necklaces and similar trifles, stuff for buffoons and mountebanks, all of which caused Agostino Chigi, who liked his whims, the greatest amusement in the world.[50]

In Sodoma's fresco, Alexander approaches the demure and chaste bride, who is seated upon a bed. A continuum between the real bedroom of Chigi and the painted bedroom is implied by a painted balustrade, which is similar in its intentions to Peruzzi's painted architecture in the *salone*. As Alexander approaches Roxanne, a host of *amorini*, fools of the boudoir and extensions of Sodoma's comic personality, fly around and caper. They relate to Lucian just as the little satyrs in Botticelli's *Mars and Venus* do. Some play with Alexan-

Figure 5-14, p. 129

46. This term was used in conversation by Detlef Heikamp, who was referring to Florentine painting.

47. For example, *The Punishment inflicted on Lemuel Gulliver*, illustrated in Ronald Paulson, *William Hogarth: His Life, Art and Times*, 1:171, pl. 57.

48. The decoration is fully discussed by Frommel, *Baldassare Peruzzi*, cat. no. 31.

49. Andrée Hayum, "A New Dating for Sodoma's Frescoes in the Villa Farnesina"; and Andrée Hayum, *Giovanni Antonio Bazzi-"il Sodoma,"* p. 171.

50. Giorgio Vasari, *The Lives of the Most Eminent Painters, Sculptors, and Architects*, trans. Gaston De Vere, 6:386–87.

Figure 6–3, p. 146

Figure 4–8. Baldassare Peruzzi. *Deucalion and Pyrrha*, Sala delle Prospettive. Villa Farnesina, Rome.

Figure 4–9. Baldassare Peruzzi. *Bacchus and Ariadne*, Sala delle Prospettive. Villa Farnesina, Rome.

Figure 4-10. Sodoma. *Marriage of Alexander and Roxanne*. Villa Farnesina, Rome.

der's armor, others play peek-a-boo above the canopy of the bed, and others twist and turn in elaborate and contorted postures, which seem almost to be variations on the twisting *putti* and *Ignudi* in the Sistine ceiling. This playful spirit is also seen closer to the nuptial bed. In contrast to the extreme modesty of Roxanne, who is being undressed, a servant to the left leans forward with a lecherous smile upon her lips, perhaps making an illusion to the sexual union of the bride and bridegroom. This slight touch of the bawdy, reminiscent of Renaissance marriage customs, is also connected to the sexual humor in Raphael's Cupid and Psyche loggia.[51]

Sodoma's bedroom fresco might again be seen in the context of Chigi's life. It has only casually been noted that Sodoma's fresco, like Raphael's Cupid and Psyche decorations, dates from the period of Chigi's wedding.[52] Indeed, the very subject of Sodoma's fresco suggests its association to a marriage, and details of the fresco again relate to the conventions of nuptial literature and art. The representation of the bashful bride at the nuptial couch, the appearance of Hymen, the sporting of cupids, and the sensual tone of the fresco all conform to the similar elements in epithalamia from Catullus to Spenser and Jonson. As we gaze at Sodoma's exalted nuptial fresco for Chigi, we should ask whether there was at least a touch of irony in the association of his own wedding to that of the ancient hero. If so, the ironic tone here might be associated to the teasing tone of other decorations in the villa, especially the Cupid and Psyche frescoes, where Cupid seems to have playfully symbolized Chigi.

The striking illusionism of Sodoma's fresco is especially apparent in the mirror painted behind the bed of Alexander and Roxanne. Here we see reflected the image of a bed, presumably a reflection of Chigi's actual bed, with the curtains drawn! As we contemplate the significance of this detail we should recall that not only had his bride, Francesca, graced Chigi's couch for years as his mistress, but the distinguished courtesan, Imperia, is reputed to have also spent some time there. Upon her death Biagio Palladio composed the witty epitaph, "Mars gave imperial rule to Rome, and Venus gave us Imperia."[53] The "reflection" of Chigi's bed in Sodoma's fresco reminds us that Chigi paid 1,592 ducats for a bed of iron and silver.[54] Sodoma's bedroom fresco and the other decorations of the villa convey something of the *pompa* that, according to Aretino, bedazzled Pope Leo X on more than one occasion ("più volte fece stupir Leone").[55] If painting during the Renaissance increasingly reflected the personality of the artist, we might also add that the decoration of an entire villa could express the personality of the patron. Chigi's *impresa* was an *amorino*, and we have seen *amorini* flying throughout Chigi's villa. Many of these little creatures still grace the facade. If we cannot witness the splendor of Chigi's banquets, the charming humor of his theatrical festivities, and the playful joking of his entourage, we can capture a fleeting glimpse

51. The vulgar character of marriage celebrations is discussed in general by Johan Huizinga, *The Waning of the Middle Ages*, p. 109.

52. Hayum, *"Il Sodoma,"* p. 171.

53. Cronin, *The Flowering of the Renaissance*, p. 60.

54. Ibid., 69.

55. Pietro Aretino, *Il primo libro delle lettere*, ed. Fausto Nicolini, p. 192.

of this life as it was celebrated and immortalized on the walls of his villa by Raphael, Peruzzi, and Sodoma.

The taste of Chigi can be associated with that of his friend, Leo X, who enjoyed the comedies of Ariosto and Bibbiena. And, as noted above, the tone of the decorations done for Chigi also brings to mind Castiglione's *The Book of the Courtier*. Too often so much attention is paid to Castiglione's definition of the ideal courtier that the pervasive playful spirit of the book is neglected. Yet Castiglione describes the continual laughter and irony of the court. Speech after speech in the book is filled with playful wit as sophisticated and pervasive as the comedy in the paintings of Castiglione's friend, Raphael. This gay spirit is typified, for example, by the ladies of the court who jocularly attack their satirical nemesis, signor Gasparo, treating him "as the bacchantes treated Orpheus."[56] And Castiglione reports that after Bembo's famous, frenzied speech on Neoplatonic love, the duchess ironically plucked Bembo by the hem of his robe, remarking, "Take care, messer Pietro, that with these thoughts your soul, too, does not forsake your body."[57] This kind of satire of the idealizing Neoplatonic philosophy of love was to be made more sharply later in the century by a young man in the entourage of Chigi, Pietro Aretino.

Let us consider a late work by Raphael that is now lost and thus has been little discussed. In 1519 Raphael is reported to have done a painting of Leo X's buffoon, Fra Mariano, as part of the decorations for the 8 March performance of Ariosto's *Suppositi* before the pope in the Castel Sant'Angelo. According to the Ferrarese ambassador, Alfonso Paolucci, the painting showed the buffoon attacked by devils and included an inscription, "Questi sono li capricci de Fra Mariano" ("These are the caprices of Fra Mariano"). Paolucci's description of the performance of Ariosto's play gives us insight into the situation in which Raphael's image was seen.

> When the audience was seated the pipers began to play, and the curtain was raised. During the music the pope looked through his glass at the stage, on which Raphael had painted the town of Ferrara in perspective. Artistic candelabra with five lights in each were arranged to form the monogram of Leo X. First of all entered a messenger, who spoke the prologue and made jests about the title of the comedy, at which the Pope and those near him laughed heartily, though I understand that some Frenchmen were offended.[58]

We may not know what Raphael's painting of Fra Mariano looked like, but we can gain some sense of its tone by considering its subject and the jocular taste of his patron, Leo X. We know from Aretino and Ludovico Domenichi, author of a Renaissance joke book, that Leo X delighted in jokes, buffoons, and jesters. According to Domenichi, Leo X's domestic *cameriere*, Serapica, "had the authority to introduce into his room at any hour, mad men, jesters, and similar diverting types."[59] Fra Mariano, who along with Serafino of

56. Castiglione, *The Book of the Courtier*, pp. 193–94.

57. Ibid., 357.

58. Ludwig Pastor, *The History of the Popes*, 8:155–56. That Raphael actually painted the *Fra Mariano* was doubted by Domenico Gnoli, "Raffaello alla corte di Leone X," p. 584.

59. Most of what follows on Fra Mariano comes from Arturo Graf, "Un buffone di Leone X," in *Attraverso il Cinquecento*, pp. 299ff. Serapica is discussed on p. 300.

Urbino was considered among the leading buffoons of his day, was praised by Bibbiena in Castiglione's *The Book of the Courtier*, and his name is also invoked by Castiglione in a discussion of the pleasure of folly: "And if the vein of folly which we discover chances to be so abundant that it seems beyond repair, we will encourage it, and according to the doctrine of Fra Mariano, we shall have saved a soul, which will be no small gain."[60]

There are countless stories of Fra Mariano's humorous *capricci*. One of them is alluded to by Bibbiena in *The Book of the Courtier*, "For I was once turned into a spring, not by any of the ancient gods, but by our friend Fra Mariano, and never since have I lacked water."[61] Castiglione continues by describing the mirth of Bibbiena's listeners, "Then everyone began to laugh, for the pleasantry alluded to by messer Bernardo was well known to all, having occurred in Rome."[62] We do not know exactly what everybody was laughing about, but we do know that Fra Mariano had a magnificent garden on Monte Cavallo filled with "1,000 caprices."[63] Could Bibbiena have been turned into a spring by a hidden fountain (a familiar Renaissance joke) in Mariano's garden? Fra Mariano was also known for his prodigious gluttony and is believed to have swallowed a pigeon in one mouthful and to have eaten twenty chickens and sucked forty-four eggs in one sitting.[64] Sometimes Fra Mariano's jests were brilliantly and elaborately contrived. Aretino tells us in the *Ragionamenti* of how Fra Mariano perpetrated a mock-heroic joust in the Piazza Navona.[65] First, the buffoon stationed himself at the corner of Piazza Navona near Maestro Pasquino, the familiar ancient statue, upon which satires or pasquinades, frequently against the popes, were placed. He then waited for some time until suddenly there were terrifying blasts from two trumpets, wonderfully described in amusing alliteration by Aretino ("una tara tara e una tantara scoppia fuori di due trombe"). Two knights in armor rushed forth through the piazza, dashing through pots, pans, and pottery, and making such a racket as to evoke the Last Judgment. The people in the piazza fled, according to Aretino, as if the flood were coming down on the ark of Noah.

The spirit of Mariano is conveyed in his reputed remark to Pope Leo X that is reported by the Venetian writer, Andrea Calmo: "Let's live, Holy Daddy [*babbo santo*], for all else is a joke."[66] And live in the spirit of Fra Mariano, Leo X certainly did! In a letter of Castiglione there is a description of a carnival performance by Sienese actors for Leo X in the Castel Sant'-Angelo, which is summarized by Pastor:

> The play began with the entrance of a woman, who in graceful verse, prayed to Venus to send her a lover. On this, to the sound of drums, there appeared eight hermits clad in grey tunics. These danced, and began to drive away a Cupid, who had appeared on the stage with his quiver. Cupid, in tears, prayed Venus to deliver him out of the hands of the hermits, who had snatched away his bow. There-

60. Castiglione, *The Book of the Courtier*, p. 21.

61. Ibid., p. 143.

62. Ibid., pp. 143–44.

63. Graf, *Attraverso il Cinquecento*, p. 312.

64. Ibid., p. 310.

65. Ibid., pp. 313–14.

66. Ibid., p. 315.

upon Venus appeared, and calling to her, the love-sick woman bade her give the hermits a charmed potion, which sent them all to sleep. Cupid now took back his bow, and waked up the hermits with his arrows; they danced around Cupid and made declarations of love to the woman, and finally casting away their grey tunics, they appeared as comely young men. When they had performed a moresca, the woman commanded them to make proof of their weapons; a combat then ensued, in which seven of them were killed, the survivor receiving the woman as the prize of victory.[67]

67. Pastor, *The History of the Popes*, 8:176–77.

The sensual and playful iconography of this performance can be related in spirit to Raphael's decorations for Bibbiena and his Cupid and Psyche loggia for Chigi, while the portrayal of hermits as young lovers in the play is reminiscent of Aretino's clerical lovers in the *Ragionamenti*. Bosch uses a harsh tone when he satirizes the carnal desires of the clergy by depicting a nun as a pig making love to a naked notary in the *Garden of Delights*. And when Julius II is kept out of heaven for his unholy activities in the dialogue *Julius exclusus*, there is also a sharp edge to the satire. But for Raphael, Leo, Aretino, Chigi, Bibbiena, and Fra Mariano, these monkish antics are more playfully joked about, as they later were by Vasari, who gives a charming and good-humored novelistic account of Fra Filippo Lippi's libidinous impulses.

The joking of Pope Leo X (who we should remember is the son of Lorenzo de' Medici) is of course legendary and is worth exploring as part of the context of the humorous art he commissioned from Raphael. Unfortunately, the fun of many jokes is lost or spoiled when they are repeated or taken out of context, as readers of Bibbiena's speech on jokes in *The Book of the Courtier* will know. But let us sample just a few of the quips of Leo and his friends. In a letter to the Emperor, who sent Leo some eagles, the pope, playing on the eagle as an imperial insignia, warned that the emperor was giving away his imperial power. On giving the cardinalate to the very young Innocenzo Cibo, Pope Leo, who himself was made a cardinal at an early age by Pope Innocent VIII, played on words when he remarked, "What I received from Innocent, I repay to Innocent." Upon receiving the lucrative job of papal *piombatore*, with its stipend of eight hundred ducats, Fra Mariano (who could afford to have a chapel decorated by Raphael's disciple, Polidoro) quipped that now he had discovered the alchemist's art, for he could make gold out of lead (*piombo*). Ferdinando Ponzetti, like Bibbiena a good friend of the pope and a patron of Peruzzi, was also made a cardinal and papal treasurer. Comparing his new cardinal's hat to that of a soldier he remarked, "Your hat cost one ducat, whereas mine cost 60,000."[68]

68. These jokes are given by Cronin, *The Flowering of the Renaissance*, pp. 69–70.

Before departing from Leonine Rome, let us look further at the playfulness and burlesque in the papal court. Leo invited the fat poetaster, Camillo Querno, to a symposium. Querno was made to drink and sing; he was crowned with vine leaves, cabbage, and laurel and solemnly named "archpoet." He wept for joy at this honor, although the pope and his entourage laughed at his absurdity. The documents indicate that Querno, whose wine was diluted with water when he made a mistake in his poetical improvisations, was paid regularly for his unwitting poetic travesties. Baraballo da Gaeta was the butt of another of Leo's jests. The latter foolishly considered himself another Petrarch and claimed the right to be crowned on the Capitol.[69] A mock-ceremony was arranged for the feast day of the Medici saints in which the unwitting Baraballo was to ride to the Capital mounted on the back of the elephant given to the pope by the King of Portugal. Baraballo, who like Fra Mariano was a cleric, dressed in elaborate robes in the classical style for the ceremony, and he was first received at the Vatican by the pope. As the poet recited, the court of Leo attempted to repress its laughter. Paolo Giovio observed, "Had I not seen it with my own eyes, I would not have believed that a man of sixty years of age, with grey hair, could have lent himself to such a comedy." Poor Baraballo never did make it to the Capitol, by the way, for as he rode across the Ponte Sant'Angelo, the elephant shied, throwing the helpless poet to the ground.[70]

The burlesque of poor Baraballo brings to mind a joke on the Medici emblem of two lions guarding the Medici laurel. This emblem was adapted in fact by Raphael in one of the tapestries for Pope Leo, who appropriated the lion, emblematic of his name, as a personal symbol. These symbolic lions abound, for example, in the grotesques of the Sala di Costantino, which was begun by Raphael and finished by his students. But what about this emblem? Filippo Strozzi is reported by Paolo Giovio to have suggested to Duke Lorenzo de' Medici that the lions guard the laurel to defend it from the fury of those poets who come running, having heard of the coronation of Baraballo in Rome. The function of the lions was to prevent the defoliation of the laurel by all of these would-be laureates.[71] One wonders if Rabelais, had he wanted to parody a Medici device, could have done better.

The elephant that Baraballo rode was the gift from the king of Portugal to Pope Leo, who in typical mock-heroic fashion called the animal Annone after the great Carthaginian general who took his forces with elephants over the Alps. It is a curious coincidence that the sound made by this animal when Baraballo rode him was reported to have sounded like "bar, bar, bar." At any rate, Annone became the object of the pope's playful delight. He was paraded through the streets of Rome bearing magnificent jewels, and as he passed the pope in the Castel Sant'Angelo, he genuflected three times. Upon his death, he was mourned by the papal court, and Aretino, who was a member of the Chigi entourage at the time, composed a humorous will for the dead elephant. The elephant was also immortalized in a portrait painted by Raphael and in an *intarsia* image in the papal apartments.[72]

Perhaps something of the character of burlesque ceremonial in Leonine Rome was also captured by Raphael in the preliminary idea for a painting

69. This account is from Pastor, *The History of the Popes*, 8:153–54.

70. Ibid., pp. 154–55.

71. Mathias Winner, "Pontormos Fresko in Poggio a Caiano."

72. Mathias Winner, "Raffael malt einen Elefanten."

Figure 4–11. Benvenuto da Garofalo. *Triumph of Bacchus*. Staatliche Kunstsammlungen, Dresden.

Figure 4–12. Martin van Heemskerck. *The Triumph of Silenus*. Kunsthistorisches Museum, Vienna.

that he never executed. This is the *Triumph of Bacchus* (a fitting deity for Leo and his court) commissioned for the *camerino* of Alfonso d'Este and known from a copy or variation, probably after a Raphael drawing, by the Ferrarese painter, Garofalo (Figure 4–11). In this playful image reminiscent of ancient reliefs and possibly inspired by Lucian's comic *Dionysius*, Raphael presents the effeminate god of wine, triumphant upon his return from India and attended by satyrs and Silenus.[73] Although Raphael's scheme was never fully realized and Alfonso had to turn to Titian for a *Bacchus and Ariadne*, his composition anticipated similar comic works of the cinquecento. Martin van Heemskerck's wonderfully riotous *Triumph of Silenus* captures much of the Raphaelesque mock-ceremonial and of course also reminds us of Piero di Cosimo's portrayals of Silenus (Figure 4–12).[74] In van Heemskerck's painting, the farce is heightened as the triumphant Bacchus is now replaced by a fat and jovial Silenus. It is as if we have before us a carnival image in which the fool is momentarily made king in a world that is upside down. Silenus is attended by a variety of satyrs and marvelous, virtuoso acrobats, who riot across the painting. At the end of the cinquecento, when Annibale Carracci painted the *Triumph of Bacchus* in the center of the Farnese gallery, he may have been referring indirectly to the earlier ideas of Raphael.[75] His great ceiling decoration was certainly in the tradition of Raphael's facetious art.

73. Edgar Wind, "A Note on Bacchus and Ariadne."

74. To my knowledge the iconography of this painting has never been systematically studied. However, both the subject and context of this work are presently being studied by Nora Wiseman, who is preparing a Ph. D. dissertation at the University of Virginia on Bacchic iconography in the Renaissance.

75. For the drawing of this subject by Raphael's follower, Perino del Vaga, see John Rupert Martin, *The Farnese Gallery*, pl. 281.

V. Mannerist Bizzarrie

The brain of this foolish, compounded clay, man, is not able to invent anything that tends to laughter more than I invent or is invented on me: I am not only witty in myself, but the cause that wit is in other men.—Falstaff in William Shakespeare, *Henry IV: Part II*

1. John Shearman, *Mannerism*.

2. Ibid., p. 68, pl. 67, and 130.

3. Ibid., p. 101.

4. Ibid., p. 133, pl. 74.

Figure 6–3, p. 146

5. Frederick Hartt has called my attention to an unpublished paper by Ludovico Borgo (on file in the Fogg Museum), which apparently deals convincingly with the subject of Rosso's work.

The wit and humor in sixteenth-century art has been noted by various writers but has not been the topic of sustained discussion. In some recent writing, the humor of the mannerists is acknowledged, but only in a cursory way. In the learned study of mannerism by John Shearman, for example, the author is usually so preoccupied with the elegance of mannerism that he has too little to say about its abundant humor.[1] This is not to say that the author of this widely read book is totally devoid of a sense of humor, for he does recognize the humor in Rosso Fiorentino's *Saturn and Philyra* and *Mars and Venus*, and in the aquatic jokes at the Medicean villa at Pratolino.[2] Yet on the whole, the richly diverse and capricious wit and humor of the mannerists, which are so basic to their temperaments and so frequently expressed in their art, is excessively rationalized and submerged by Shearman beneath stylistic analysis. Although Bronzino's *Venus, Cupid, Folly, and Time*, for example (see Figure 6–3), is filled with subtle wit, Shearman ignores this wit and concentrates instead on the polished colors, artifice, and ornament of the work.[3] When Shearman mentions Giovanni da Bologna's statue of Venus in the Boboli Gardens as part of an elaborate mannerist garden art, he does not even comment on the playful caricature of the four satyrs who lecherously peer at the naked Venus over the basin of the fountain.[4] Giovanni da Bologna plays here on voyeurism, in the same manner as Raphael and Peruzzi, and this humor is an important aspect of the work as is its elegance of style. Finally, in his emphasis on the elegance of mannerism, Shearman ignores one of the important traits of mannered, sixteenth-century culture: its taste for humorous vulgarity. The mannerists were eager to play with and laugh at what is coarse and vulgar.

A vein of strange and sometimes disturbing wit runs throughout the work of Rosso Fiorentino, the early mannerist, who along with Pontormo, was one of the first artists to react to High Renaissance classicism. This wit appears in Rosso's bizarre and macabre drawing in the Uffizi, the *Allegory of Death* (Figure 5–1). Although the precise symbolic meaning of this drawing has yet to be explained, the meaning of its form is apparent.[5] Rosso has created

Figure 5–1. Rosso Fiorentino. *Allegory of Death*. Gabinetto dei Disegni, Uffizi, Florence.

a caricature of death through a series of grotesque images, which suggest the influence of Northern art. Skeletons and other figures surround a reclining skeleton, suggesting the traditional compositional arrangement of a *Pietà* or *Entombment*. Is it not possible that Rosso conceived of the composition as a parody of this kind of subject?

A similar strangeness is found in Rosso's fresco of the Assumption of the Virgin, painted in the *cortile* of Sta. Annunziata. The faces of the Apostles are caricatures, some having the semblance of wild men, especially the St. James on the extreme left; and the angels who swirl around the Virgin have facetious expressions on their faces.[6] The satirical tendency of Rosso is especially apparent in his so-called S. M. Nuova altarpiece, done for the *spedalingo* of S. M. Nuova and eventually placed in the hospital of that church, but originally intended, as a neglected document reveals, for an altar in Ognissanti (Figure 5–2).[7] According to Vasari, the painting was criticized by Rosso's patron, who

6. Bottari identified the figure of James as a portrait of the satirical poet, Francesco Berni; see Giorgio Vasari, *Le vite dè più eccellenti pittori scultori et architettori*, ed. Gaetano Milanesi, 7:157, n. 3. Rosso's painting is illustrated by Sydney J. Freedberg, *Painting of the High Renaissance in Rome and Florence*, 2: pl. 665.

7. The document, called to my attention by Anne Jukkola, is in Vasari, *Le vite*, 9:263.

Figure 5–2. Rosso Fiorentino. *Madonna and Child with Saints*. Uffizi, Florence.

condemned Rosso's *santi diavoli*, and the above-mentioned document which has been little considered by Rosso scholars indicates that there probably was indeed a dispute between Rosso and his patron.[8] In fact Rosso seems not to have finished the painting, and the document indicates the possibility that Granacci and Bugiardini were asked to finish it by the dissatisfied patron. The *spedalingo*'s response to the painting suggests the possibilities that he was offended either by Rosso's travesty of the religious subject matter or offended by the artist's unorthodox and caricatural style. Most of the saints have strange expressions, and the gesticulating, seemingly angry St. Jerome, who seems to be debating rather than discoursing with St. John, might especially have been offensive. Rosso's saints also imply a parody of the dignified, idealized decorum of High Renaissance art.[9] We need only compare Rosso's altarpiece to Sarto's *Madonna of the Harpies* or Pitti *Trinity* to sense how Rosso could have been mocking the classical style.

We should note that the issue of parody in Renaissance art has received relatively little attention, and this is not surprising since it is exceedingly difficult to speak with certainty about an artist's stylistic intentions. But was Rosso's S. M. Nuova altarpiece in fact a parody? It would seem that the hypothesis that this painting is, to an extent, parodic is supported not only by the eccentricities of the painting and our knowledge of Rosso's personality gained from Vasari but by the general context of sixteenth-century art and literature in which parody flourished. Let us consider for a moment the parody of Rosso's literary contemporaries. Parody of medieval romance pervades the writing of Pulci, Boiardo, Ariosto, Berni, Folengo, Rabelais, and Cervantes, to name several notable writers. We find frequent parodies of Neoplatonism in the writing of Aretino, Sansovino, and Doni (see Chapter 7). We have already noted that Petrarchan conventions were frequently mocked, and we noted examples by Michelangelo and Lorenzo de' Medici, who also parodied Dante. Parody could also refer not only to general literary traditions or genres but to specific works. Thus, Berni seems to have parodied a particular sonnet by Bembo, and later Shakespeare made light of euphuistic passages from Lily in his *Henry IV: Part I*.[10] Analogies can be found in music and the visual arts; for example, Giovanni Gabrieli's parody of a Cipriano de Rore madrigal, or Dürer's drawing of dancing monkeys, which seems to make a mocking reference to the classicizing Italian prints of dancing figures.[11] And these examples could be multiplied. Moreover, parody was common in the courts of Europe where chivalric ceremonies and the Mass were mocked by court fools and jesters, echoing medieval conventions; indeed we have already considered some of this parodic jesting in the court of Leo X. Thus, the possibility of specific parody in Italian art and, in particular, in Rosso's altarpiece cannot be simply dismissed. Parody is based on an acute awareness of style or manner, and it is just at this moment in the early sixteenth century in the work of

8. Ibid., 5:157.

9. The parody in Rosso's art is brought out by Freedberg, *Painting of the High Renaissance*, 1:539ff.

10. Francesco Berni, *Rime facete*, pp. 26, 179; and William Shakespeare, *Henry IV: Part I*, act II, scene iv, ll. 399ff.

11. H. W. Janson, *Apes and Ape Lore in the Middle Ages and the Renaissance*, pp. 271–72, pl. 47a.

12. This self-consciousness is especially brought out by Sydney J. Freedberg, "Observations on the Painting of the Maniera."

Raphael and his followers and the early mannerists that a keenly heightened consciousness of style developed.[12] It would appear that artists adapted the style of others with acute self-awareness and that, like contemporary writers, they sometimes delighted in mocking these adapted styles.

Parody, it should further be stressed, was not simply the negative response of one artist to the style of another. Throughout the sixteenth century, artists made light of Michelangelo's style, but at the same time their responses were based on deep respect and admiration for Buonarroti. Similarly, when Cervantes parodied the romantic tradition in *Don Quixote*, it is clear that he still regarded this tradition with great affection. One can also speak of a tendency in the sixteenth century to create unwitting parody. Cellini's heroic exploits, seemingly modeled on the romantic ideals of the period, make of him a laughable, almost Rabelaisian character. Similarly Baccio Bandinelli's *Hercules*, which in all of its pomp was intended to surpass the work of Michelangelo, became an unwitting self-parody, eliciting the ridicule of Florentine sonnet writers. The same unwitting parody is found in Ammanati's *Neptune*, which was eventually erected in front of the Palazzo Vecchio in Florence for Duke Cosimo. This gigantic statue may have stood for the naval ambitions and power of the duke, but the absurdity of its Michelangelesque gigantism and rhetoric were probably the subject of cinquecento humor.[13] The familiar jingle on the *Neptune*—"Ammanato Ammanati che bel pezzo di marmo hai sciupato" (Ammanato Ammanati what a beautiful piece of marble you have ruined)—may well be rooted in a cinquecento response to the work, a response similar to that of many Florentines to Baccio's *Hercules*.

13. The often-neglected political significance of Ammanati's *Neptune* is discussed by Giorgio Spini, "Architettura e Politica nel Principato Mediceo," pp. 839–40.

Rosso's eccentric humor is also apparent in his drawing of a woman (Figure 5–3). The drawing is done in the manner of those exquisite female heads, the *teste divine*, of Michelangelo. But whereas Michelangelo's figures have an air of grace and dignity, Rosso's woman peers bizarrely over her shoulder at the viewer. Rosso's lady is suggestive of the frequent satire of women in Renaissance literature, as for example, in Machiavelli's roughly contemporary *novella, Belfagor*. In this satirical tale by the brilliant author of the comedies *La Mandragola* and *La Clizia*, Machiavelli humorously indicates how even a devil cannot deal with woman, a situation also humorously illustrated by Bruegel in his *Proverbs*.[14]

The humor in Rosso's drawing of a woman is expressed through the subtly playful treatment of physiognomy. This playful handling of facial expression is also evident in Rosso's design for the *Saturn and Philyra*, which was engraved by Caraglio as part of the series of *Loves of the Gods*.[15] If Raphael had already given a human quality to a horse in his *St. George* (Washington), Rosso now fully exploits this pathetic fallacy in his charmingly ridiculous image of a horse in love. This print might remind us that horses are frequently

14. Gustaf Glück, *Pieter Breughel The Elder*, pl. 11, proverb 16: "She would bind the devil himself."

15. Shearman, *Mannerism*, p. 68, pl. 67.

Figure 5–3. Rosso Fiorentino. *Study of a Woman*. Metropolitan Museum of Art, New York.

16. Fern Rusk Shapley, *Paintings from the Samuel H. Kress Collection*, 2: fig. 287.

the subject of visual joking in the Renaissance. Earlier in quattrocento Florence we find a comically buck-toothed steed dominated by a nude female in a mysterious allegory attributed to Piero di Cosimo (Washington).[16] In the same period Biagio di Antonio included a comical equestrian detail in his *Triumph of Scipio*, also in Washington. Here the triumphant entry of Scipio is portrayed with magnificent pomp and chivalric splendor, yet in the background we find the ludicrous detail of a horse kicking wildly in response to a dog sniffing at its genitals. Horses are of course played upon later in the cinquecento, and finally, we will encounter the more sedate, if not silly, humor of the horse who appears in the boudoir of Mars and Venus in a painting by Veronese.

Resuming our analysis of Rosso, we find that even when his art is highly refined, its mocking character persists. His *Marriage of the Virgin* is on the surface a very elegant painting of a religious subject. But one becomes aware of another level of meaning in the painting. The saint in the right foreground draws attention to Joseph and the Virgin by pointing at them. But his pointing finger happens to project in front of Joseph's groin, subtly or perhaps not so subtly, indicating the bridegroom's sexual excitement. Given Joseph's lack of involvement in the conception of Christ, the phallic joke takes on a rather curious significance. Rosso's phallic wit has been observed by various art historians, but they have not commented upon it in print.[17] Perhaps they thought it indecorous. But it is worth commenting upon, for it reflects attitudes of the artist and perhaps the patron, who in this case was Cardinal Ginori. Playful sexual innuendo occurs in another religious work done by Rosso in the same period as the *Marriage of the Virgin*, the painting of Moses and the daughters of Jethro, now in the Uffizi. Rosso's composition is filled with violent, twisting Michelangelesque nudes, and the degree of *furia* in Rosso's rhetorical picture is so great that once again we have to wonder whether Rosso was not making parody here, in this case, of Michelangelo's *terribilità*. Rosso also focuses our attention on the sexual parts of his figures, and he plays on this feature of the painting by contriving to place the genitals of one furious Michelangelesque figure at the center of the composition (Figure 5-4).[18]

The phallic humor in Rosso's religious works is only slightly more subtle than that in his profane works such as his *Juno* (Figure 5-5). This drawing is one of a series of twenty *Antique Deities* which, like the *Love of the Gods*, was designed to be engraved by Caraglio. The peacock is of course the symbol of Juno. But given the way in which the goddess strokes the bird's neck, it would also seem that Rosso is playing on the iconographical tradition of the bird as phallus. We might cite here another example of this tradition, a North Italian print that depicts a ludicrous, giant, winged phallus.[19]

17. Rosso's playful, phallic allusion was brought to my attention by Robert Munman. Frederick Hartt has informed me that other art historians have noted this detail in the past.

18. This detail was brought to my attention by Marla Price. Robert Munman has informed me that this detail was also discussed in a lecture given at Harvard in 1962 by Federico Zeri.

19. Jay Levenson, et al., *Early Italian Engravings from the National Gallery of Art*, pl. 527. The phallic character of bird symbolism in Northern art has been discussed by E. De Jongh, "Erotica in Vogelperspektief," *Simiolus* 3 (1968–1969): 22–74.

Figure 5–4. Rosso Fiorentino. *Marriage of the Virgin*. S. Lorenzo, Florence.

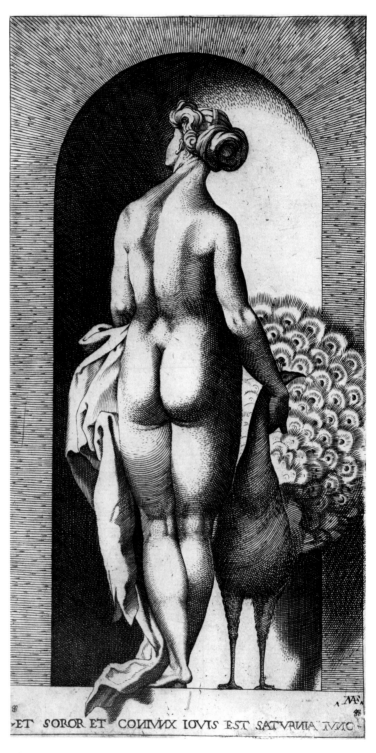

ET SOROR ET CONIVNX IOVIS EST SATVRNIA IVNO

Figure 5-5. Rosso Fiorentino. *Juno* (engraved by Iacopo Caraglio). British Museum, London.

The priapean allusions in Rosso's art are related in general to the phallic comedy that is ubiquitous in the art that we have already discussed and in secular Renaissance literature. One finds this kind of humor in late quattrocento Florence in Alessandro Braccesi's *Ad Laurentium Emporianum Cultorem*, which explicitly extols the virtues of Lorenzo's phallus: "You may well be cockier even than Priapus himself—/ For you really are, Lorenzo, one wholly languid prick—:/ And I think you'd really like to surpass the holy name/ and private parts of the Hellespontian god Priapus."[20] In the *capitolo* on the needle by Rosso's contemporary, Francesco Berni, the subject of the poem is an obvious symbol for the penis, which is defined as the instrument of all instruments: "è l'instrumento de gli altri instrumenti."[21] The same idea is treated by Rosso's friend and Berni's literary enemy, Pietro Aretino, who in a letter to the physician Battista Zatti extols the virtues of the male organ:

> It seems to me that the images of the organ which nature gives us for our preservation should be worn around the neck as a pendant and in the hat as a medal. It is that which has made you, who are among the first physicians. It has produced the Bembos, the Sansovinos, the Titians, and the Michelangelos. It has generated popes, emperors, and kings.[22]

This kind of priapean humor also occurs in Bronzino's *capitolo* on the radish for which women "howl like lions and dragons/ if they don't have it enough,"[23] and in Rabelais's humorous description of Gargantua's codpiece: "On one point I will inform you now, however, that not only was it long and capacious, but well furnished within and well victualled, having no resemblance to the fraudulent codpieces of many young gentlemen which contain nothing but wind, to the great disappointment of the female sex."[24] These sexual jokes also frequently appear in religious contexts. In his *Ragionamenti*, for example, Aretino mocks the sexual appetites of the clergy by describing a monastic orgy in a brilliant sequence of images in which the sounds and actions of the lovers are compared to the hammering of smiths, the do re me of the musical scale, and the shaking houses during an earthquake:

> When they had pushed and squirmed and twisted for half an hour, the General suddenly cried: "Now all at the same time, and you my dear boys, kiss me and you too, my dove!" and holding one hand on the lovely angel's box and with the other fondling the cherub's behind, now kissing him, now kissing her, he wore that funny look the marble statue at the Vatican Museum gives the snakes that are strangling him between his sons. In the finale the nuns on the bed with the young men, the General and the sister he was mounted on, together with the fellow at his behind, and last of all, the nun with her Murano prodder, all agreed to do it together as choristers sing in unison, or more to the point, as blacksmiths hammer in time, and so each attentive to his task, all that one heard was "Oh my God, oh my Christ!" "Hug me!" "Ream me!" "Push out that sweet tongue!" "Give it to me!" "Take it into me!" "Holy God!" "Hold me!" and "Help!" Some were whimpering, others were moaning loudly, and listening to them you would

20. Alessandro Bracchi, *Carmina*, p. 90. I am indebted to Malcolm Bell for this translation.

21. Berni, *Rime facete*, p. 145.

22. Translated in James Cleugh, *The Divine Aretino*, p. 71.

23. Il Bronzino, *Li Capitoli Faceti*, p. 402.

24. François Rabelais, *The Histories of Gargantua and Pantagruel*, trans. J. M. Cohen, p. 55.

have thought they were running the scales, *sol, fa, me, re, do*—their eyes popping out of their heads, their gasps and groans, their twistings and turnings making the chests, wooden beds, chairs, and chamber pots shake and rattle as if the house had been hit by an earthquake.[25]

25. Pietro Aretino, *Aretino's Dialogues*, trans. Raymond Rosenthal, p. 29.

It would seem that Rosso treated sexuality not only playfully but also ironically. In Rome he painted the hauntingly beautiful *Dead Christ* for Bishop Tornabuoni of Arezzo. There is of course nothing humorous about this stark, eucharistic image, but as Freedberg suggests, there may well be elements of aesthetic and theological irony in the painting.

Even more in its psychological content, Rosso's image perverts the classicism of his exemplars, equivocating with brilliant irony—or effrontery, perhaps—between deference and outrage. The equivocation is not only between the authority of past artistic style and Rosso's individuality, but also seems to be between that individuality and the beliefs required by the Catholic religion. The theme that Rosso's picture illustrates is a vital dogma of the Church, one that especially in these years was the subject of defense against heretical assault. The palpable body of Christ, neither dead nor alive but eternal is exposed to us on the altar, around which the angels are the acolytes; this is a demonstration of the Eucharistic miracle of Christ's real presence. But the presence here asserted to the senses is described with a sensuality that contradicts a value more essentially Christian than the specific dogma, and the sensuality is confounded with an aestheticism that seems more important than the picture's meaning of religiosity. The ambivalence in content of the theme is all the more remarkable when we recall that the picture was painted for the bishop of a major see, Leonardo Tornabuoni of Arezzo. The *Dead Christ* may reflect more than Rosso's private state of mind; it may be the most immediate evidence we possess of religiously as well as morally cynical attitudes within elite circles of contemporary Rome.[26]

26. Sydney J. Freedberg, *Painting in Italy: 1500–1600*, p. 131, pl. 83.

Rosso's irony is related to attitudes pervasive in cinquecento Rome, which were sometimes expressed in satirical terms. For example, Paris de Grassis tells us of a seemingly playful sermon given at a mass celebrated before Pope Leo X in 1519 by a scholar from Narni.

On the day of St. John, in the papal chamber, in the presence of the pope with all the cardinals . . . (a cardinal) . . . celebrated the mass, and the sermon was given by a certain scholar from Narni more in the gentile fashion than in the Christian. He invoked (the immortal) gods and goddesses in an exclamation, so that many people laughed and became angry. The Pope patiently tolerated (the blunder) in keeping with his very patient and very kind nature.[27]

27. Bonner Mitchell, *Rome in the High Renaissance*, pp. 88–89.

From what we know of Leo X we might suspect that he more than tolerated the scholar's invocation of the pagan gods.

The satirical strain of Roman society is also described by Benvenuto Cellini in his autobiography. Cellini describes an almost Aretinian party held by a company of artists, including Raphael's followers, Penni and Giulio Romano, to which each brought a lady friend. Cellini decided to play a trick on his friends by dressing up a sixteen-year-old boy, Diego, as a woman. Cellini's deception is also reminiscent of the ambiguities of sex in the Plautine comedies like Bibbiena's *La Calandria* that was performed in Rome during the early cinquecento. Diego, whose head and face (like that of Rosso's Christ) "were far more beautiful than those of the antique Antinous," was admired by Cellini's fellow artists, and Michel Agnolo of Siena, the founder of this company of artists, made everyone bow down before Diego.

> . . . while, he, on his knees upon the floor, cried out for mercy, and called to all the folk in words like this: "Behold ye of what sort are the angels of paradise! though they are called angels, here shall ye see that they are not all of the male gender." Then with a loud voice he added:
> "Angel beauteous, angel best,
> Save me thou, make thou me blest."

Cellini continues to describe this satirical and ironical scene that turns out to be a travesty of the church.

> Upon this my charming creature laughed and lifted the right hand and gave him a papal benediction, with many pleasant words to boot. So Michel Agnolo stood up and said it was the custom to kiss the feet of the Pope and cheeks of angels; and having done the latter to Diego, the boy blushed deeply which enhanced his beauty.[28]

Although I will leave other parts of Cellini's tale for the reader to pursue on his own, it might be noted here that the courtesans at the supper party eventually discovered who, or rather what, Diego was. Giulio Romano's consort, feigning to feel the supposedly pregnant belly of Diego, reached down, "discovering the real sex" of Cellini's companion. As Cellini tells us, "The whole room rang with laughter."

In Rosso's devilish early works and his later, more refined works there is a nasty wit that relates to the general mood of skeptical humor in early sixteenth-century Italy. Rosso's Apostles in the early *Assumption of the Virgin* can be likened to the rather devastating caricatures done by the pessimistic Leonardo. His negative view of things might be compared to the pessimism in the writings of Machiavelli and Guicciardini. His mocking attitude brings to mind the ridicule of human nature in Machiavelli's *La Mandragola* and *La Clizia* and in Guicciardini's biting *Ricordi*. Rosso's caustic humor is especially close in tone to that of Gaspar Pallavicino in Castiglione's *The Book of the Courtier*. Careful attention should be paid to the fact that signor Gasparo, a close friend of Castiglione, often mocks the idealized attitudes toward the perfect courtier put forward by various other speakers. Gasparo provides a satirical critique of Renaissance decorum which in its skeptical tone is related to Rosso's satires of the idealized decorum in classical art. We have already observed that the ladies of the court "attacked" signor Gasparo for his satirical comments. These remarks, which were on love, relate in spirit to the mocking

28. For the whole episode, see Benvenuto Cellini, *The Life of Benvenuto Cellini*, trans. John Addington Symonds, pp. 102ff.

tone in Rosso's work, as they do to the satire of women in the writing of Machiavelli:

> I do not deny that the purpose, the labors, and the dangers of lovers should be chiefly directed to the conquest of the beloved's mind rather than the body. But I say that these deceits, which you call treacheries in men and tricks in women are excellent means of attaining this claim, for whoever possesses a woman's body is always master of her mind also.[29]

After the sack of Rome, Rosso traveled to Venice where he did a drawing of Mars and Venus for Pietro Aretino (Figure 5–6). According to the anonymous author of *The Whore's Rhetoric* (London, 1683), a certain Philo-Puttanus, Aretino "had an exquisite knowledge in the nature of Mars and Venus . . . and the varieties of their conjunction."[30] Aretino was also an artistic advisor to King Francis I, and he may have commissioned the composition for the king as a commemoration of the latter's wedding, reminding us that Botticelli's painting of the same subject and Mantegna's *Parnassus*, including Mars and Venus, may also have alluded to marriages. According to Adhémar, "Mars relinquishing his arms to devote himself to Venus can be taken, therefore, as an allegory of Francis I."[31] Recently, Rosso's drawing has been discussed by Shearman as a manifestation of mannerism:

> The subject itself is mocked; for example the ring of flying *putti* above . . . loose off a great deal of ammunition and threaten to empty their cornucopias on the lovers, but Mars is revealed by Cupid as improbably triumphant and anything but master of the situation. What the work stimulates positively is not belief in a narrative, not the evocation of something real outside of itself, but fascination in itself, in its complexities, its visual jokes, its *tours de force* of manipulation and technique, and its accumulated demonstration of artistic capacity.[32]

One suspects that both Rosso and Aretino would have chuckled, as Francis I might have, at this slightly elliptical discussion of the drawing in which the subject is all but described. In Rosso's drawing, Mars and Venus are being undressed before their lovemaking. Like Botticelli, but even more emphatically, Rosso mocks the frail Mars, who is a parody of the heroic god of war. The teasing is perhaps amplified by Rosso in the foreground where an *amorino* gazing up at Mars plays with a phalluslike sword between his legs. Weapons were common sexual metaphors in Renaissance literature, as we have seen, for example, in Lorenzo de' Medici's *Amori di Marte e Venere*, and the *amorino* who gazes up at Mars seems to be endowed with the "weapon" that Rosso's helpless Mars lacks.[33] The sexual joke here is reminiscent of the humor in Rosso's earlier religious works. It is nasty and explicit like the jokes in Aretino's *Ragionamenti*, and one cannot but wonder whether Aretino himself provided Rosso with the idea for the drawing. While the *amorino* playing peek-a-boo with Mars's armor and the *amorini* flying above recall Sodoma's

29. Baldesar Castiglione, *The Book of the Courtier*, trans. Charles Singleton, p. 192.

30. Philo-Puttanus, *The Whore's Rhetoric*, p. 129.

31. Jean Adhémar, "Aretino: Artistic Adviser to Francis I."

32. Shearman, *Mannerism*, p. 68.

33. Lorenzo de' Medici, *Opere*, 2:17.

Figure 5–6. Rosso Fiorentino. *Mars and Venus*. Cabinet des Dessins, Louvre, Paris.

Figure 4-10, p. 93

Figure 2-12, p. 39

34. Erwin Panofsky and Dora Panofsky, "The Iconography of the Galerie François I at Fontainebleau."

Marriage of Alexander and Roxanne (see Figure 4-10) and Botticelli's *Mars and Venus* (see Figure 2-12), the charm of the earlier works is now spiked by Rosso's more caustic wit.

Rosso worked at Fontainebleau during the last phase of his career, decorating a gallery in fresco and stucco for Francis I. The elaborate and highly contrived iconography of these decorations, with mythological and historical scenes alluding to the king and celebrating his rule, have been partially elucidated by the Panofskys.[34] The precise meaning of these decorations is not immediately apparent but must be deciphered like a puzzle. Accompanying the narrative scenes are fantastic marginal decorations, including an elaborate sequence of nudes and *putti*, who in their various postures and embraces suggest a play on Michelangelo's inventions. Rosso's decoration abounds in surprising and strange marginal details that are reminiscent of the marginalia in medieval illuminated manuscripts. An entire essay could be written on the wit of Rosso's decoration, but we might note here just a few examples such as the bizarre animals and masks surrounding the fresco of a naval battle (Figure 5-7). One detail itself has a mock-Michelangelesque *terribilità* about it, recalling the playful mock-heroism of so much romantic literature and art of the period. As figures battle furiously on the high seas, we find an element of elegant play when we discover one curious head emerging casually from the waves and spouting water in a lovely arc.

In many respects Rosso's witty decorations can also be compared to Rabelais's *Gargantua*, which was first published in France during the period when Rosso worked on the gallery. Rabelais's writing, with its formal complexities, wit, and delightful wordplay, conforms in various respects to recent definitions of mannerism. Just as Rabelais plays with rhetoric and the words and literary styles of Church Latin, Rosso plays with the "language" of his art in his playful variations on High Renaissance art, especially that of Michelangelo. Rosso's elaborately contrived frieze is filled with ingenious scrolls, frames, masks, nudes, festoons, and other details that are comparable in their wit to the liter-

Figure 5–7. Rosso Fiorentino. Gallery of François I (detail). Fontainebleau, France.

35. Leo Spitzer, "Die Wortbildung als stilistiches Mittel exemplifiziert an Rabelais . . . ," *Beihefte zür Romanische Philologie.* Shearman, *Mannerism,* discusses the relationship of literary mannerism to mannerism in the visual arts. He does not, however, discuss Rabelais.

36. Rabelais, *Gargantua,* p. 155.

37. Ibid., p. 684. This quotation and many others below are from Book 5 of Rabelais's *Gargantua.* Rabelais's authorship of this book has sometimes been questioned, but it is now generally agreed that even if he did not write it (or all of it), it is based on Rabelais's ideas. For a full discussion of the problem, see Donald Frame, *François Rabelais,* pp. 86ff.

38. Rabelais, *Gargantua,* p. 686.

ary embellishments in Rabelais's language. Rabelais's writing has sometimes been compared to the painting of the period, especially Bruegel's. But art historians have not discussed in any detail the ways in which Rabelais's language relates to mannerism. Philologists such as Leo Spitzer have analyzed the complexities of Rabelais's word formation, and it should now be apparent that Rabelais's ingenious and delightful wordplay has much in common with the manerism of Italian writing during this period, as well as with the wit of mannerist artists such as Rosso.[35] The delightfully contrived iconography of Rosso's decorations also relates in spirit to Rabelais's playful fascination with puzzles, paradoxes, and conundrums. Both the artist and the writer were addressing themselves to the same courtly society that delighted in arcane jokes and *recherché* meanings, as well as sumptuous decorations. Rabelais's description of the Abbey of Thélème, which could almost be a description of Fontainebleau itself, may not simply reflect an ideal of court life but possibly suggest a play on the taste of the French court:

> In the middle of the first court was a magnificent fountain of fine alabaster, on the top of which were the three Graces with horns of abundance, spouting water from their breasts, mouths, ears, eyes, and other orifices. The rooms of the building above this first court stood upon stout pillars of chalcedony and porphry, with magnificent old-fashioned arches between; and inside were fine, long spacious galleries decorated with paintings, with horns of stags, unicorns, rhinoceroses, and hippopotami, with elephant tusks and with other remarkable objects.[36]

These "remarkable objects" appealed to the courtly reader just as Rosso's grotesques appealed to the beholder at Fontainebleau. There is an underlying humor in Rabelais's description of exotic animal parts (verbal grotesques!) that is like the humor in Rosso's bizarre festoons, masks, and animals. Rabelais's attention to bodily orifices and his general interest in bodily functions also relate to the attitudes of Rosso's delightful, embracing nudes at Fontainebleau.

Rabelais is continually describing witty decorations filled with paintings, mosaics, and grotesques, which are related iconographically to much Renaissance art and art theory. An especially good example is the Temple of the Bottle. The vault of the temple entrance included "a dance of women and satyrs around an old laughing Silenus on his ass," which recalls similar images painted by Peruzzi, Piero di Cosimo, and others.[37] The marble staircase to the temple is a spoof of the Pythagorean and Neoplatonic numerology that influenced various philosophers and theorists on art during the period. Here is a sample from Rabelais's description of this tetradic staircase: "And note most carefully that this is the true psychogony of Plato, which was so highly praised by the Academicians, but so little understood. The half of it is made up of unity, of the first two plain numbers, two squares, and two cubes."[38]

After describing the marvelous emblems and mosaics of the temple, Rabelais tells us of the lamp of the temple, with its sculptural grotesques worthy of Rosso's Fontainebleau work. Rabelais's grotesques include "a brisk and jolly battle between little naked boys, mounted on little hobby-horses with little whirling lances and shields cunningly made of grape-bunches, interlaced with leaves."[39] Rabelais then gives us an elaborate detailed description of the temple fountain in terms that evoke and possibly reflect the highly symbolic fountains of Colonna's influential *Hypnerotomachia Poliphili*, a work known to Rabelais. Playing with traditional cosmological symbolism, he tells us of this domed heptagonal structure that consisted of columns in precious stones, surmounted by astrological figures. "Its edge, base, and structure were of the purest alabaster, a little more than a foot high, heptagonal in shape, and divided into equal parts on the outside, with a number of column-bases, miniature altars, mouldings, and Doric undulations all round it."[40] Rabelais also does a delightful, if hard-to-follow, mock-analysis of the fountain's geometry which was worked out "according to the instructions given of old by Euclid, Aristotle, Archimedes, and others."[41] His analysis sounds almost like a parody of the mathematical exegeses in architectural treatises of the period. Had Rosso known Rabelais's description of the Temple of the Bottle, he no doubt would have enjoyed its playful artistry and Rabelais's mock-pedantic commentary on it. Finally, we might add that shortly before the description of the temple, Rabelais has Friar John make a joke on theological dogma and women, which would have tickled Rosso:

> But I read in my Breviary, in the Book of Revelation, that a woman was seen with the moon under her feet, and it was reckoned a marvelous sight. The significance of it, as Bigot explains to me, is that she was of a different race from the rest of women, who are quite contrary by nature. They have the moon in their heads and consequently their brains are always moon-struck.[42]

As Mikhail Bakhtin has pointed out, Friar John has his roots in the literature of the Middle Ages in which religious parodies ("drunkards' masses," etc.) and travesties of sacred texts were pervasive.[43] We may also eventually discover that, at least in part, Rosso's parodic humor has similar medieval bases.

Rabelais's book, like Aretino's writing and Rosso's art, was created for a society that delighted in laughing at itself. His *History of Gargantua*, in part a satire of the kind of perfect courtier defined by Castiglione, deals with the education, dress, and manners of Gargantua, the young courtier. Through exaggeration and caricature, Rabelais (like Castiglione's friend, signor Gasparo) mocks the very notion of the ideal courtier. This satire occurs, for example, in Rabelais's description of the dress of the young courtier, Gargantua.

> And he was already beginning to exercise his codpiece, which his governess decorated every day with fine garlands, lovely ribbons, pretty flowers, and gay silken

39. Ibid., pp. 695, 696.

40. Ibid., p. 696.

41. Ibid., p. 697.

42. Ibid., p. 684.

43. Mikhail Bakhtin, *Rabelais and His World*.

44. Rabelais, *Gargantua*, p. 63.

tufts. And they amused themselves by rubbing it between their hands like a roll of pastry, and then burst out laughing when it raised its ears, as if the game pleased them. One of them called it my pillock, my ninepin, another my coral-branch, another my stopper, my cork, my quiver, my drawing pin, my crimping iron, my little red sausage, my sweet little cocky.[44]

The joking here recalls Rosso's earlier work as well as the humorous, erotic innuendoes in the Fontainebleau decorations. This joking is not simply Rabelaisian fantasy but would seem to reflect the sometimes amused openness of the French court toward sexuality. This openness persisted into the seventeenth century, and we find it described by Heroard in his account of the young King Louis XIII. The playful and comic fictions of Rosso and Rabelais relate to the play on sexuality in the court:

> It was a common joke, repeated time and again to say to him: 'Monsieur, you haven't got a cock.' Then he replied: "Hey, here it is!"—laughing and lifting it with one finger. These jokes were not limited to the servants, or to the brainless youths, or to women of easy virtue such as the King's mistress. The Queen, his mother, made the same sort of joke: 'The Queen touching his cock, said: "Son I am holding your spout."'
>
> The court was amused in fact, to see his first erections: "Waking up at eight o'clock, he called Mlle Bethousay and said to her: 'Zezai, my cock is like a drawbridge; see how it goes up and down.' And he raised it and lowered it."[45]

45. Philippe Ariès, *Centuries of Childhood*, p. 101.

Like his companion Rosso, Pontormo had a distinct sense of the bizarre; however, Pontormo's wit seems less biting and perhaps somewhat less contrived than Rosso's. Pontormo's Visdomini altarpiece, for example, is a highly urgent and expressive work, but in it Pontormo depicts Christ and the surrounding angels with strange, leering smiles on their faces. Like Rosso's early religious works (and the angels in Rosso's *Assumption of the Virgin* come to mind), Pontormo's painting seems to undermine the restrained, dignified decorum of the High Renaissance. And there may well be an element of parody in it.[46] Although there are no humorous activities depicted in Pontormo's painting, the expressions on the faces of the figures and some of their contrived postures reveal a bizarre humor. In his well-known painting of Joseph in Egypt, now in London, Pontormo again exhibits this peculiar wit, especially in his depiction of an ambiguous space, a bizarre spiral staircase, and various statues, including the *putto*, which seems to be alive.[47] The ambiguities of these statues recall Mantegna's caryatid-angels and Filippino Lippi's lifelike Mars but are even more subjective and eccentric than their quattrocento precedents. The effects of ambiguity and strangeness are not necessarily the symptoms of a mannerist crisis, and they are not simply the detached musings of an artist preoccupied with formal complexities for their own sake. They reflect a witty, if troubled, attitude toward reality.

46. Walter Friedlaender, *Mannerism and Anti-Mannerism in Italian Painting*, pp. 21–22.

47. Frederick Hartt, *History of Italian Renaissance Art*, pl. 609.

Pontormo's wit is especially manifest in his decoration of the lunette in the *salone* of Poggio a Caiano (Figure 5–8). This work, along with the political allegories of Sarto and Franciabigio at Poggio and Michelangelo's contemporary work at San Lorenzo, celebrate the imperial aspirations of the Medici house.[48] The program of this cycle was, according to Vasari, furnished by Paolo Giovio, who we remember described his amazed and amused response to the poet Baraballo, mocked by Leo X. The imagery of the fresco may also have been associated with a poem by Ariosto celebrating the Medici and the Golden Age of their rule. The precise theme of the lunette has been the subject of considerable discussion, but recent iconographical investigations seem to support Vasari's identification of Vertumnus and Pomona in the fresco. An inscription at the top of the lunette, alluding to Virgil, indicates the presence of gods and goddesses in a garden, which at once is appropriate to the setting of the villa in the country and is evocative of the Golden Age, associated with the Medici ascendency by Leo X as it was by his father, Lorenzo de' Medici. The iconography of the gods in a garden of course recalls the tradition of the *Primavera* by Botticelli (see Figure 2–9), an artist for whom Pontormo seems to have had considerable sympathy. The precise identification of Pontormo's figures is still conjectural, but we can nevertheless observe their bizarre tone. Their attitudes and postures are especially eccentric, as Pontormo plays on the roughness of the ugly *contadino*-like figure at the left, the intense, ambiguous gazes of the languid and somewhat odd ladies at the right, and the capricious attitudes of the lackadaisical, seemingly dazed *putti*. Pontormo attenuates and exaggerates forms in strange ways, as in the elongated toes of many of his protagonists. And he plays on the relationship of his fresco to the decoration by Andrea del Sarto below, as Shearman has noted, by making his dog, at the left of the lunette, respond to the excitement in Sarto's fresco of the tribute to Caesar.[49]

In a way, the characters in Pontormo's decoration are evocative of the bucolic poetry of Lorenzo de' Medici. They are related to the comic rustics who appear in a great deal of the art and literature of the period, as in Renaissance festivities. For the wedding of Duke Cosimo de' Medici a number of allegorical figures were dressed in bizarre rustic costumes, and at a wedding feast for Charles the Bold, a female dwarf of Madamoiselle of Burgundy entered dressed like a shepherdess mounted on a gold lion.[50] Pontormo's strange characters not only evoke this pastoral travesty but also the comic Arcadia of Shakespeare's *As You Like It* or Cervantes's *Don Quixote* where Touchstone and Sancho Panza make farce of pastoral conventions or Bruegel's *Dirty Bride* where odd rustics make a travesty of Virgil.[51]

Pontormo did further decorations for the Medici at Poggio a Caiano for which there still are a number of drawings. The decoration consisted of nude

48. Mathias Winner, "Pontormos Fresko in Poggio a Caiano."

Figure 2–9, p. 32

49. John Shearman, *Andrea del Sarto*, 1:65.

50. Andrew C. Minor and Bonner Mitchell, *A Renaissance Entertainment*, pp. 176ff. Johan Huizinga, *The Waning of the Middle Ages*, p. 26.

51. Barnouw's interpretation of Bruegel's Virgilian travesty is given by H. A. Klein, *Graphic Worlds of Peter Bruegel The Elder*, p. 123, pl. 26.

Figure 5–8. Iacopo Pontormo. *Vertumnus and Pomona.* Poggio a Caiano.

Figure 5–9. Iacopo Pontormo. *Study of a Nude Playing Calcio.* Gabinetto dei Disegni, Uffizi, Florence.

figures playing football or *calcio*.[52] The iconography of the game is puzzling, but it may be that the subject of the game, the ball or *palla*, was intended emblematically as a reference to the Medici coat of arms (one might think of an analogous situation in the lost Vatican decoration by Tibaldi for Pope Julius III where *putti* played with mounts, emblematic of the del Monte pope).[53] In one marvelous drawing for the fresco, now in the Uffizi, a large, awkward nude lies on the ground, arms extended and mouth opened, as if he is bellowing in frustration (Figure 5–9). Perhaps he is a comic goalie who has just missed a shot? We might note in this context that *calcio* was also a subject for treatment later in the century when Giovanni dè Bardi of the Florentine *camerata* wrote a treatise, *Discorso sopra il gioco del calcio fiorentino.* Spoofing Aristotelian logic, Bardi observed that the final cause of the game is the passage of the ball through the goal of your opponent more times than through your own; the material cause is the player; and the efficient cause is the rich nobleman who pays for the uniforms. As Eric Cochrane has observed, the "clever juxtaposition of neat logical deductions and rough-and-tumble brawling" in dè Bardi's discourse was intended to elicit a smile from the reader.[54]

We also find Pontormo's bizarre wit exhibited in a late drawing, now in the Uffizi, of the Three Graces, that may also have been done for a Medicean decorative cycle (Figure 5–10).[55] Pontormo's oddly attenuated, wobbling, and

52. Janet Rearick-Cox, *The Drawings of Pontormo*, cat. nos. 307ff.

53. A. E. Popham and Johannes Wilde, *The Italian Drawings of the XV and XVI Centuries . . . at Windsor Castle*, no. 945, pl. 111. The relationship of the Windsor drawing to decorations for Julius III was brought to my attention by John Gere.

54. Eric Cochrane, "A Case in Point: The End of the Renaissance in Florence," in *The Late Renaissance*, p. 62.

55. Rearick-Cox, *The Drawings of Pontormo*, cat. no. 321.

Figure 5–10. Iacopo Pontormo. *Study of the Three Graces*. Gabinetto dei Disegni, Uffizi, Florence.

dazed figures are a bizarre travesty of the classical ideal that had been expressed in a more serious way by artists like Raphael and Correggio. It would almost appear that Pontormo's beauties are like young school girls self-consciously learning to dance, a striking contrast, for example, to the suave dancing Graces in Botticelli's *Primavera*.[56]

Pontormo's tendency to make caricature is also apparent in his religious works, including the small painting of the Madonna and Child with Saints Jerome and Francis (Uffizi), which seems to reflect the influence of Rosso's S. M. Nuova altarpiece.[57] Like Rosso, Pontormo tends to ridicule the noble decorum of High Renaissance religious art. His hump-backed, bald, and toothless St. Francis is a charmingly grotesque caricature. And the lion at the feet of St. Jerome peers out with an engaging but strange expression that reinforces the tone of the painting. Although the intense expressiveness and sincerity in many of Pontormo's religious works (including the Certosa Passion series and the Capponi Chapel altarpiece) may stand apart from the more cynical works of Rosso, it nevertheless is important to remember that, like Rosso, Pontormo was frequently capable of brilliant satire and parody. Both artists sustained the facetious strain found in the art of their important precursor, Piero di Cosimo.

In the same period that Rosso and Pontormo were exhibiting their bizarre wit, Francesco Parmigianino was creating equally bizarre and playful works, both in his native Emilia and in Rome. Before his voyage to the papal city, Parmigianino decorated a bedroom at Fontanellato (near Parma) with the legend of Diana and Acteon, inventing an illusionistic scheme derived from the playful allegories in Correggio's Camera di San Paolo (Figure 5–11).[58] The *putti* in his work, like Correggio's playful *putti*, are intended to add a tone of levity to the chamber. Parmigianino manipulates the shapes of their bodies, warping them in relation to the curving vault into highly contrived patterns that are delightfully bizarre. These playful deformations are analogous to the strange distortions of form in Pontormo's Poggio a Caiano frescoes.

When Parmigianino traveled to Rome in the 1520s, he brought with him a self-portrait in which he depicted himself as seen in a convex mirror (Figure 5–12). The exaggerated shapes and distortions of this painting reflect a bizarre and eccentric wit related to the eccentricities at Fontanellato. In both of these works Parmigianino seems to be playing on the conventions of illusionism. When one considers that the current style of art in Rome during the 1520s was one of exquisite grace, based to a considerable degree on Raphael's late work, the exaggerations of the portrait (especially in the hands) can be seen as an extension and, ironically, as an extreme expression of this refinement. It is perhaps not an exaggeration to see his self-portrait as a kind of parody of conventional portraiture. This is not to say that Parmigianino regarded the elegance of his art in a frivolous way. Yet the attitude underlying its conception

56. I owe this way of describing Pontormo's *Graces* to Beth Turner. Sydney Freedberg has pointed out to me that Pontormo's figures are poignant. However, poignance and parody are not necessarily incompatible.

57. Luciano Berti, *Pontormo*, pl. 78.

58. Augusta Ghidiglia Quintavalle, *Gli affreschi giovanili del Parmigianino*, pp. 74ff.

Figure 5-11. Parmigianino. *Diana and Acteon* (detail). Fontanellato.

Figure 5-12. Parmigianino. *Self-Portrait*. Kunsthistorisches Museum, Vienna.

59. Vasari, *Le vite*, 5:221.

60. A. E. Popham, *The Drawings of Parmigianino*, no. 43.

61. Vasari, *Le vite*, 5:230.

62. This interpretation was partially suggested to me by Konrad Oberhuber. To my knowledge the iconography of Parmigianino's painting has never been fully discussed.

63. John Charles Nelson, *Renaissance Theory of Love*, p. 104; and Edgar Wind, *Pagan Mysteries of the Renaissance*, p. 92.

seems to be ironic. Vasari would have appreciated this irony, and he did remark on its bizarre character.[59] In short, we may well compare the seeming irony and parody implicit in Parmigianino's painting to the similar qualities we have already noted in works of the period by Michelangelo and Rosso.

Like Rosso Fiorentino, Parmigianino would play at times on the humorous aspects of sex. In a drawing in the British Museum, Parmigianino represented Vulcan (with the other gods) pulling Diana forward to witness a sight repugnant to her chaste eyes (Figure 5-13).[60] In the background is a bed where figures of Mars and Venus may have been depicted before they were rubbed out by a puritanical collector. Parmigianino's sadistic joke on the virginal Diana has a nasty tone like that in Parmigianino's strange painting of Cupid done for a Parmesan gentleman (Figure 5-14). The subject of Cupid carving his bow and looking out, smiling at us, is puzzling. In the background one *amorino* twists the arm of another, who resists in pain. According to Vasari, the one *amorino* is scorching the hand of the other on the hot body of Cupid.[61] The humor here is rather sadistic, as the *amorino* who is inflicting considerable pain on his companion peers out at the beholder with a smile of satisfaction. The sadism of the painting is rather disturbing, but it is something which we might expect to find in the art of early mannerism. Within this bizarre, sadistic context Parmigianino's painting seems to illustrate a conventional theme, which is generally ignored in discussions of the painting. Cupid is, of course, the god of love, and the conjunction of love and pain here would no doubt have brought to mind for the sixteenth-century beholder the cliché, sometimes beautifully expressed in poetry and other literary genres, that love involves pain.[62] One thinks, for example, of Petrarch's sonnets and countless imitations, or more immediately, of Bembo's play on words in *Gli Asolani* where the association of love and bitterness (*amore* and *amaro*) is discussed.[63] Thus, the theme of Parmigianino's painting is conventional, although Parmigianino's manner of presenting this theme is somewhat bizarre.

One of the most notable of the early mannerists, Giulio Romano, was heir to Raphael's shop after the latter's death in 1520. Giulio completed Raphael's work in the Sala di Costantino, painting scenes from the life of Constantine that embody the political and religious ideals of Pope Leo X (Figure 5-15). The character of the illusionism used in these frescoes is a highly contrived synthesis of elements from Michelangelo's Sistine ceiling, Raphael's Loggia di Psiche, and other sources. The narrative scenes are painted on fictive tapestries (recalling Raphael's loggia for Chigi), flanked by popes, caryatids, and other allegorical figures. These figures are placed on different imaginary planes, and it is difficult to identify the location of the wall upon which the illusion of their reality is projected. The wit of this illusionism is related to the elaborate illusionistic frescoes by Peruzzi in the *salone* of the Farnesina (also influenced by Raphael), but Giulio's is more highly contrived. In Peruzzi's frescoes, the

Figure 5-13. Parmigianino. *Study of the Gods before the Bed of Mars and Venus*. British Museum, London.

Figure 5-14. Parmigianino. *Cupid Carving His Bow*.
Kunsthistorisches Museum, Vienna.

Figure 5–15. Giulio Romano. *Battle of Constantine*, Sala di Costantino. Vatican Palace, Rome.

wall is easy to locate once the viewer recognizes the illusion. In Giulio's frescoes, the complicated, overlapping surfaces of tapestries, painted figures, and fictive architecture create an ambiguity, causing the beholder's vision to oscillate before he finds the ultimate plane of the wall. Giulio's frescoes are a witty commentary on the artfulness of art and ultimately imply the fictional character of illusionism. Although passages in the narrative scenes are naturalistic, we are reminded that they are fictions since they are depicted on painted tapestries. These fictive tapestries project off the wall realistically, suggesting the reality of these objects which had implied the falseness of the reality in the narrative scenes. Like his contemporary, Parmigianino, Giulio is making a witty comment on the conventions of illusionism. Moreover, his frescoes have the quality of paradox about them, and in this respect they relate to the highly sophisticated paradoxical effects in Renaissance literature.[64] In Erasmus's ironic *The Praise of Folly*, for example, the author presents a view of folly in the world, but since these thoughts are expressed by Folly, we cannot be sure of the meaning of these foolish words. Giulio's art shares with Erasmus's rhetoric the ambiguities of paradox, which delighted the sophisticated and learned society of the sixteenth century. In this period, artists, as well as writers such as Erasmus, Rabelais, and Cervantes, began with increasing frequency to consider the ways in which man deceives himself in his perception of reality. Giulio Romano's frescoes and much of the decorative art of the cinquecento are witty, if not deeply serious, reflections of this issue. We have already considered the wit underlying the earlier illusionism of Mantegna and Peruzzi, and we should bear in mind that the elaborate mannerist decorations of the sixteenth century are also based on various witty manipulations of form. Giulio's Sala dei Giganti frescoes at Mantua, Perino del Vaga's Sala Paolina frescoes in the Castel Sant'Angelo, and Francesco Salviati's Palazzo Farnese and Palazzo Sacchetti frescoes are but a few of the more distinguished and wonderful examples of this kind of ingenious illusionism. These fresco cycles belong not only to the history of mannerist art but also to the story of wit in Renaissance culture.

Large-scale decorative works frequently include humorous details alluding to the life of the courts for which they were made, many of their pictorial incidents humorous in intent. In Giulio's dramatic *Vision of Constantine* in the Sala di Costantino, for example, a row of soldiers rushes forward dramatically across the composition toward the emperor. But in the meanwhile, in the right foreground of the fresco we find the leering and comically grotesque dwarf of Cardinal Ippolito de' Medici, Gradasso Berettai da Norcia, lifting his helmet. As Hartt has observed, the dwarf's activity might have been an allusion to his surname, "hatter."[65] The court of Pope Leo might have recognized his activity as a pictorial pun. In any case, the incongruity between the Medici dwarf and the scene's serious and dramatic event would no doubt, like the

64. Paradox in the Renaissance is discussed by Rosalie Colie, *Paradoxica Epidemica: The Renaissance Tradition of Paradox*. See also Walter Kaiser, *Praisers of Folly: Erasmus, Rabelais, Shakespeare*.

65. Frederick Hartt, *Giulio Romano*, 1:47.

little boy in Mantegna's St. James frescoes, have elicited a smile from the courtly observer. Berettai belongs to the world of Fra Mariano and Baraballo.

Much of the comedy in Giulio's art is gross. He drew a series of designs for engravings, now lost but known from woodcuts, to accompany a sequence of erotic sonnets, the *Sonnetti lussoriosi* by Pietro Aretino. Giulio's athletic figures, who make love in various improbable positions worthy of Aretino's ingenuity, could almost be parodies of the twisting *Ignudi* of Michelangelo. The humor in these prints is coarse, like the exchange between lovers in Sonnet III:

> Let him who hath it small play sodomite.
> But one like mine, both pitiless and proud,
> should never leave the female nest of joy.
>
> Ay but we girls, boy,
> so greedy are of what we hold so glad
> a thruster that we'd take him whole behind.[66]

This sexual comedy caused something of a scandal. Raimondi, who made the engravings from Giulio's *invenzioni*, was imprisoned, and Aretino, as Symonds put it, "discreetly retired from Rome for a season."[67]

Something of the flavor of these prints is still apparent in a painting of two lovers in the Hermitage which has been attributed to Giulio Romano (Figure 5–16). In this jewel-like, highly polished work, two lovers seated upon a bed embrace and are about to make love. Their bed has various decorations in relief, including a satyr making love with a woman, which contributes to the lascivious tone of the work. In the background an old lady enters the room. Is she a *ruffiana* or procuress of the sort that we might meet in Italian comedies of the period? A dog jumps up at her side, frightening the cat in front of the bed and drawing the viewer's attention to a ring of keys hanging from her waist. These keys may not be the keys which she uses to open doors, but they may also have another meaning. The Italian word for key (*chiave*) is frequently used colloquially in a sexual sense. In Act III, scene x of Bibbiena's *La Calandria*, for example, when Samia remarks to Ferensio, who is outside the door, that the "key hole is full" and that she has "oiled the key so that it might function better," she is not talking about what Ferensio thinks she is but about her lovemaking behind the door.[68] In Anton Francesco Doni's treatise, *La chiave*, which is related to other mock-pedantic discourses of the period on figs and chestnuts, the author discourses with extraordinary erudition on the sexual implications of *chiave*. He tells us that the key "is the sweetest, most dear, most necessary thing in the world" in a passage reminiscent of Aretino's above-cited apostrophe on the penis. He also suggests, with ludicrous learning, that Chiavasso, Chiasso, Chiaveri, and Chiavenna are towns all named after sexual events explicit in *chiavare*.[69] The same kind of joking

66. Quoted by Cleugh, *The Divine Aretino*, p. 70.

67. John Addington Symonds, *Renaissance in Italy*, 2:389.

68. Bernardo Dovizi da Bibbiena, *La Calandria*, in *Commedie del Cinquecento*, 2:64–65.

69. Anton Francesco Doni, *La mula la chiave e madrigali satirici del Doni fiorentino*, p. 24.

Figure 5–16. Giulio Romano. *Two Lovers*. Hermitage, Leningrad.

70. Seigneur de Brantôme, *Recueil des Dames*, p. 110.

71. Klein, *Graphic Worlds of Peter Bruegel The Elder*, pl. 45.

is found in Aretino's *Ragionamenti* where the "key in the lock," as in Bibbiena's *La Calandria*, is clearly understood in the sexual sense; and in the writings of the French Aretinesque author, Brantôme, mention is made of the *dames de Rome* who *chiavano*.[70] When we find a key placed prominently in the center of Bruegel's print of Lechery, its sexual connotations should be rather obvious to us.[71] Given then the sense of *chiave* or key in the works of Bibbiena, Doni, Aretino, Brantôme, and Bruegel (and we will stop here!), might not the key have the same playful sexual connotation in Giulio's erotic picture?

When patronage declined in Rome during the pontificate of Pope Adrian, Giulio traveled to Mantua, where he built and decorated the Palazzo del Te, the magnificent villa of Federigo Gonzaga. The mannerist architecture of the villa has frequently been remarked upon (Figure 5–17). On the facade of the inner court, triglyphs sag from the architrave, pediments appear above niches without shafts, and a seemingly random rustication creates a disconcerting effect. These witty architectural devices, superficially analogous to Michelangelo's unorthodox and more oppressive and powerful inventions in the Laurentian Library vestibule and the playful fantasies of cinquecento grotesque decorations, reflect the taste of the court for playful wit. Like the contemporary paintings of Rosso and Pontormo, Giulio's architecture makes light of High Renaissance classicism and has an element of parody in it. Giulio's

Figure 5–17. Giulio Romano. Courtyard. Palazzo del Te, Mantua.

play of architectural forms can also be likened to the verbal play in the word games that were so common in the Italian courts and which are embodied in Castiglione's *The Book of the Courtier*. Just as Giulio plays, for example, with the classical triglyph, deliberately misquoting it to create a new and witty effect, Bibbiena, in *The Book of the Courtier*, plays on a passage from Virgil's *Aeneid* (VI, 605–606), changing its meaning:

> It is also amusing to quote a verse or so, putting it to a use other than that intended by the author, or some other well-known saying, used in the same way or with a word in it changed. As when a gentleman who had an ugly and disagreeable wife, when asked how he was, replied, "You can imagine when *Furiarum maxima juxta me cubit*."[72]

72. Castiglione. *The Book of the Court-ier*, p. 159.

As Singleton points out in the notes to his translation of *The Book of the Court-ier*, the gentleman is playing on Virgil's *Furiarum maxima iuxta accubat*. The slight change is from "reclining hard by the greatest of Furies" to "The greatest of the Furies sleeps beside me."[73]

73. Ibid., p. 364, n. 25.

The various rooms of the Palazzo del Te are filled with decorations that, like the architecture, have a playful and often witty tone. The various humorous aspects of these decorations are worthy of a chapter in their own right, but we can only stop here to note a few details. The voluptuous decorations in the Sala di Psiche, for example, which evoke the palace of Cupid as described by Apuleius (as Chigi's villa had) have been appropriately called "Aretinian" by Gombrich.[74] In this room Giulio depicted scenes from the fable of Cupid and Psyche and related mythological subjects. We also know from a letter of Aretino to Federigo Gonzaga that a statue of Venus was also planned for the room. Hartt has suggested that the program for the decorations my have been invented by Paolo Giovio, the author of a book on emblems who had also invented the program for Pontormo's lunette fresco at Poggio a Caiano.[75] Giulio's decorations combine elegant, sensuous images with sometimes rather coarse, comic details. In the vault of the chamber, Giulio depicted a nude female figure (one of the Graces?) pouring water from a pitcher, as if on the spectator below (Figure 5-18). Next to her a *putto pisciatore*, also seems to be watering the spectator. If Mantegna had joked with the beholder by placing a pot precariously above the beholder in the Camera degli Sposi, Giulio carries the implications of Mantegna's earlier decoration to a coarse extreme. Although Giulio's foreshortened *putto* is inspired by Mantegna's Camera degli Sposi creatures, the activity of Giulio's *putto* is the product of his own ingenious, if gross and parodic wit.

74. E. H. Gombrich, *Symbolic Images*, p. 227, n. 40.

75. Hartt, *Giulio Romano*, 1:126ff, 2: pls. 265ff.

As in Raphael's loggia of Cupid and Psyche, which clearly influenced Giulio's frescoes, Giulio's decorations include the matrimonial banquet of the two lovers, Cupid and Psyche. This scene was depicted in the vault of Raphael's loggia but is magnificently and prominently illustrated on a lower wall in Giulio's chamber. We know that the iconography of Giulio's room actually

Figure 5-18. Giulio Romano. *A Grace and a Putto*, Sala di Psiche. Palazzo del Te, Mantua.

pertained to its function, for a banquet was held in the Sala di Psiche in honor of the imperial visitor, Charles V.[76] One can well imagine the delight of the emperor (known for his prodigious appetite, by the way), enjoying his feast and gazing at the equally sumptuous banquet of the gods, with its playful details, and the other entertaining decorations of the chamber.

One of the most capricious rooms in the villa is the fantastic Sala dei Giganti. In the ceiling, Jupiter flies through the air, unleashing thunderbolts on the giants below (Figure 5-19). The eagle of Jupiter was the emblem of Charles V, and the fresco may have been intended to flatter the Jovian Holy Roman Emperor during his visit to the villa. The eagle of Jupiter had also been adapted as an *impresa* by Frederigo Gonzaga himself, following Charles V.[77] In Giulio's fresco the giants are crushed by massive stones that appear to be part of the very architecture, giving the illusion that the room is collapsing on

76. Ibid., 1:106.

77. Ibid., 1:157–58.

Figure 5-19. Giulio Romano. *Fall of the Giants* (detail), Sala dei Giganti. Palazzo del Te, Mantua.

the beholder. The effect was thus described by Vasari: "whoever enters into that room, seeing the windows, and other things crumbling, and nearby in ruin, and the mountains and buildings falling, cannot but fear that everything is going to fall down in ruins upon him."[78] The playful effects of Giulio's painted architecture are similar to his witty manipulations of actual architecture, and his highly contrived illusionism is reminiscent of the witty effects in the Sala di Costantino frescoes. When Vasari says that the effect of the room is "horrible and frightful" his description, like the frescoes themselves, is rhetorical. There is nothing really frightening about this room. It is a delightful expression of fantasy, like the giant beasts done for the Orsini at Bomarzo or the exotic horrors in Ariosto's *Orlando Furioso*. Giulio's creatures are also related to the gigantic caricatures of Rabelais and the giants who are the ridiculous figments of Don Quixote's imagination.

Giulio's giants not only seem to celebrate the grandeur of Michelangelo's art but they also seem to mock the noble ideal of Michelangelo's nudes, implicitly making a travesty of the great artist's *terribilità*. Giulio's gigantic oafs might also be compared in their mocking caricature to the vulgar and hideous characters in Folengo's mock-romance, *Orlandino*, which was in fact dedicated to Giulio's patron, Federigo Gonzaga. When Folengo describes his hero, Orlandino, as a little boy in Sutri, the spirit of his mock *terribilità* is like Giulio's: "He hits, smashes, damages, and dismembers;/ Bears, lions, tigers, without fear,/ Fearlessly, he takes them on."[79] Folengo's kitchen and bedroom scenes have an earthy humor to them that is not only related to Giulio's work at Mantua but is similar to the general taste of the mannered courts of Europe, including the elegant French court that enjoyed Rabelais. A fascination with the humor of vulgarity is, as we have observed, one of the salient features of the mannerist sensibility.

78. Vasari, *Le vite*, 5:543.

79. Teofilo Folengo, *Orlandino*, in *Opere italiane*, ed. Umberto Renda, 1:128.

VI. The Lighter Side of Cosimo de' Medici's Court

That's exactly what I was saying—there's no room at Court for philosophy.
—Thomas More, *Utopia*

When we gaze at Benvenuto Cellini's fierce portrait of Duke Cosimo de' Medici, now in the Bargello, contemplate Baccio Bandinelli's severe busts of the duke, or consider Bronzino's equally grave portraits of Cosimo, we are reminded of the observations made by the Venetian ambassador to the Medici court, Vincenzo Fedeli, who underscored the harshness and severity of the duke's regime.[1] Fedeli tells us of Cosimo's severe legislation and penal system and of his terrifying system of spying on the Florentines. The severity of Cosimo's government was evident even to such a casual visitor to his court as William Thomas, who comments briefly on it in his *History of Italy* (1549).[2] It might, therefore, seem odd to look for humorous art in the court of a man who caused so much *terrore* and *spavento*. Yet the duke, for all severity and harshness, was a man who could laugh and be amused. His sense of humor is evident in a variety of works of art and literature done for and around him.

If Fedeli remarks on the duke's *terribilità*, he also tells us that the duke enjoyed joking (*burlando*) with his servants.[3] We also know that the duke kept a court dwarf, Morgante, and had court jesters such as the one whose death was lamented, according to a letter of the court painter, Bronzino, at the ducal villa, Poggio a Caiano.[4] Cosimo's sense of humor could be rather blunt. Seemingly annoyed by the lack of security in his court, he caustically remarked at one point, "that no one opens his mouth or even pisses in my house without its first being known down there [Rome]."[5] We know that the duke was frequently amused by the activities of Benvenuto Cellini, as the latter tells us, and the following story told by Cellini reflects both his and the duke's sense of humor.

> . . . one morning, after I heard mass at San Piero Scheraggio, that brute Bernardone, broker, worthless goldsmith, and by the Duke's grace purveyor to the mint, passed by me. No sooner had he got outside the church than the dirty pig let fly four cracks which might have been heard from San Miniato. I cried: "Yah! pig, poltroon, donkey! is that the noise your filthy talents make!" and ran off for a cudgel. He took refuge on the instant in the mint; while I stationed myself inside my house-door, which I left ajar, setting a boy at watch upon the street to warn me when the pig should leave the mint. After waiting some time, I grew tired, and my heat cooled. Reflecting then, that blows are not dealt by contract, and that some

1. Vincenzo Fedeli, *Relazioni degli ambasciatori veneti al Senato*, ed. Arnaldo Segarizzi, 3: part 1, pp. 123–74.

2. William Thomas, *History of Italy*, p. 105.

3. Fedeli, *Relazione*, p. 145.

4. Michael Levey, *Painting at Court*, p. 105.

5. Eric Cochrane, *Florence in the Forgotten Centuries, 1527–1800*, p. 44.

disaster might ensue, I resolved to wreck my vengeance by another method. The incident took place about the feast of our San Giovanni, one or two days before; so I composed four verses, and stuck them up in an angle of the church where people go to ease themselves. The verses ran as follows:-

> "Here lieth Bernardone, ass and pig,
> Spy, broker, thief, in whom Pandora planted
> All her worst evils, and from thence transplanted
> Into that brute Buaccio's carcass big."[6]

Both the incident and the verses were circulated throughout the palace, giving the duke and duchess much amusement. Cellini, who carried on at times like a court buffoon before Cosimo, no doubt amused the duke with his brilliant characterization of Baccio Bandinelli's Lysippean sculpture of *Hercules and Cacus* (Florence):

> Well, then, this virtuous school says that if one were to shave the hair of your Hercules, there would not be skull enough left to hold his brain; it says that it is impossible to distinguish whether his features are those of a man or of something between a lion and an ox; the face too is turned away from the action of the figure, and is so badly set upon the neck, with such poverty of art and so ill a grace, that nothing worse was ever seen; his sprawling shoulders are like the two pommels of an ass's packsaddle; his breasts and all the muscles of the body are not portrayed from a man, but from a big sack full of melons set upright against a wall.[7]

In this confrontation with Bandinelli before the duke, who assumes an almost Solomon-like role in settling the dispute between the two artists, Cellini continually jests, especially in defending himself against the charge of sodomy leveled at him by Bandinelli. After Cellini's retort, "the Duke and his attendants could control themselves no longer, but broke into such shouts of laughter that one never heard the like."[8]

Satire, comedy, and wit pervade the literature written for Cosimo. There is much playful humor, for example, in the comedy, *Il Commodo* by Antonio Landi, which was performed as part of the festivities celebrating the wedding of the duke to Elenora da Toledo in 1539.[9] This comedy belongs to the tradition of Renaissance comedies that was influenced by ancient Roman theater, including the works of Ariosto and Bibbiena performed earlier for Leo X. In the following decade, Giovanni Battista Gelli, who also wrote for Cosimo's wedding, dedicated his satirical *Circe* to the duke.[10] In these biting dialogues, which were influenced by Lucian and which relate to the skepticism of Guicciardini and Machiavelli (who translated Lucian), human beings turned into animals by Circe explain why they would prefer to remain animals rather than return to their dismal human form. Although serious issues concerning the human condition are raised, the arguments of the various creatures, such as the oyster and the mole, are quite witty. In the same period, Giorgio Vasari, the painter and superintendent of arts for Cosimo, produced his masterful

6. Benvenuto Cellini, *The Life of Benvenuto Cellini*, trans. John Addington Symonds, pp. 453ff.

7. Ibid., pp. 423–24.

8. Ibid., p. 425.

9. Andrew C. Minor and Bonner Mitchell, *A Renaissance Entertainment*.

10. The 1549 translation by Thomas Brown of *The Circe*, ed. R. Adams.

11. Giorgio Vasari, *Le vite dè più eccellenti pittori scultori et architettori*, ed. Gaetano Milanesi, 5:160.

Lives of the artists for the duke, a book that is filled with delightful tales about the humorous sayings and antics of artists. Vasari relied heavily on the trecento *novella* tradition of Boccaccio, which was continued by Florentine writers such as Firenzuola and Il Lasca. Vasari used humorous tales about artists not merely as casual anecdotes but to interpret and evoke the personality of the artist. For example, by relating a story about Rosso Fiorentino's pet baboon who wreaked havoc in the garden of a friar, Vasari expresses Rosso's satirical bent and attitude toward religion.[11]

A strong current of wit can be found in the work of Bronzino, one of the principal painters in the court of Cosimo. Bronzino was also a poet, and we should not neglect the ways in which the wit of his paintings relates to the literature of the period. We find a rather restrained wit in Bronzino's *Portrait of a Man* (Figure 6–1). The man portrayed by Bronzino is elegantly posed and aloof, the suave and graceful embodiment of the perfect Renaissance courtier. But despite the decorum of the painting, on the legs of the table next to the man there is an almost Michelangelesque cloth mask with a mocking expression on its face, and on the arm of the chair to the right is a grotesque animal head. We might ask why Bronzino has included these grotesque elements in his dignified portrait. For all of the portrait's seriousness, the witty grotesques create a tone that ironically runs counter to the overall tone of the painting. These coarse and bizarre elements suggest the ironic self-awareness of the courtier who poses or postures so elegantly, both aware of their presence and aloof from them. This sense of irony relates to the keenly ironic viewpoint found in the writings of Castiglione, Machiavelli, and Michelangelo, and in the *Essays* of Montaigne, which acknowledge and scrutinize the dichotomy between outer appearances and inner realities.

The kind of irony implicit in Bronzino's portrait can also be found in the widely read etiquette book, *Il Galateo*, written by the Florentine *letterato* and papal nuncio, Giovanni della Casa. This book ostensibly describes the elegance and grace of the perfect man of manners (like the man in Bronzino's portrait), and from the first word, *consciosiacosachè*, to the very last it is written in an elegant, mannered style. But what is frequently overlooked is the irony implicit in della Casa's continuous contrasts between vulgar habits and refined behavior. Della Casa's remark, "Again when you have blown your nose, you should not open your handkerchief and inspect it as though pearls and rubies had dropped out of your skull," is not only good advice but is intended to be amusing in its vulgarity.[12] One can well imagine Bronzino's aloof man, next to his own grotesques, smiling at della Casa's "grotesque" advice. He might also have been amused by the similarly ironic humor in Montaigne's tale:

> One French gentleman always used to blow his nose in his hand, a thing very repugnant to our practice. Defending his action against this reproach (and he

12. Giovanni della Casa, *Galateo*, trans. R. S. Coffin, p. 26.

Figure 6–1. Bronzino. *Portrait of a Young Man.* Metropolitan Museum of Art, New York.

13. Michel de Montaigne, *The Complete Essays of Montaigne*, trans. Donald Frame, p. 80.

14. Edi Baccheschi, *L'opera completa del Bronzino*, pl. 64.

15. Montaigne, *The Complete Essays*, p. 648.

16. Ibid., p. 644.

17. Leo Steinberg, "Michelangelo's Florentine *Pietà*: The Missing Leg," pp. 342–49.

18. *Burlington Magazine* 117 (1975):132.

19. James Holderbaum, "A Bronze by Giovanni da Bologna and a Painting by Bronzino," pp. 439–45.

was famous for his original remarks), he asked me what privilege this dirty excrement had that we should prepare a fine delicate piece of linen to receive it, and then, what is more, wrap it up and carry it carefully on us; for that should be much more horrifying and nauseating than to see it dropped in any old place, as we do all other excrements.[13]

One can suppose that Montaigne's tale would have amused many of the countless gentlemen and ladies during the cinquecento who elegantly posed for portraits with handkerchiefs in their hands.

We cannot fail to note that Bronzino's young man, like his *Gino Capponi* in the Frick Gallery and many other gentlemen in the sixteenth century, wears a codpiece.[14] Although this fashionable appendage appears to have been prevalent in the cinquecento, the codpiece hyperbolically symbolized sexual prowess and virility, and in this respect its prominence can be related to the pervasive priapean impulses in Renaissance literature. It also became the subject for considerable joking and satire. We can easily suppose that Bronzino's idealized gentleman (with his idealized phallus), who belonged to the world of Berni, Gelli, Doni, Firenzuola, della Casa, and of course, Bronzino, would have been amused by Montaigne's quotation from Juvenal in his *On Some Verses of Virgil*: "There is destiny that rules/ The parts of our clothes; for if the stars abhor you/ Unheard of lengths of member will do nothing for you."[15] Montaigne's comment in the cinquecento about the "sexual act" is applicable to current art historians' references to sexuality in Renaissance art: "What has the sexual act, so natural, so necessary, and so just, done for mankind, for us not to dare talk about it without shame and for us to exclude it from serious and decent conversation?"[16] We have an extensive iconography of Neoplatonic love in Renaissance art and literature, yet notwithstanding the current fashionable interest in erotic and pornographic art, we scarcely have a complete iconography of erotica in Italian Renaissance art. A few years ago an imaginative scholar put forward a controversial interpretation of Michelangelo's Florence *Pietà* that dealt with the erotic implications of the slung leg in the original conception of the statue and its theological bases.[17] Recently, on the anniversary of Michelangelo's birth, the editor of a distinguished art history journal dismissed this interpretation, calling for more careful scholarship in studies on Michelangelo.[18] Even if the erotic interpretation of the *Pietà* is open to question, one cannot but wonder whether the editor was offended by its allegedly poor scholarship or by its concern with sexuality.

In contrast to Bronzino's graceful portrait of a man, the artist's double-sided painting in the Uffizi of Cosimo's dwarf, Morgante, is more unequivocally unrefined (Figure 6–2).[19] By showing Morgante on two sides of the panel from two points of view, Bronzino is seemingly revealing that painting, like sculpture, can show more than a single point of view. It was just a few years before that Cosimo's court historian, Benedetto Varchi, had made his famous

Figure 6–2. Bronzino. *Morgante*. Uffizi, Florence.

inchiesta, asking notable Florentine artists, including Michelangelo, Bronzino, Cellini, and Pontormo, their opinions on the relative merits of painting and sculpture. A standard argument asserting the superiority of sculpture over painting (noted by Leonardo da Vinci, Castiglione, and others) was that painting, unlike sculpture, could not represent multiple points of view. It would seem that by painting Morgante from the front and then from the back that Bronzino was making a witty pictorial defense of painting. The issue was also explored in the same period by Daniele da Volterra whose two-sided David and Goliath (now at Fontainebleau) was painted for none other than Giovanni della Casa, who according to Vasari, wrote a treatise on painting and sculpture.[20] But leaving aside theoretical issues for the moment, we might note that the grossness of Bronzino's subject, who takes his name from Luigi's Pulci's giant, was intended to be laughable. Bronzino's work demonstrates again how the highly mannered society of the court appreciated this kind of vulgar comedy. Just as Bronzino could shift from a portrait of an exquisite gentleman to a coarse dwarf, a contemporary writer in Florence like Varchi could write elegant pages on Petrarch and Neoplatonism on the one hand, and comic poetry on pockets on the other: "If there were no pockets, every gentleman,/ Every rascal would always have his hands full of keys, papers, and thousands of twigs."[21]

Perhaps the best known of Bronzino's witty paintings is the *Venus, Cupid, Folly, and Time*, a work originally done for Duke Cosimo, who later gave it to Francis I (Figure 6–3). Bronzino's exquisite and lascivious painting, which shows Venus and Cupid kissing and surrounded by various allegorical figures, seems to be exceedingly complex in its meaning, and it has been subjected to a vast number of interpretations, the most influential of which has been Panofsky's in his *Studies in Iconology*.[22] In discussing all of the figures in the painting in relation to the moralizing iconographic tradition of the sixteenth century, Panofsky observed that Bronzino's work, "perfectly in harmony with the spirit of the Counter-Reformation, is an allegory of the 'Exposure of Luxury.'" But is the painting necessarily a seriously moralizing work as Panofsky and most art historians following him have assumed?

Michael Levey has recently suggested that in past discussions of the work, part of its narrative meaning has been overlooked. Not only are Venus and Cupid kissing, but Venus is stealing one of Cupid's arrows. Levey briefly surveyed a long iconographic tradition for this theft, from ancient cameos through the paintings of Fragonard, including an immediate precedent in a drawing by Michelangelo that was adapted for a painting by Pontormo.[23] Bronzino's painting is thus not only about the lovemaking of Venus and Cupid but about Venus's deceit. Bronzino has depicted Venus's deceit with such subtle wit and cunning that the viewer is more aware of the elegant pose of Venus's arm than of the fact that she is removing the arrow from Cupid's

20. Vasari, *Le vite*, 8:61.

21. Francesco Berni, *Opere burlesche*, 2:24.

22. Erwin Panofsky, *Studies in Iconology: Humanistic Themes in the Art of the Renaissance*, pp. 86ff.

23. Michael Levey, "Sacred and Profane Significance in Two Paintings by Bronzino," *Studies in Renaissance and Baroque Art presented to Anthony Blunt on his 60th birthday*, pp. 30ff.

Figure 6–3. Bronzino. *Venus, Cupid, Folly, and Time*. The National Gallery, London.

quiver and is thus disarming him. Indeed, many a beholder has been deceived by Bronzino's ingenious invention. Both the playful wit and lasciviousness of Bronzino's painting seem hardly in accord with the serious moralizing of the Counter-Reformation, as found for example in Giglio da Fabriano's *Degli errori della pittura* or Ammanati's famous penitent letter on the blatant nudity in his art. If the sixteenth-century beholder looked for a moral allegory in Bronzino's painting, what he in fact found was a lascivious seduction, incest, and theft. In discussing Bronzino's ironic painting, Freedberg wryly observes that it "pretends a moral demonstration of which its actual content is the reverse."[24]

Venus's deception of Cupid is a subtle variation on the familiar ironic theme of deception that can be found, for example, in Metsys's *Ill-Matched Lovers* (Figure 6–4). In the Northern painting an old lecher, seemingly in control of the situation, fondles the breast of a young woman, while she and an accomplice lift his purse. The pervasive irony of sixteenth-century art, which is related to the ironic literature of the period, has frequently been neglected. Nevertheless this irony is found in familiar works, even if it is rather basic. Thus, in Bosch's *Haywain* (Madrid) we find a simple irony as peasants, prelates, and knights all greedily grasp for hay, as if it were treasure, while unbeknownst to them the hay-filled wagon they follow is being pulled by demons into hell.[25] While Bosch ridicules human vices there seems to be no such moral allegory in Bronzino's painting. Or, rather, if Bronzino's painting does suggest a moral allegory, it seems not to take the allegory very seriously. Yet both Bosch and Bronzino do agree in their mocking of human folly.

The ambivalent humor in Bronzino's painting is especially apparent in the female figure at the right, identified by Panofsky as Deceit, and by Levey, following Vasari, as Pleasure. She is a cunning invention:

> She offers a honeycomb with one hand while she hides a poisonous little animal in the other, and moreover the hand is attached to her right arm, that is the hand with the honeycomb is in reality a left hand, while the hand attached to her left arm is in reality a right one, so that the figure offers sweetness with what seems to be her "good" hand but is really her "evil" one, and hides poison in what seems to be her "evil" hand but is really her "good" one.[26]

This "perverted duplicity," described perhaps not completely accurately but with mannered virtuosity by Panofsky, is related to the duplicity of Venus who steals the arrow from Cupid and to the perversion in the erotic embrace between mother and son.

In many respects, Bronzino's painting is like the elaborate decorations done by Rosso for Francis I and the witty emblems of the period that were meant to be deciphered. Bronzino's painting can be seen as a kind of painted emblem meant to amuse the duke. Even the smallest details in the painting are

24. Sydney J. Freedberg, *Painting in Italy: 1500–1600*, p. 299.

25. Carl Linfert, *Hieronymus Bosch*, pp. 56ff.

26. Panofsky, *Studies in Iconology*, p. 90. Difficulties with Panofsky's interpretation were initially pointed out in reviews of his book by Allan Gilbert and H. W. Janson, *Art Bulletin* 22 (1940):172–75.

Figure 6–4. Quentin Metsys. *The Ill-Matched Lovers.* National Gallery of Art, Washington, D. C.

meant to be understood in relation to the general meaning of the painting. Take, for example, a detail such as the centerpiece of Venus's headdress. It includes a naked figure in gold, which is seemingly Venus. Thus we gradually become aware as we scrutinize the painting that Venus is wearing a crown adorned by an image of herself, the epitome of *ricercato* wit. Cupid, who by the way, was known for his various tricks and deceits as we learn from Ovid, Tibullus, Apuleius, and others, seems to be fondling his mother's crown; and as they kiss and his mother disarms him, it seems possible that he is not simply grasping her bejeweled crown but is in fact in the act of removing it.[27]

At the right of Bronzino's painting a tone of levity is created by the figure identified by Vasari as Giuoco (Play), who smiles knowingly at Venus as he is about to scatter roses.[28] Giuoco wears bells, which were frequently worn by fools or jesters in courts like Cosimo's. And indeed there is an etymological connection between Giuoco and the court jester seen in the Joker that is still

27. I owe this observation to Andrew Ladis.

28. Vasari, *Le vite*, 7:598–99.

29. The possible allusion to Horace's ode was suggested to me by Andrew Ladis. For the use of "Sparge rosas" on the occasion of Duke Cosimo's wedding, see Minor and Mitchell, *A Renaissance Entertainment*, p. 121.

Figure 5-14, p. 129

30. Max Friedlaender and Jacob Rosenberg, *Die Gemälde von Lucas Cranach*, pls. 202–3.

31. Freedberg, *Painting in Italy*, p. 501, n. 13.

32. This kind of paradox is discussed by Sydney J. Freedberg, "Observations on the Painting of the Maniera."

evident in a modern deck of playing cards. As Cosimo watched Giuoco scatter roses he would perhaps have been made to think of "Sparge rosas," a motto from an ode by Horace that had been used several years earlier as part of the decorations for his wedding.[29] Bronzino is ironic even in his juxtaposition of figures, as Giuoco's outer levity only partially obscures the more ominous, deceitful figure behind him. Across from both of these figures we find the anguished figure generally identified as Jealousy, and when this figure is seen in relation to the deceitful action (or acts?) of the painting, we become more aware of how Bronzino has painted a satire on the pitfalls of love. The more playful aspects of Bronzino's commentary on the dangers of love might be compared in tone to Rabelais's satirical discussion of love in Book 3 of the *Histories of Gargantua and Pantagruel*, which would have amused Francis I, who, as we noted above, was the eventual recipient of Bronzino's painting. The sardonic tone of Bronzino's pictorial treatise on love might also be related to the satirical remarks of Gasparo, who makes a travesty of the more idealized views of love presented by others in *The Book of the Courtier*. The dangers of love evoked by Bronzino recall the similar themes in Parmigianino's *Cupid Carving His Bow* (see Figure 5-14) and the Lucianesque dialogues of Aretino. And Bronzino's cool and cunning Venus might almost be compared to Cranach's treacherous vamp in his various paintings of Venus and Cupid.[30] The honeycombs in both Bronzino's and Cranach's paintings remind us of the sting as well as of the sweetness of love.

Finally, as we might expect, the wit in Bronzino's painting can also be found in its very style. For instance, it has been noted that Bronzino's Venus is ingeniously based on the authoritative example of the Virgin in Michelangelo's Doni *tondo*.[31] Given the basic tone of Bronzino's painting it seems scarcely possible that Bronzino was alluding to an association between the Virgin and Venus. Rather, Bronzino's drastic shift in the function and context of the figure might suggest a certain element of parody. Moreover, the masks at the lower right of the painting not only function allegorically, alluding to deceit, but they also appear to be as natural as the actual figures in the painting, which on the other hand are highly artificial.[32] In short, the very premises of Bronzino's style are based on the wit and irony which were surely prized by Duke Cosimo and his court.

Among the artists who worked along with Bronzino, Vasari, and Cellini, for Duke Cosimo, Francesco Salviati is among the most notable. Although Salviati did not work as extensively for Cosimo as did other artists, he was exceptionally gifted and had an uncommonly fertile imagination. His illusionistic wit is not only abundantly present in the Palazzo Vecchio decorations and his frescoes in Rome in the Palazzo Sacchetti and the Palazzo Farnese but also in various drawings. Many of these include grotesque devices like those in Giulio Romano's studies for plates and utensils and are similar to the *invenzioni* of Cellini such as the *saliera* for Francis I. Salviati's pen-and-ink study of a helmet is teeming with seemingly alive creatures reminiscent of Filippino's grotesques and the living grotesques in the sculpture of Michelangelo and Cellini (Figure 6–5). The position of the eye on the helmet suggests that the contours of the helmet form a human profile. Salviati's delightful invention recalls Michelangelo's transformation of the profile of a pilaster base into a face. Yet if there was a fierce intensity in Michelangelo's poetical profile, there is a more bizarre effect in Salviati's. The eye of Salviati's helmet peers out almost surreptitiously in a way that evokes the eccentric gaze of the woman in Rosso Fiorentino's drawing (see Figure 5–3).

Playfulness and jest are found throughout the palatial apartments and gardens of Duke Cosimo. Some rather gross joking takes place, for example, in the Palazzo Vecchio. In the magnificent *salone* of the palace, Cosimo had Vasari decorate the walls and ceiling with scenes celebrating the might and grandeur not only of the Florentine state but ultimately of the Medici house and of Cosimo himself. As the duke indicated in a letter to Vasari, he wanted the *salone* to be more splendid than anything ever done for the popes or the Venetian Republic.[33] At the north end of the *salone* Baccio Bandinelli carved highly formal statues of Cosimo's illustrious Medici predecessors; and Michelangelo's *Victory* was eventually placed at the opposite end of the great room. The stress in Vasari's gigantic battle paintings is on the *fortezza* of Duke Cosimo, whose apotheosis was painted at the center of the ceiling. Ducal power is also expressed in the monumental *Labors of Hercules* done for the *salone* by the sculptor, Vincenzo de' Rossi. Hercules, who had been a symbol of the Florentine Republic in the Middle Ages, was appropriated as a symbol of ducal strength by Duke Alessandro (Bandinelli's *Hercules*) and by Cosimo.[34] But de' Rossi's statues are perhaps a bit ridiculous. Not only are they Michelangelesque but their contrived musculature and movements suggest an almost unwitting parody of Michelangelo's fierce style. They can almost be compared to Cellini's Herculean description of himself in his autobiography. To the reader Cellini's ferocity is somewhat ridiculous, although Cellini seems to take himself seriously. In de' Rossi's *Hercules and Anteus* there is, however, an unequivocal joke (Figure 6–6). As Hercules defeats Anteus by lifting him off the ground, Anteus holds firmly on to Hercules' penis, and it appears that Anteus is about to rip the mighty hero's genitals off. The comic theme that Hercules' sexuality is in jeopardy reflects general concerns in Cosimo's Florence that can also be found in literature of the period. In a tale told by Firenzuola, for example, a libidinous monk loses his genitals, and in a tale recounted by Il Lasca, a joke is played on an unpleasant tutor, who is dismembered.[35]

Figure 5–3, p. 106

33. Vasari, *Le vite*, 8:363.

34. L. D. Ettlinger, "Hercules Florentinus," pp. 119–42.

35. Agnolo Firenzuola, *Ragionamenti d'amore*, ed. Bartolomeo Rosetti, pp. 113ff; and Il Lasca, *Le cene*, pp. 15–20.

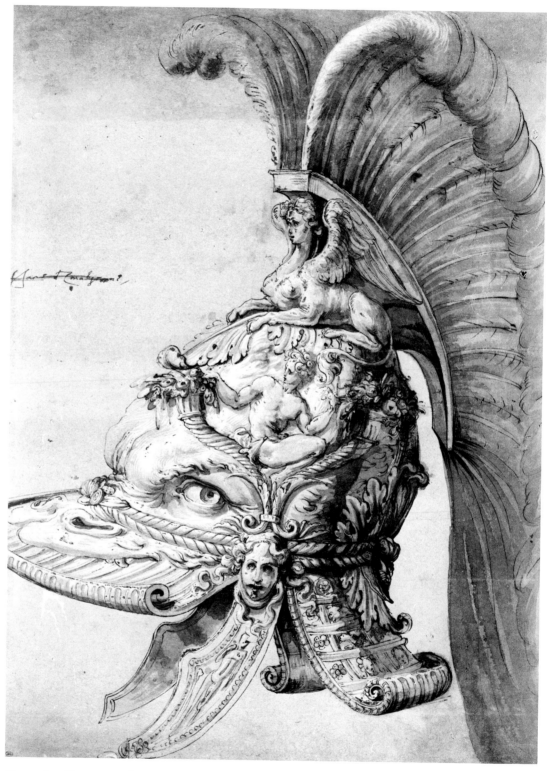

Figure 6–5. Francesco Salviati. *Study of a Helmet.* Cabinet des Dessins, Louvre, Paris.

Figure 6–6. Vincenzo de' Rossi.
Hercules and Anteus.
Palazzo Vecchio, Florence.

Once again we are reminded of the English poet's words: "We laugh at deformed creatures."

When Cosimo and Elenora moved out of the Palazzo della Signoria, which then became the Palazzo Vecchio, into the recently acquired Palazzo Pitti, they commissioned a number of works at their new residence, some of these both witty and amusing. In the gardens of the Palazzo Pitti, there is a sculpture by Valerio Cioli of Cosimo's dwarf, Morgante, astride a turtle who spouts water into a basin below (Figure 6–7). Cioli's magnificently paunchy Morgante is reminiscent of the fat Silenus as Piero di Cosimo and Peruzzi had painted him. It has also been suggested that the gesture of Morgante's hand extended over the water may be a mock-heroic reference to Neptune's calming the waters. When we recall that the giant *Neptune* in the Piazza della Signoria had just been done for Cosimo by Ammanati, the possible allusion to Neptune in the Cioli statue may take on a further mock-heroic implication.[36] Cioli's statue brings us back once again to Giovanni della Casa's *Galateo*. The plump, nude Morgante, whose phallus lines up with the turtle spout, is meant to amuse, as do della Casa's observations on nudity.

> No one must take off his clothes, especially his lower garments, in public, that is, in the presence of decent people, because that is not the right place for undressing. Besides, it might happen that the parts of the body which are normally hidden should be laid bare, and this would embarrass both the man himself and the onlookers.[37]

Throughout his *Galateo*, della Casa describes in vivid detail, no doubt to the delight of his courtly readers in the sixteenth century, the kinds of vulgarity to be avoided. He thus creates a comic image not only related to Cioli's and Bronzino's *Morgante* but also to Bruegel's peasants, Gargantua, Caliban, and Sancho Panza.

When we stroll from Cioli's *Morgante* back toward the Boboli Gardens, we reach the grotto begun by Vasari. The play between "nature" and "art" is a pervasive theme in Renaissance art and literature, and it is wittily expressed in the facade of the grotto where tufa is used to give a natural look to the highly artificial structure. Within the grotto we come upon Giovanni da Bologna's exquisite fountain statue of Venus, who is perched on a basin (Figure 6–8). As we have already noted, the lecherous satyrs, who peer up at Venus from below the basin, like the excited satyrs of Raphael and Peruzzi, were meant to amuse. Also within the grotto, Bernardo Poccetti painted a witty illusionistic view of playful satyrs and animals, evoking the bucolic world idealized in courtly literature (Figure 6–9). They are depicted above men and animals, shaped by Buontalenti in tufa, once again evoking the character of natural grotto forms. Beyond the ostensible visual wit in this decorative

36. Holderbaum, "A Bronze by Giovanni da Bologna," pp. 439ff.; and Eve Borsook, *A Companion Guide to Florence*, p. 287.

37. Della Casa, *Galateo*, p. 102.

Figure 6–7. Valerio Cioli.
Morgante Astride a Turtle.
Boboli Gardens, Florence.

Figure 6–8. Giovanni
da Bologna. *Venus*.
Boboli Gardens, Florence.

Figure 6–9. Bernardo Buontalenti. Grotto. Boboli Gardens, Florence.

38. Detlef Heikamp, "La Grotta Grande del Giardino di Boboli," pp. 27–43.

39. Heikamp's remark was made in a lecture given at Harvard in 1965.

40. Virginia Bush, *The Colossal Sculpture of the Cinquecento*, p. 293, pls. 320–21.

41. This detail was pointed out to me by Detlef Heikamp.

42. Cellini, *The Life of Benvenuto Cellini*, pp. 358–59.

ensemble, there is also an iconographical wit that was only recently rediscovered by Detlef Heikamp.[38] According to Bocchi's late sixteenth-century *Le bellezze di Firenze*, the decorations refer to the catastrophe described by Ovid in the beginning of *Metamorphoses* when mankind was turned into stone. The witty conceit underlying the work is this catastrophe, and Buontalenti's creatures appear appropriately in stone. The wit of this decoration is also expressed in the very decision of placing Michelangelo's unfinished slaves for the tomb of Pope Julius II (now replaced by copies) in the corners of the chamber. Their straining, heroic postures are implicitly parodied as now they are made within their new context to resist the mock-calamity, reminding us of Giulio's giants at Mantua. Informally, Heikamp has suggested that the joking in the Medici grotto is a kind of antecedent to similar devices used in the contemporary amusement park. One could almost say that the ducal **grotto** built for the Medici was a kind of courtly "fun house."[39] Strange as it might at first seem, it may be that many gimmicks in the fun houses and tunnels of love of the modern amusement park are related to the decorations of Renaissance villas and gardens.

The Medici filled the gardens of their villas with hidden fountains and playful sculptures, including the delightful decorations at Pratolino which were described in the sixteenth century by Montaigne. One of the most stupendous and amusing of these is the gigantic statue by Giovanni da Bologna symbolizing the Appenines done at Pratolino.[40] The statue is so gigantic (nineteen meters high) that, according to Federico Zuccaro, Cosimo's son, Francesco, fished from the giant's eye.[41] Like the creatures of Don Quixote's imagination, Giovanni da Bologna's statue is a testimony to the fantasy of the sixteenth century. This fantasy is also apparent in Benvenuto Cellini's "highly comic" tale of the colossal statue of Mars, which Cellini did for Francis I. This statue, like Giovanni da Bologna's, was so huge in fact that Cellini's *garzone*, Ascanio, kept his lover in the giant's head. With considerable delight and amusement Cellini tells us:

> The girl, while she sojourned in the statue's head, could not prevent some of her movements to and fro from being perceptible through its eye-holes; this made stupid people say that the ghost had gotten into the body of the figure, and was setting its eyes in motion, and its mouth as though it were about to talk. Many of them went away in terror; others, more incredulous, came to observe the phenomenon and when they were unable to deny the flashing of the statue's eyes, they too declared their credence in a spirit—not guessing that there was a spirit there and a sound young flesh to boot.[42]

VII. Laughter from The Venetian Boudoir

This chapter will be in the boudoir.—Michel de Montaigne, *On Some Verses from Virgil*

In Venice the greatest painters often tease the amorous activities of the gods. This lovemaking frequently occurs in the bedroom, but sometimes it takes place *al fresco*. Take, for example, Bellini's *Feast of the Gods*, which is one of the most beautiful paintings of the Italian Renaissance (Figure 7–1).[1] It was originally painted for the *camerino* adjacent to the bedroom of Alfonso d'Este in Ferrara. Like Mantegna's *Parnassus*, which was done for the *studiolo* of Alfonso's sister, Isabella, at Mantua, Bellini's painting belongs to a series of paintings.[2] Bellini placed the Olympian protagonists of his painting in a sensuous, dreamlike, woodland setting. Initially, Bellini apparently only hinted that his protagonists were gods by including just a few of their attributes.

Titian, who made changes throughout the painting when he completed it, especially in the landscape at the upper left, seems to have diminished the subtlety of Bellini's original conception by adding additional attributes.[3] In this charming and delicate work, the gods sit quietly, caress, and drink, as voluptuous nymphs attend them with wine. The painting is a sensuous, lyrical idyll, yet upon closer inspection it becomes a delightfully amusing work. When we look carefully at Jupiter, for example, we are amused by the slightly dazed look of the seemingly potted god, who reminds us of Piero di Cosimo's tipsy Bacchus in the *Discovery of Honey*. Jupiter's eagle (probably added by Titian) is "so bedraggled a fowl that it could be mistaken for a black goose."[4] It is reminiscent of Jupiter's comically crushed eagle painted by Raphael in the Farnesina. We might note that just a few years after Bellini's painting, Raphael, who had been commissioned to do a painting for Alfonso's camerino, which was never executed, painted a humorous feast of the gods as part of his Cupid and Psyche decorations for Chigi. The explicit joke in Bellini's painting, as Wind pointed out, is based on a passage in Ovid's *Fasti*. As the drowsy gods drank, Priapus approached the sleeping Lotis and began to "draw the garment from off her feet."[5] As Rabelais later put it, "Priapus, full of priapism, was about to priapize her."[6] Bellini shows Priapus at the right approaching the sleeping Lotis, and the beholder needs not only to look at the

1. The implicit humor in this painting is discussed by Edgar Wind, *Bellini's Feast of the Gods*, pp. 27ff.

2. The literature on the *camerino* is vast and controversial. A summary of it is given by Harold Wethey, pp. 29ff, and cat. nos. 12–15. See also Philipp Fehl, "The Worship of Bacchus and Venus in Bellini's and Titian's Bacchanals for Alfonso d'Este," pp. 37–95.

3. John Walker, *Bellini and Titian at Ferrara*.

4. Wind, *Bellini's Feast of the Gods*, p. 6.

5. Ibid., p. 29.

6. François Rabelais, *The Histories of Gargantua and Pantagruel*, trans. J. M. Cohen, p. 693.

Figure 7–1. Giovanni Bellini. *The Feast of the Gods*. National Gallery of Art, Washington, D. C.

painting but to listen to it, for according to Ovid, at the very moment of Priapus's approach, the ass of Silenus brayed, awakening Lotis and frustrating Priapus—a source of amusement to the other gods. The humor in Bellini's work is dependent upon the beholder's knowledge that the wanton Priapus is about to be disappointed, and the beholder knowingly joins the gods in the amusement that follows his frustration in Ovid's story. The joke, we might add, was amplfied by Titian who seems to have added the lyre held by Apollo between the legs of the excited Priapus. The rather unsubtle detail is reminiscent of the various priapean jokes we have already noted in abundance.

If Bellini's painting is facetious, its tone is at the same time rather grave and somber. Despite the erotic meaning of the painting, there is an almost spiritual aura that pervades the figures, who are gently bathed in the darkness before dawn. This tone is perhaps accounted for if we remember that the tale illustrated by Bellini is told by Ovid as part of his account of the cult of Priapus. Each year, according to Ovid, an ass was sacrificed as part of the annual offering to Priapus. This offering was illustrated in Colonna's *Hypnerotomachia Poliphili*, and perhaps Bellini, like Colonna, sought to evoke the spirit of these sacred mysteries.[7]

7. Wind, Bellini's *Feast of the Gods*, p. 30.

In considering Bellini's painting, it might be appropriate to note here two of the fundamental limits of visual humor. First, the painter presents the image directly to the beholder, unlike the writer who describes his subject in words. Thus, there is always the danger that the artist will be obvious in the creation of images, leaving too little to the imagination of the beholder. Second, the artist can only represent a single moment in time, whereas the writer conveys the flow or passage of time.[8] Much humor or effective telling of jokes is based on "timing," an element that is not part of the painter's repertoire. Bellini, with characteristic wit and delicacy, successfully confronted these limitations. By presenting Priapus at the side of the composition he does not overstress the central joke of the painting, and by presenting his subject in an abstracting if sensuous style he maintains a delicacy of tone. Bellini also approaches his subject in a literary way, describing the approach of Priapus to Lotis, but only suggesting the climactic bray of the ass and laughter of the gods at Priapus. The beholder is still in the position of the reader having to imagine for himself the next moment when Priapus is frustrated and ridiculed. The highly literary and delicate humor of Bellini's work can be compared to the implicit humor in the ensemble of Raphael's *Galatea* and Sebastiano del Piombo's *Polyphemus*. Although clearly the oafish Cyclops was meant to be ridiculed, the humorous aspects of this tale are not so much emphasized as suggested to the beholder, who, familiar with the story, would have been made by the images to remember its details. The beholders of Bellini's *Feast of the Gods* and of the contemporary frescoes by Raphael and Sebastiano del Piombo,

8. Gotthold Lessing, *Laocoön*, trans. E. Frothingham.

in appreciating the humor of these works, would in part have been "reading" into them what they already knew from texts.

Titian, who completed *The Feast of the Gods*, also did paintings for the *camerino* of Alfonso, the *Festival of Venus*, the *Andrians*, and the *Bacchus and Ariadne*. These paintings are based on various classical texts by Ovid, Catullus, and Philostratus.[9] The *Festival of Venus*, in particular, is based on the description of a painting in Philostratus' *Imagines* (Figure 7-2). If Philostratus had sought to demonstrate his literary virtuosity by describing an imaginary painting of the festival of Venus in brilliant and vivid detail, Titian would almost seem to have been trying to surpass the literary account of a painting with his own visual rhetoric. His playful and good-humored work portrays, with extraordinary virtuosity, a hoard of *amorini* beneath a statue of Venus, exploding across the canvas in a variety of playful activities. They hug, they dance, they wrestle, they fly, and they chase a hare. Their generally playful manner is reminiscent of innumerable other capricious *putti* who set a similar tone in Mantegna's Camera degli Sposi frescoes, Raphael's Loggia of Cupid and Psyche, Sodoma's bedroom decoration for Chigi, Correggio's Camera di San Paolo frescoes, Parmigianino's Fontanellato decorations, and Giulio Romano's Sala di Psiche frescoes at Mantua. In contrast to Bellini's languid and quiet comedy in the *Feast of the Gods*, Titian's is dynamic, joyous, and boisterous. One can almost hear the chatter of his gleeful *putti*.

The *Bacchanal of the Andrians*, also painted by Titian for Alfonso d'Este, is about love, music, and drinking, themes related to Bellini's *Feast of the Gods* (Figure 7-3). But in contrast to the quiet and dreamy tone of Bellini's painting, the spirit of the *Andrians*, like that of the *Festival of Venus*, is more exuberant. The dancing and drinking in Titian's painting are described and evoked by pulsating rhythms and dynamic brushwork that is especially apparent in the glittering, sensuous garments worn by the protagonists. To the right of this revelry and near a voluptuous, sleeping nude, recently identified as an allegory of Revelry, we find a *putto pisciatore*, who shows the effects of the wine. This amusing little character has recently been associated with Laughter, who is mentioned by Philostratus.[10] The image had already been adapted in Venice by Colonna in his *Hypnerotomachia Polifili*, which had a considerable influence on Venetian art in general and on details of Titian's *Sacred and Profane Love*, in particular.[11] Colonna described his *putto pisciatore* or *Riso* (Laughter) as part of a fountain, which in fact squirted Polifilo in the face, provoking laughter.[12] Rosso had included at least one *putto pisciatore* in his decoration for Francis I at Fontainebleau, Michelangelo depicted one in his drawing of a bacchanal of children, Giulio Romano adapted one at Mantua, and long after in the North, another one, the famous *Manniquin Pis* (an almost benevolent demon like Donatello's *Genius*) became a symbol

9. The iconography of these paintings is discussed by Erwin Panofsky, *Problems in Titian, Mostly Iconographic*, pp. 98ff.

10. Harry Marutes, "'Personifications of Laughter and Drunken Sleep in Titian's 'Andrians,' " p. 518. The identification of Laughter is disputed, however, by Fehl, "The Worship of Bacchus and Venus," pp. 37ff.

11. Walter Friedlaender, "La tintura delle rose," pp. 320–24.

12. Marutes, "Personifications of Laughter and Drunken Sleep," p. 518.

Figure 7–2. Titian. *Festival of Venus*. Prado, Madrid.

Figure 7–3. Titian. *Bacchanal of the Andrians*. Prado, Madrid.

Figure 7–4. Titian. *Venus and a Musician*. Prado, Madrid.

of Brussels. The *putto pisciatore* is, at any rate, a stock comic character in Italian Renaissance art, a counterpart to the comic dwarfs and buffoons of the Renaissance court. We encounter him in a drawing for a fountain by Correggio (British Museum), reminding us that the pissing *putto* of Colonna, whose book was known to Correggio, was also on a fountain.[13] The subject of the pissing *putto* could easily become a pictorial cliché or hackneyed formula as it did in countless Renaissance prints, but it escaped this pitfall in great works such as the Farnese ceiling decoration where Annibale Carracci painted (in a genuine tour de force) a *putto*, reclining on his back and pissing, with the utmost virtuosity, in a perfect arc.[14] This micturial comedy in the art of Titian, Giulio, Correggio, Carracci, and others has its analogue in the literature of the period. We have already met Lorenzo de' Medici's Bertoldo Corsini, "who

13. A. E. Popham, *Correggio's Drawings*, cat. no. 3.

14. John Rupert Martin, *The Farnese Gallery*, pl. 41.

Figure 7-5. Titian. *Venus and a Musician*. Prado, Madrid.

15. Rabelais, *Gargantua*, p. 74.

pissed like a mule," and we also encountered the most awesome *pisciatore* of the entire Renaissance, Rabelais's overgrown *putto*, Gargantua, who knew how to *faire un pipi*. Gargantua pissed on Paris *par ris*, hence the great city's name.[15]

    A great deal of Venetian art is of course erotic, and some of this erotic art was meant to be funny. This is certainly true of two paintings conceived by Titian of Venus and a musician which belong to a large series of paintings of Venus and a musician done by Titian and his assistants (Figures 7-4, 7-5). This group of pictures has been subjected to a highly detailed and serious Neoplatonic interpretation by Otto Brendel, which in large measure was followed and popularized by Panofsky.[16] Yet there is evidence that this interpretation is improbable and that the two Madrid paintings are satires rather than Neoplatonic allegories. But before analyzing these paintings it might be helpful to make a few observations on the place of Neoplatonism in the art historical literature.

16. Otto Brendel, "The interpretation of the Holkham Venus," pp. 65–75. See also Panofsky, *Problems in Titian*, pp. 121ff. The entire group of Venus paintings is discussed by Wethey, *Titian*, 3:195ff.

Now it is an indisputable fact that the Neoplatonic ideas of Ficino, Pico, and others had an extensive influence in Renaissance Italy as Robb, Kristeller, and others have demonstrated.[17] It seems apparent that the art theory of the period reflects this Neoplatonic thinking, as Gombrich and Panofsky have persuasively shown.[18] Nevertheless, there has been a tendency in the scholarly literature, as is the case in the interpretation of Titian's two Madrid paintings, to find Neoplatonic intentions in works of art where there is no firm evidence to justify such interpretations. We have already suggested, for example, that even if Botticelli's *Mars and Venus* alludes to an astrological passage in the writing of Ficino, we can scarcely refer to this playfully erotic work as Neoplatonic. This gradual tendency to over-Neoplatonize Renaissance works, which still persists, has only recently been called into serious question by a number of art historians. For instance, Hartt, followed by others, has argued that the Neoplatonic interpretations put forward by De Tolnay and Panofsky of Michelangelo's Sistine ceiling, his tomb of Pope Julius II, and the Medici Chapel decorations are exaggerated.[19] This is not to say that these works by Michelangelo cannot be analyzed in the Neoplatonic language of the artist's poetry. But evidence for a Neoplatonic intention or program in these works is open to question. Panofsky's suggestion that Raphael's Loggia of Cupid and Psyche was "invented in a Neo-Platonic spirit" has justifiably not been followed by the succeeding generation of Raphael scholars.[20] And arguments for reconsidering Hartt's Neoplatonic interpretation of Giulio Romano's Sala di Psiche frescoes have been offered.[21] In addition, Panofsky's widely disseminated Neoplatonic interpretation of Titian's *Sacred and Profane Love* does not take into account the fact that in the bucolic landscape behind the foreground figures there is a rabbit hunt, a subject that in the Renaissance had explicit sexual implications, as in the voluptuous rabbit hunt described by Shakespeare in *Venus and Adonis*.[22] Moreover, the rabbit in Titian's painting leads the viewer's eye to a rustic couple making love. This activity, too, stands quite apart from the idealized Neoplatonic concept of love.[23] Overly zealous Neoplatonizers of the twentieth century have tended to ignore the fact that, like Petrarchan conventions, as Neoplatonism became pervasive in the sixteenth century, it became the subject of fashionable or casual quotation and of playful satire.[24] They have, therefore, tended to neglect the analogous, satirical aspects of the visual arts. It is in this neglected satirical context, I believe, that we should approach Titian's Madrid paintings.

Brendel cited passages from Ficino, Bembo, Leon Ebreo, and Castiglione, to point out that, according to this Neoplatonic tradition, the senses of sight and hearing were the most noble and the means to the perception of beauty. According to Brendel's interpretation, the music played by the organists in Titian's paintings alludes to the sense of hearing, and the glances of the mu-

17. Nesca Robb, *Neoplatonism of the Italian Renaissance*; and Paul Oskar Kristeller, *Renaissance Thought*, pp. 48ff.

18. Erwin Panofsky, *Idea: A Concept in Art Theory*; and E. Gombrich, *Symbolic Images*, pp. 123ff.

19. Frederick Hartt, *History of Italian Renaissance Art*, pp. 488ff.

20. Erwin Panofsky, *Renaissance and Renascences in Western Art*, p. 191, n. 3.

21. Egon Verheyen, "Die Malereien in der Sala di Psiche des Palazzo del Te," pp. 42–43.

22. Erwin Panofsky, *Studies in Iconology: Humanistic Themes in the Art of the Renaissance*, pp. 150ff.

23. Recently emphasis has been placed in the scholarly literature on the nuptial significance of the painting; see Wethey, *Titian*, 3:175ff.

24. This kind of Neoplatonism is discussed by Robb, *Neoplatonism*, pp. 177ff.

sicians at Venus refer to the sense of sight. This Neoplatonic concept is clearly stated by Bembo in his speech on love in *The Book of the Courtier*:

> [The courtier] must consider that just as one cannot hear with the palate or smell with the ears, so too can beauty in no wise be enjoyed, nor can the desire which it excites in our minds be satisfied by means of touch, but by that sense of which this beauty is the very object, namely the power of vision.
>
> Therefore, let him shun the blind judgment of sense, and with his own eyes enjoy the splendor of his lady, her grace, her amorous sparkle, the laughs, the ways, and the other pleasant ornaments of her beauty. Likewise, with his hearing let him enjoy the sweetness of her voice, the concord of her words, the harmony of her music (if his beloved be a musician). Thus he will feed his soul on sweetest food by means of these two senses.[25]

Brendel's interpretation was qualified considerably by Middeldorf, who suggested that the paintings may refer to more than the senses of sight and hearing in the perception of beauty.[26] Not only does Cupid touch Venus in one painting and Venus touch a dog in the other, but the foot of Venus in each painting touches or appears to touch the musical courtier. Middeldorf also traces an extensive tradition from antiquity through Brantôme's *Dames Galantes* in which the importance of touch is stressed. Moreover, in some of Titian's related paintings, including a later painting in the Uffizi of Venus in which flowers are present, Titian evokes the beholder's sense of smell. In many of these paintings we have a veritable appeal to all or many of the senses, which can be compared to the similar intentions in Renaissance poetry such as Chapman's *Ovid's Banquet of Sence*. Middeldorf's point is sustained by mid-sixteenth-century literature in Venice, which is little known or read today. In his *Pistolotti amorosi*, love letters addressed to courtesans, Anton Francesco Doni frequently speaks of the manner in which all of his senses respond to the celestial beauty of his lovers. All of his senses are inebriated by the sight of them. In one letter to the distinguished courtesan, Francesca Baffo, Doni remarks that seeing and hearing her affected all of his senses: "dal vedere e udire voi trahevano i sensi miei."[27] The spirit is the same in Ludovico Domenichi's *La nobilità delle donne* in which Francesco Grasso speaks of the female body, appealing to the sense of touch as well as of sight. Grasso's observations on the female body closely parallel Titian's sensuous descriptions of Venus: "From this, it follows that the female body is very delicate to see and touch; the very tender flesh, the fine pale neck, the luminous and fine hair, the beautiful head . . . the full breasts, dressed abundantly in flesh to form solid mounds . . . the very fleshy thighs."[28]

It might be suspected that, according to these writers, the sense of sight is not necessarily related to the Neoplatonic philosophy of love. In Bartolommeo Gottifredi's *Specchio d'Amore*, for example, the old bawd, Coppina, instructs the young Maddalena that the sight of any part of her body ("ogni

25. Quoted by Brendel, "The Interpretation of the Holkham Venus," pp. 65ff.

26. Ulrich Middeldorf, *Art Bulletin* 29 (1947):65–66; see also the letter of Alfred E. Hamill, p. 65, of the same issue. I have been informed that similar approaches to the erotic character of Titian's paintings were also recently taken in lectures delivered by Charles Hope at the Johns Hopkins Symposium and by D. M. Davidson at the Middle Atlantic Symposium in the History of Art (April 1976).

27. Anton Francesco Doni, *Pistolotti amorosi*, 29v, 115r, 48v.

28. Ludovico Domenichi, *La nobilità delle donne*, 21r.

particella del tuo corpo veduto ignuda") will inflame her lover. Coppina is talking about physical passion, not Neoplatonic ascent.[29] In his *La piazza universale di tutte le professioni del mondo* Tommaso Garzoni observes that courtesans attract the lascivious eye of their beholders, thus inciting them to libidinous acts.[30] And Thomas Coryat, an English visitor to Venice, warns his readers against the allurements of the Venetian courtesans: "As for thine eyes, shut them and turne them aside from these venerous Venetian objects. For they are also double windows that conveigh them to thy heart. Also thy must fortifie thine ears against the attractive inchaunments of their pleasurable speeches."[31] In Venice sight and hearing lead to passion and lascivious acts! This is the city in which, as Shakespeare intimates, Cupid, "king of codpieces," has spent much of his quiver, and it is also the city of Ben Jonson's libidinous Volpone.[32]

So many paintings done in Venice by Titian and his followers, such as Lambert Sustris, were erotic and were meant to be titillating.[33] Their character and the bemused responses to them is known from contemporary accounts. Thus, Paolo Pino, the painter and art theorist who was a contemporary of Titian, remarked with what Gilbert has called "sly frankness" on an erotic painting that excited desire ("Vi se ricciava l'appetito"). And Giovanni della Casa, who was papal nuncio in Venice, remarked characteristically with tongue in cheek that a nude by Titian would excite Cardinal San Silvestro ("che faria venir il diavolo adosso al Cardinale San Silvestro").[34]

Erwin Panofsky, who accepted Brendel's Neoplatonic interpretation of Titian's paintings with qualifications, remarked that "The Neoplatonic doctrine of love and beauty thus filled the very air which Titian breathed."[35] But these Neoplatonic vapors must not, alas, have been breathed (in their purest form) by men like Titian, Doni, Calmo, Domenichi, Gottifredi, and Aretino, and by women such as Veronica Franco and Angela Zaffetta. In the sixteenth century a famous visitor to Titian's city, Montaigne, remarked: "My page makes love and understands it. Read him Leon Ebreo and Ficino; they talk about him, his thoughts, and his actions, and yet he does not understand a thing in it."[36] Montaigne's satirical comment on Neoplatonic theories of love is closer to Venetian attitudes toward Neoplatonism than the modern art historian's observation would lead one to believe. There was a strong and pervasive tradition in Venice of humorous anti-Neoplatonism, to which Titian's paintings are, I believe, related. Some of this neglected writing, much of which was published in Venice, is very good satire and is worthy of our attention. In his *Ragionamenti*, for example, Francesco Sansovino satirizes Neoplatonism in his discussion of the art of seduction. Sansovino, whose model is Ovid rather than Plato, claims that "woman was born solely for our pleasure."[37] He facetiously pokes fun at the improbabilities of Neoplatonic love. Sansovino's *Ragionamenti* is similar to and was perhaps influenced by Alessandro

29. Published in Florence by Doni, who wrote and usually published in Venice; see Giuseppe Zonta, ed., *Trattati d'Amore*, p. 263.

30. First published in 1585, Tommaso Garzoni, *La piazza universale di tutte le professioni del mondo*, p. 441.

31. The reprint of the 1611 edition of Thomas Coryat, *Coryat's Crudities*, 1:406.

32. William Shakespeare, *Much Ado About Nothing*, act III, scene iii, ll. 133–35.

33. For example, Bernard Berenson, *Italian Pictures of the Renaissance: Venetian School*, 2: pl. 1242.

34. Both quotations are from Creighton Gilbert, "Antique Frameworks for Renaissance Art Theory: Alberti and Pino," p. 97.

35. Panofsky, *Problems in Titian*, p. 109.

36. Michel de Montaigne, *The Complete Essays of Montaigne*, trans. Donald Frame, p. 666.

37. Published in Venice in 1545; see Zonta, *Trattati d'Amore*, esp. pp. 153ff., and pp. 160, 165.

38. Published in 1539; see Alessandro Piccolomini, *La Raffaella*, ed. Dino Valeri.

39. Rita Casagrande, *Le Cortigiane veneziane nel '500*, p. 171.

40. Zonta, *Trattati d'Amore*, p. 207.

41. Nicholas James Perella, *The Kiss Sacred and Profane*, p. 202.

42. Andrea Calmo, *I piacevoli et ingegnosi discorsi*, p. 42.

Piccolomini's *La Raffaella*, published earlier in Venice. In Piccolomini's dialogue, Raffaella receives a complete recipe from the older Margherita on how to take a lover when her husband is away. Sometimes using the idealized language of Neoplatonism (and thus parodying it), Piccolomini plays ironically on the outer "modesty" and "honesty" of the perfect young seductress and her subtle, yet sensual techniques.[38] In one of his *Pistolotti amorosi*, Anton Francesco Doni remarks to his lover that he and she, "two old foxes," do not need all of those theorists of love. Love for Doni is being beside and above his lover.[39] When he remarks in the letter cited above that his seeing and hearing the courtesan Francesca Baffo overwhelmed his senses, he is clearly not speaking in a Neoplatonic way. Another distinguished courtesan, Tullia d'Aragona, who lived in Venice for several years, wrote an elaborate dialogue, *Della infinità di amore*, in which she learns from Benedetto Varchi about Neoplatonic love, a rather ironic situation given her profession. In fact, at one point in the dialogue, which rehearses so many Neoplatonic clichés, Tullia reminds Varchi that because of her experience she really does know more about love than her mentor.[40] Titian's friend, Aretino, the king of comic erotica, whose writings set the tone for much Venetian literature, mocked the Neoplatonic soul kiss in various passages, including the following one from his *Ragionamenti*:

> Their breasts were now joined so firmly together that the hearts of both of them kissed one another with equal affection. Whereupon they fed themselves gently in each other's spirit that had rushed to their lips because of the pleasure, and drinking them (the spirits) in, they tasted the sweet pleasures of heaven, and the aforesaid spirits gave signs of happiness during the "ohs" and "ahs" and "life" "soul of mine," "my heart," "I'm dying," "wait for me" were over. Whereupon both he and she sank slowly down, expiring their souls into one another with a sigh.[41]

It seems possible, as Brendel suggested, that Titian's paintings of Venus with a musician allude to the senses of sight and hearing. Yet they (and especially the Madrid versions) clearly refer to more than that. The spirit of these paintings does not relate simply to the serious Neoplatonizing texts of Ficino, Bembo, Leon Ebreo, and Castiglione, but to the playful treatment of Neoplatonism that one finds in the humorous, if vulgar writings of Aretino and his circle. After all, the aperture of Venus's body at which Titian's musicians are looking in the two Madrid paintings is clearly not the Neoplatonic "window" to the soul. Even more to the point we are reminded by Titian's musicians of yet another Venetian love letter, this one written by Andrea Calmo to Madonna Taffuri in which Calmo asks for the privilege of the lady's "melliflous concavity": "vi domando il fausto, et trionpho, el privilegio de la vostra concavitae meliflua."[42] The subject of the courtier's concern in Titian's painting is, like Calmo's, what the anonymous sixteenth-century

French poet referred to as the *bien suprême*.[43] Titian would have smiled knowingly had word later reached him in Hades during the seventeenth century of
The Antiplatonick by John Cleveland, who wrote, "Love that's in contem-
plation plac't, Is Venus drawn but to the waist."[44] In the backgrounds of both
of Titian's paintings there are fountains with satyrs on them, related to the
actual fountain done by Giovanni da Bologna for the Medici. Might these
satyrs refer not only to the lasciviousness of the painting's subject but also to
the painter's satirical intention?

In a well-known essay on the influence of Neoplatonism, "Icones Sym-
bolicae," Gombrich observes that "the search for recondite symbolism should
not blind us to the more obvious qualities of 'bedroom art.' But the one approach does not necessarily exclude the other. Perhaps even this type of art
was thought sometimes to exert an influence beyond its erotic appeal."[45] Perhaps this observation applies to some paintings, but one can well imagine what
Titian or Aretino would have thought had such a suggestion been made about
the two Madrid paintings. Gombrich is nevertheless suggestive when he uses
the term *bedroom art,* for he reminds us, as Middeldorf had, that Titian's
Venus paintings and other related works were possibly hung in bedrooms.
Coryat tells us that courtesans had their portraits hung in their bedrooms, but
we want to know more about the destiny and context of the large group of
Venus paintings done by Titian and his followers.[46] Venus was of course the
goddess who was reputed to have taught courtesans their art, as was her sister
goddess, Flora. Now Titian and Palma Vecchio had painted portraits of
women in the guise of Flora, which have reasonably been identified as courtesans.[47] But we might further consider the various paintings of Venus done
in cinquecento Venice in light of the fact that Venice was the abode of a
prominent and celebrated group of courtesans such as Francesca Baffo and
Veronica Franco, highly talented ladies, who sang, composed poetry, and
seemingly set the tone of fashionable Venice.[48] Their status was such that
Henry III sought out and visited Veronica Franco during his state visit to
Venice in 1574, which by the way is magnificently described by Francesco
Sansovino in his *Venetia città noblissima*.[49] Madonna Franco later sent her
portrait to the French monarch. It is also highly suggestive that the Venus in
Titian's *Venus of Urbino* is reclining in a room filled with magnificent tapestries and decorations that invite comparison with the voluptuous *ambiente* of
the courtesan in the anonymous cinquecento poem, *Il vanto della cortigiana*.[50]
One supposes that the paintings of Venus were made for men, and indeed we
know that one of the Madrid paintings was owned by Charles V.[51] But still
we might ask to what extent do these paintings reflect or relate to the ambience
of the Venetian courtesans, who were the friends of Titian and Aretino. Perhaps further research and study of these paintings will provide us with answers

43. Jacques Bosquet, *Mannerism*, p. 185.

44. *The Metaphysical Poets*, ed. Helen
Gardner (Baltimore, 1957), p. 218.

45. *Journal of the Warburg and Courtauld Institutes* 11 (1948): 185. The note
is expunged from the reprinted version of
the essay in Gombrich, *Symbolic Images*,
p. 123.

46. Coryat, *Coryat's Crudities*, 1:403.

47. Julius Held, "Flora, Goddess and
Courtesan," in *De artibus opuscula XV:
Essays in Honor of Erwin Panofsky*, ed.
Millard Meiss, 1:201–18.

48. Much fascinating information concerning the Venetian courtesans is given by
Arturo Graf, "Una cortigiana fra mille:
Veronica Franco," *Attraverso il Cinquecento*, pp. 177ff; and by Casagrande, *Le
cortigiane*.

49. First printed in 1563; Francesco Sansovino, *Venetia città nobilissima et singolare*, pp. 441ff.

50. Graf, *Attraverso il Cinquecento*, pp.
285ff. On the other hand, it has been argued
that this painting was made for the marriage of the Duke of Urbino; Theodore
Reff, "The Meaning of Titian's *Venus of
Urbino*," pp. 359–66.

51. For all of these paintings, see Wethey,
Titian, 3: 195ff. The painting owned by
Charles V is listed as cat. no. 47.

52. Casagrande, *Le cortigiane*, p. 156.

53. The *poesie* are illustrated by Wethey, *Titian*, 3: pls. 141ff.

to the question. But for the moment we must rest content, imagining that the lovely music, sensuality, and humorous satire of the two Madrid paintings reflect comic and erotic aspects of evenings like the one spent in December 1547 by Titian and Aretino visiting the courtesan, Angela Zaffetta.[52]

Titian also exhibited his playfulness in the *poesie* done for Philip II.[53] Sometimes the humor in these works is incidental, that is, subordinated to a larger expressive purpose. Thus, the garter and grotesque sandals worn by Adonis in the *Venus and Adonis* are incidental to the intense passion of the scene. Similarly, although one may suppose that the benign docility expressed on the face of Titian's beflowered bull in the *Rape of Europa* might have been intended to elicit a smile, again this detail has minor importance in terms of the painting's overall dramatic purpose. Titian's humor is, however, more boisterous when he illustrates Jupiter's seduction of Danae (Figure 7–6). On the one hand his painting, echoing Correggio's for Federigo Gonzaga, is a voluptuous and sensuous image of the chaste maiden seduced by Jupiter in the form of a gold shower. But while Titian focuses our attention on the yielding flesh of Danae, he also plays with the myth by stressing Danae's servant greedily collecting the gold coins that descend as part of Jupiter's shower. One might imagine that this *invenzione*, worthy of Titian's friend, Aretino, could have originated in farcical presentations of the myth in court festivities. It might be noted here that Titian's joke is carried to a ridiculous extreme in a painting now in Lucca of the same subject by the Bolognese mannerist, Calvaert (Figure 7–7). In a painting that verges on heavy-handed farce Calvaert not only shows the servant eagerly reaching up for the gold coins but also Danae herself reaching up for them. Calvaert's painting, which is similar in tone to much unsubtle humor in countless cinquecento *novelle* and comedies, is worth noting as a contrast to the more subtle and charming humor of a master like Titian. The transformation of the classical myth into farce has its parallels in Italian comedy of the period. In Alessandro Piccolomini's *L'amore costante*, the ridiculous tutor, Ligdonio, makes passionate love to his student, Margherita, by comparing his own passion for her to that of Jupiter, who descended to his lover in a golden shower. Not only is Ligdonio's comparison of himself to the Olympian god rather ridiculous but the foolish pedant gets his mythology mixed up, confounding the myths of Jupiter and describing the god as gold passing into the lap of the sweet Leda! ("Scennesse Iove e, diventato oro lustrantissimo, se n'ando de passo in passo in grembo della zuccarata sua Leda)![54]

54. Alessandro Piccolomini, *L'amore costante*, in *Commedie del Cinquecento*, Nino Borsellino, ed., 1:368.

Piccolomini's Ligdonio is one of the countless pedants ridiculed during the Renaissance. They are usually mocked in literature and only rarely in the visual arts as in Bruegel's ironic *Temperance*, which shows a wonderfully absurd, almost Aristophanesque astronomer standing upon a globe, improbably

Figure 7–6. Titian. *Danae*. Prado, Madrid.

Figure 7–7. Dionisio Calvaert. *Danae*. Pinacoteca, Lucca.

Figure 7–8. Niccolò Boldrini. *Parody of the Laocoön* (woodcut after Titian). British Museum, London.

and intemperately measuring the distance to the moon with a compass.[55] Ligdonio and the astronomer are joined by Belo's *pedante*, Rabelais's Hippothadeus, Rondibilis, and Wordspinner, and Shakespeare's Holofernes, all babbling *pedantesco*. Even the greatest men of learning from antiquity are mocked. We find the lecherous and silly Virgil dangling in a basket and Aristotle ridden by Phyllis in prints by Lucas van Leyden and others.[56] These supposedly wise men, mocked for their lust or false learning, are to be measured against the great men of learning idealized by Raphael in the Stanza della Segnatura.

Titian's humor is not always so delicate. In a drawing, known from a print by Boldrini, he mocks the great *Laocoön* statue unearthed in Rome in 1506 (Figure 7–8). This work had inspired a poem by Sadoleto and had influenced Michelangelo.[57] Innumerable copies of it were made, including a

55. H. A. Klein, *Graphic Worlds of Peter Bruegel The Elder*, pl. 54.

56. Other examples are given by Jane Campbell Hutchinson, "The Housebook Master and the Folly of the Wise Man," pp. 73–78. I am grateful to Christie Stephenson for calling this satirical tradition to my attention.

57. Sadoleto's poem is given in Lessing, *Laocoön*, p. 207.

Figure 7–9. Iacopo Tintoretto. *Venus and Vulcan*. Alte Pinakothek, Munich.

58. H. W. Janson, *Apes and Ape Lore in the Middle Ages and the Renaissance*, pp. 355ff.

version by Baccio Bandinelli, now in the Uffizi, and a bronze cast was done by Primaticcio for Francis I, which is now in the Louvre. But whereas the Hellenistic statue embodied a heroic concept of humanity that inspired Michelangelo's *Ignudi*, Titian depicted the Trojan priest and his sons as apes! Titian's intention may have been to parody not only the statue itself but also the fashionable interest shown by contemporary artists who "aped" its style.[58] Titian's parody of the ancient work that was so admired recalls some of the nasty jokes of Aretino and Rosso. It is related to various other parodies of style that we have already discussed, in particular the travesty of the *Laocoön* in a passage from the *Ragionamenti* written by his friend Pietro Aretino. Aretino describes a *Generale* of the church making love with a nun. He calls her his dove, he places one hand between her legs, the other on her breasts, and as he kisses her, his face has "that funny look the marble statue at the Vatican museum gives the snakes that are strangling him between his sons."[59]

Iacopo Tintoretto, who appropriated the drama of Titian's painting, transforming it into his own highly rhetorical and theatrical art, is one of the masters of bold, unsubtle Venetian comedy. Perhaps his best-known humorous painting is the *Venus and Vulcan* (Figure 7–9). As Venus reclines upon a bed, almost naked, the clumsy cuckold, Vulcan, moves slowly forward, pulling away a drapery from between her legs. Tintoretto seems to have put as much stress on the clumsiness of Vulcan as on the erotic charm of Venus. His god of the forge is mocked in the same spirit by Niccolò Franco, secretary of Aretino, who laughs at Vulcan in his *Dialoghi piacevoli*: "I don't know who could stomach looking at you, as you are lame, crippled, black, and with all the curses of mankind. We wonder then how Madame Venus can even put up with you."[60] In Tintoretto's painting, Venus seems scarcely interested in her husband, who to borrow Franco's term, is *Zoppo*, the Cripple. Our attention is also drawn by the yapping dog on the floor to the figure of Mars hiding under the furniture. This is not the triumphant Mars of Mantegna's *Parnassus*, in harmony with Venus, but the absurd figure of her lover, clinking around in his armor, hiding from Vulcan. As the mighty god of war cowers on the floor, we are reminded of the joking of Aretino, especially of his satires of the infidelities of wives in the *Ragionamenti*. The Aretinesque joking here is also comparable to farcical, Boccaccesque bedroom scenes in cinquecento comedy in which lovemaking is witnessed by a concealed voyeur.[61]

Tintoretto also exhibits a spirit comparable to that of cinquecento comedy, in his painting, *Susannah and the Elders* (Figure 7–10). On a superficial level the painting seems to have been intended as an allegory condemning vanity or lasciviousness, yet in a way related to the effect of Bronzino's *Venus, Cupid, Folly, and Time*. Tintoretto's voluptuous nude (like similar figures in the work of Titian) seems also to have been intended for the voyeuristic pleasure of the beholder, who is in the position of the elders. As Tintoretto's beautiful and luminous maiden sits by her bath, surrounded by garments and jewels, two lecherous elders peer at her around a trellis of roses. The bald, bearded elder in the foreground, sneaking a peek at the young beauty, looks absurd carrying on in such a fashion at his age. He is like Giannotti's *Vecchio amoroso*, Amerigo, and the other *vecchi rimbambiti* of the Italian cinquecento comedy such as Cecchi's Ambrogio (*L'Assaiuolo*) and Caro's Marabeo (*Gli Straccioni*) whose passions, like those of the old lechers in ancient Roman comedies, are ludicrous.[62] The old lecher, Marabeo, is in fact called "Vecchiaccio di

59. *Aretino's Dialogues*, trans. Raymond Rosenthal, p. 29.

60. Niccolò Franco, *Dialoghi piacevoli*, 17r.

61. The farcical element in Tintoretto's paintings is discussed by Carla Lord, "Tintoretto and the *Roman de la Rose*," pp. 313–17.

62. These comedies are included in Borsellino, *Commedie del Cinquecento*.

Figure 7–10. Iacopo Tintoretto. *Susannah and the Elders*. Kunsthistorisches Museum, Vienna.

Susanna" by the servant, Nuta, who ridicules his lust.[63] In his interpretation of a subject that is frequently painted seriously, Tintoretto dwells on the grotesque quality of the lecherous old man. He seems to be making the same point that Montaigne made in his essay, *On Some Verses from Virgil*: "Nature should have contented herself with making this age miserable without making it also ridiculous . . . . This appetite should belong only to the flower of beauty and youth."[64] A close parallel to Tintoretto's *vecchio rimbambito* appears in the Giustiniana, a type of song popular in Venice in which old men stutter out their passionate pleas to young lovers. Andrea Gabrieli's three-part Giustiniana of 1570 is a wonderful example in which the singers tremble and stutter: "Ancho-no-no-nor che col patire/ Ma se-ne-ne-ne-ne sento sgagliare,/ Scamper vorave ogni-hora nome-ne-ne-ne nento." As Alfred Einstein has pointed out, Gabrieli's Giustiniana is also a parody of both the music and the text of Cipriano de Rore's *Anchor che col partire*.[65] We might further note that Tintoretto's foolish old lechers can be compared to the ludicrous old men who were inflamed by young women in Northern paintings by Metsys and others. In the sixteenth century there is a related iconography in the comic emblem discussed by Alciati in which old people are accidentally wounded by the arrows of Love rather than of Death and are thus ludicrously inflamed.[66] This emblem was adapted in the seventeenth century by Peachem in his *Minerva Britanna* and was humorously dramatized in the same period by James Shirley in his masque, *Cupid and Death*.[67] This iconographic tradition persists through Thomas Rowlandson's comic-erotic drawings of libidinous old men and in the late prints of Picasso where the aged artist appears as lover and voyeur.[68]

Tintoretto's humorous bent appears again in his painting, now in the Uffizi, *Leda and the Swan* (Figure 7–11). In Tintoretto's painting the fleshy body of Leda is presented openly to the viewer (voyeur?) as the swan snakes forward from the right toward the subject of his passion. To the left a servant holds the top of a cage with a duck in it, and behind her there is a caged parrot. The presence of these other caged birds underscores the absurdity of the divine lover as an uncaged bird. As a dog yaps at the approaching swan, a cat to the left eyes the duck in the cage. Both the caged duck and the parrot may function here in a symbolic way, just as the key probably did in Giulio Romano's painting of two lovers. There is an extensive tradition in the works from Bosch to Steen in which caged birds have a sexual meaning; and we have already noted the giant, winged, birdlike phallus in the North Italian print of the late quattrocento.[69] Given both Tintoretto's subject and the implications of the word *bird* (*uccello*) it seems possible that this sexual symbolism is present as part of Tintoretto's erotic comedy.

The playful implications of the myth of Mars and Venus have been seen

63. Ibid., 2:221.

64. Montaigne, *The Complete Essays*, p. 676.

65. Alfred Einstein, *The Italian Madrigal*, 1:374.

66. Edgar Wind, *Pagan Mysteries of the Renaissance*, p. 163.

67. The reprint of the 1612 edition of Henry Peachem, *Minerva Britanna*, p. 172; and James Shirley, *Cupid and Death*.

68. An example is given in Gert Schiff, *The Amorous Illustrations of Thomas Rowlandson*, pl. 6.

69. Jay Levenson et al., *Early Italian Engravings from the National Gallery of Art*, pl. 527.

Figure 7–11. Iacopo Tintoretto. *Leda and the Swan*. Uffizi, Florence.

Figure 7–12. Paolo Veronese. *Mars and Venus*. Private Collection, Turin.

in various works of the Renaissance which we have already encountered, and we find them again in the work of that delicate and charming Venetian humorist, Paolo Veronese. Veronese's playfulness is only marginal in his masterful and voluptuous allegorical *Mars and Venus*, now in New York, where Cupid binds the two gods, evoking the allegory of Harmony. Venus squeezes milk from her breast, and there may be in the painting, as Wind suggested, a deliberate allusion to *fortezza* (Mars) submitting to *carità* (Venus).[70] There is a basic decorum in the painting as Mars covers Venus's pudenda with a drapery. In the background, however, Veronese depicts a faun, conventionally associated with lasciviousness, and the bridled horse of Mars, who is charmingly checked by Cupid, holding up Mars's sword. Veronese seems to be playing here on the sexuality of Mars and Venus, restraining it on the one hand and thereby intensifying the viewer's awareness of it. Horses are conventionally powerful erotic symbols (used, for example, by Shakespeare in *Venus and Adonis*), and Veronese seems to make a most delicate play on this tradition by realizing Mars's steed as so demure and docile. Veronese is more overtly humorous in his painting of the same subject now in Turin, a work which is neglected but which deserves to be better known (Figure 7–12). Here Mars and Venus are seated in bed, holding hands and about to begin lovemaking when Cupid strolls into the room, coaxing along Mars's bridled horse, which improbably descends a staircase. Mars's horse is rather absurd, made up with elegant, curly eyelashes and a coiffure worthy of Venus herself. Whether Veronese is playing on the bridled horse as a symbol of Mars's momentarily restrained passion, or whether he makes Mars's beautified steed allude to the taming and implicit feminizing of the god of war, there is an element of teasing in the interruption of this clandestine affair. Moreover, the bizarre image of a horse descending a staircase into the boudoir is at least incongruous, if not silly.

Veronese's humor is no less charming in his delightful *Rape of Europa*, which is in the Palazzo Ducale (Figure 7–13). If Titian's depiction of the myth, showing Europa carried across the waters, had been dramatic, Veronese has injected an almost rococo delicacy and preciosity and into his telling of the story. Veronese's picture is almost the scene of a toilette (like Tintoretto's *Susannah*), as Europa's attendants ironically, it would seem, dress her in preparation for her ride on the bull. The bull is of course Jupiter in what Shakespeare referred to as a "heavy descension."[71] There is a certain charm in the fact that our Olympian rapist seems to be so entirely overlooked amidst the busy preparations for Europa's trip. Now Ovid tells us in *Metamorphoses* that Jupiter kissed Europa, and Veronese has realized the ridiculous implications of this vague image by showing Jupiter implanting a moist bovine smooch on Europa's foot.[72] Veronese's bull, which recalls the artist's pretty horses, is adorned

70. Wind, *Pagan Mysteries*, p. 89.

71. Shakespeare, *Henry IV: Part II*, act II, scene ii, ll. 174–75.

72. *Metamorphoses*, 2:862.

Figure 7–13. Paolo Veronese. *Rape of Europa*. Palazzo Ducale, Venice.

with ringlets of flowers around each horn, and Veronese might just have been playing on the same image, appropriate to the subject of the painting, that Shakespeare did in *As You Like It* when he sang of a "lusty horn."[73] In the background of Veronese's painting we see a later moment when the bull, carrying Europa on his back, slowly descends a hill leading to the water. Finally, in the distant waters we see them again; and Europa bids us *addio* as Jupiter carries her off to his Olympian boudoir.

73. Shakespeare, *As You Like It*, act IV, scene ii, l. 18.

VIII. *The Grotesque and Mock-heroic in North Italy*

So suddenly have you cleared your brows, and with so frolic and hearty a laughter given me your applause, that in truth as many of you as I behold on every side of me no less than Homer's gods drunk with nectar and nepenthe: whereas before, you sat as lumpish and pensive as if you had come from consulting an oracle.—Erasmus, The Praise of Folly

1. Frederick Hartt, *History of Italian Renaissance Art*, pl. 395.

During the early cinquecento, Castiglione observed the delightful wit in the various courts of Italy, especially Urbino. The members of Duchess Elisabetta's court, including Giuliano de' Medici, Bibbiena, and Signor Gasparo, discussed the ideal courtier whose qualities had been embodied in the illustrious former duke of Urbino, Federico da Montefeltro. Duke Federico, who had built the magnificent palace at Urbino (where the discussions in *The Book of The Courtier* took place), was extolled by his contemporaries for his military prowess, learning, and piety, qualities symbolized in various works done for him, including Pedro Beruguette's portrait of the duke and his son. Federico was also a man of considerable wit whose taste is clearly reflected in the stunning illusionistic intarsia work of his *studiolo*.[1] In this room, which later must have impressed Pope Julius II during his visit to Urbino and which might have influenced plans for the Stanza della Segnatura, the great men of learning, whose books were in the ducal library, were depicted. In the intarsia work of this chamber, pieces of wood are minutely juxtaposed to create illusionistic vistas strikingly like those actually seen from the ducal palace: views of the gentle, rolling hills around Urbino that were also recorded by Piero della Francesca in his portraits of the duke and his wife. The wit of this intarsia work is especially apparent in the illusion of cabinets with doors that are seemingly swung open. This witty illusionism, a kind of visual play that is analogous to the illusionism of Mantegna's work at Mantua and to work done in the Palazzo Schifanoia at Ferrara, also anticipates the kind of illusionism found in the villa of Agostino Chigi, who adapted the trappings of ducal splendor. The intarsia books and musical instruments of Federico's *studiolo* evoke the sophisticated literary ideals of the court and in this respect invite comparison to later works such as the *studiolo* of Isabella d'Este at Mantua and the Stanza della Segnatura decorations, which also included intarsia work.

In contrast to the refined and mannered art done for the Northern courts, the humor of provincial artists in the North is frequently bizarre and eccentric. The late quattrocento itinerant painter, Carlo Crivelli, for example, whose playfully illusionistic fly we have already considered, was capable of the most peculiar humor. Crivelli, who worked in the Marches in the shadow of Bellini and Mantegna, populated the armor of his plaintive *St. George* (Figure 8-1) with lion heads, recalling the teeming animal life of Filippino's warrior in the Strozzi Chapel (see Figure 2-10), and he included below St. George a charmingly ferocious dragon, who roars at the indifferent saint.[2] His series of saints now in the Musée Jacquemart-André is also wonderfully bizarre in its mock-ferocious and pensive attitudes and gestures, especially the sword-swinging St. Paul and the pensive St. Basil, who deep in thought, sucks on his index finger.[3] Crivelli's rich decorative inventions, which owe a great deal to Mantegna but which are frequently even more fantastic than those of the great Lombard master, include improbable details such as the wonderful elephantine creature on the throne behind the Virgin in the London *Immaculate Conception*.[4] It is difficult to tell whether these creatures, which in their fantasy evoke the similar *bizzarrie* of the bronzes by the Paduan, Riccio, are elephants with acanthuslike ears and trunks, or whether they are in fact part of an acanthus scroll that has incipiently been transformed into elephants.

If the soul of Raphael, as it was said, had transmigrated into the body of Parmigianino, it might also have been said that the soul of Crivelli passed to the body of Lorenzo Lotto. Lotto, who like Crivelli worked in the Marches, projected an odd, if marginal, humor into his well-known works of the early cinquecento such as the Recanati *Annunciation* (Figure 8-2). In a composition influenced by Titian, the Virgin, commanding the viewer's immediate attention, turns away from the angel and directly toward the viewer in a manner that evokes her troubled response as described in the Gospel. Yet in the midst of the painting's dramatic urgency, Lotto depicts an amusingly frightened cat, perhaps an allusion to the devil, who darts away from the angel.[5]

The number of humorous provincial works done in North Italy is considerable, but as just one further example we might note a detail in the dome decoration of Santa Maria dei Miracoli in Saronno, done by the Piedmontese painter, Gaudenzio Ferrari.[6] As the Virgin is borne heavenward in the dome, the joyous event is celebrated by intense, music-making angels, who move in eccentric, excited rhythms, conveying a kind of provincial religious urgency as Lotto's characters do. One of these angels, just above the drum of the dome, is an exceedingly sweet and disarming figure, who seems transfixed as it plays the bagpipes. We cannot help becoming aware of the fact that this rapt, heavenly musician holds its instrument in such a position as to allude to two breasts. The sweetness and charm of this figure are indicative of Gaudenzio at his best.

Bagpipes frequently have humorous connotations. According to the an-

Figure 2-10, p. 34

2. Anna Bovero, *Tutta la pittura del Crivelli*, pls. 28 and 30.

3. Ibid., pp. 110-11.

4. Ibid., pp. 131-32.

5. The possibility of this diabolical symbolism was suggested to me by Gail Gibson.

6. Emanuel Winternitz, *Musical Instruments and Their Symbolism in Western Art*, chapter 10, pl. 21c.

Figure 8–1. Carlo Crivelli. *St. George*.
Metropolitan Museum, New York.

Figure 8–2. Lorenzo Lotto.
Annunciation. Recanati,
Chiesa dei Sopra Mercanti.

cient myth, the goddess Minerva played the pipes, delighting the gods at an Olympic banquet. However, Juno and Venus smiled at her distorted and puffed cheeks as she played, and the embarassed goddess eventually cursed and threw away her pipes, which were later snatched by Marsyas. The tale is told by Giovanni della Casa, who remarks that "some people have a way of pursing their lips from time to time, or screwing up their eyes, or puffing their cheeks, and blowing out their breath, or making various similar grimaces. . . . They ought to desist entirely from these habits." Della Casa concludes that because playing the pipes caused Minerva to distort her face, she did well to abandon this instrument which is unsuitable for ladies and men, "except for those poor wretches who are paid to play them and make a trade of it."[7] Della Casa's "poor wretches" might almost be the comic bagpipe players in works by Bruegel, including the *Dance of Peasants* and the *Fat Kitchen.*[8]

Let us return from the ruder areas of the Marches and Piedmont to the refined world of the court, this time the court of Ferrara. Unfortunately, most of the art work done for this court in the quattrocento has been destroyed, including what must have been a wonderful fresco cycle of the myth of Cupid and Psyche in the *zardin secreto* of the villa, Belriguardo. The magnificent astrological fresco cycle done by Francesco Cossa and others in the Palazzo Schifanoia for Borso d'Este, however, still exists, giving us a glimpse at the splendor of the Ferrarese court.[9] These frescoes include various playful and amusing passages such as the image of the duke surrounded by smiling courtiers and the court fool, Scofula, a scene that evokes the joking of the court. One of the best-known frescoes in the cycle, commemorating April, shows Mars enchained by Venus atop a barge and attended by smiling, good-humored courtiers and ladies, who chat, make music, whisper sweet nothings, or make love as we might expect them to do in the realm of Venus. We again might listen to painting and hear the trumpeting of the swans who pull the barge, actually a kind of triumphal chariot for Venus, who dominates over Mars, as she does in other paintings we have seen. In the less well known but even more erotic fresco of May, Mars and Venus are shown making love, and again as we have come to expect, the erotic subject is treated playfully. The artist has painted the empty dress of Venus by the side of the bed, as if it were occupied by a kneeling body. The empty dress (occupied by a *dama inesistente*, to transform Calvino's recent hero) seems amusingly to kneel in veneration to the divine lovers. This humorous tradition at Ferrara was continued in the early cinquecento when Bellini's *Feast of the Gods* (see Figure 7–1) and Titian's mythologies (see Chapter 7), were done for the *camerino* of Alfonso. The lovemaking, music, and humor of Titian's *Bacchanal of the Andrians* (see Figure 7–3), for example, recall the themes and tone of Cossa's allegory of April.

7. Giovanni della Casa, *Galateo*, trans. R. S. Pine-Coffin, pp. 102–3.

8. H. A. Klein, *Graphic Worlds of Peter Bruegel The Elder*, pls. 24 and 36.

9. Paolo d'Ancona, *The Schifanoia Months at Ferrara.*

Figure 7–1, p. 159

Figure 7–3, p. 163

Figure 8–3. Dosso Dossi. *Bacchanal*. The National Gallery, London.

10. Some scholars believe that the London *Bacchanal* comes from the *camerino*. The problem is reviewed by Felton Gibbons, *Dosso and Battista Dossi*, cat. no. 127.

11. Selected translations of Pulci's *Morgante* are given in John Addington Symonds, *Renaissance in Italy*, 2: 483ff.

12. Gibbons, *Dosso and Battista Dossi*, pls. 23–25.

13. The iconography is summarized in ibid., cat. no. 78.

Dosso Dossi was another artist who did work for the *camerino* of Alfonso d'Este. The son of a *fattore* at the Ferrarese court, Dosso eventually became a court aritst. Although his *Bacchanal* for the *camerino* is apparently lost, his London painting of the same subject is indicative of the playfulness in the Ferrarese court (Figure 8–3).[10] Reflecting the influences of Bellini, Giorgione, and Titian, his painting depicts satyrs and nymphs who quietly embrace and make love, or sit as if feeling the effects of the wine that they have been drinking as it courses through their veins. Some of the protagonists are still eating and drinking, and Dosso pokes gentle fun at the charmingly indulgent *putti*, first cousins of Giulio's creatures, one of whom is asleep and presumably drunk, the other eating enthusiastically. The former creature—perhaps a play on Bellini's sleeping Lotis in the *Feast of the Gods?*—is a diminutive counterpart to the prodigious comic eaters of the Renaissance such as Gargantua and Sancho Panza and Pulci's Margutte, who can tell you "How best to grease your jaws and stuff your belly."[11]

Under the influence of Giorgione, Dosso created at Ferrara lyrical and dreamy landscape paintings that are evocative of the fantastic landscapes conceived by the court poet, Ariosto, in his great *Orlando furioso*. Like Ariosto, whose playfulness and wit are apparent in his plays as well as in his great romance, the "affable" Dosso had a delightful sense of humor. This humor is abundantly manifest in a number of his works such as his painting in Modena of the smiling court buffoon, his *Laughing Youth* (Longhi Collection) and his so-called *Riso, Ira, Pianto, e Paura* (Cini Collection), where various emotions are comically mixed.[12] It is not inconceivable that the humor in this last painting alludes to the imbalance of the "humors" in its various characters. Like Ariosto, Dosso could be disarmingly charming in his presentation of a humorous situation. In a painting in Vienna he depicted Jupiter, Mercury, and a virgin in front of an exquisitely fantastic, Ariosto-like landscape which seems almost to vanish into mist before one's eyes (Figure 8–4). The picture, which is presumed to have astrological significance, conceivably alluding to the artist's birthdate, and which is also perhaps based on a dialogue of Lucian, reveals to us the improbable image of the mighty, all-powerful *Jupiter tuonans* so absorbed in his painting of delicate butterflies that he is too busy to hear the pleas of the virtuous virgin. Meanwhile, Mercury mediates between the two figures by indicating to the virgin that she should maintain silence. The tone of the painting, notwithstanding its pathos, is delicately mock-heroic, like Ariosto's poetry which gently parodies the pomp and prowess of chivalric heroes.[13] In its mixture of pathos and comedy, Dosso's painting seems almost to evoke the great comic mythologies later painted by Velasquez.

If Ariosto's literary humor could at times be exceedingly gross, as it was in his *Suppositi*, Dosso's pictorial comedy could also reflect a coarser impulse.

Figure 8–4. Dosso Dossi. *Jupiter, Mercury, and Virtue*. Kunsthistorisches Museum, Vienna.

This less refined humor is apparent, for example, in Dosso's highly satirical and curious mythological painting in the Uffizi, the *Bambocciata* or *Stregoneria*, which may have been done for Duke Ercole (Figure 8–5). According to Felton Gibbons's recent interpretation of the painting, the aged figure at the left with a ring of roses round his head is Hercules.[14] The distaff held up by the figure to the right alludes to the fact that Hercules has been tamed and feminized by Omphale. If Hercules' virility is the subject of Shakespeare's jest when he speaks of Hercules' codpiece as "massy as his club," here in Dosso's painting it is Hercules' loss of masculine powers that is made ridiculous.[15] The mock-heroic tone of the painting is sustained by the leering figures

14. Felton Gibbons, "Two Allegories by Dosso for the Court of Ferrara," pp. 493–99.

15. William Shakespeare, *Love's Labor's Lost*, act III, scene iii, l. 181.

Figure 8–5. Dosso Dossi. *Bambocciata*. Uffizi, Florence.

behind Hercules who, evoking the comic types of Jan Steen, seem to jeer at the once-mighty Hercules. Closely parallel to Dosso's painting are the various versions of Hercules and Omphale painted in the same period by Lucas Cranach, who stresses the feminine dress of Hercules (Figure 8–6).[16] Hercules is not the only great personage from antiquity to be ridiculed. Lucas van Leyden illustrated the comic tale of Virgil in a basket pursuing the emperor's daughter. The tale of Phyllis taming Aristotle, who is made to appear ridiculous and thus laughable in numerous prints by the Hausbuch Master, Hans Burgmair, Baldung Grien, Lucas van Leyden, and others, similarly mocks an ancient sage. A related subject in a drawing perhaps done in Ferrara and attributed to Cossa (Uffizi) shows a comical old hag beating down a man.[17] Dosso's absurd hero is also related to the comic image of Hercules in prints by Dürer and Goltzius and in Spranger's *Hercules and Omphale*, and we should not fail to recall the grotesquely comical sexual problem of de' Rossi's Hercules in the Medici court.

It is perhaps not unreasonable to associate Dosso's painting to the words of Sidney, who writes in his *Defense of Poesie*: "So in Hercules, painted with his great beard, and furious countenance in a woman's attyre, spinning, at Omphale's commandement, it breedes both delight and laughter; for the representing of so strange a power in love procures delight, and the scornefulnesse of the action, stirreth laughter."[18] Perhaps for Dosso, as for Sidney, Hercules was a symbol of idle luxury. But even if Dosso's painting is an allegory on effeminate idleness, thus relating it to an extensive moralistic tradition in the sixteenth-century literature, which in turn has its roots in ancient literature, Hercules' situation nevertheless "stirreth laughter."[19] And laugh we do at Dosso's sexual comedy, which is grossly expressed in a visual pun in an almost Rabelaisian way by the woman who holds a bowl of fruit, which includes strategically placed apples, below her naked breasts. In the Renaissance apples were a common symbol for breasts; for instance, Ronsard, in his *Fantasy to His Lady*, speaks of "This body, this belly, and this bosom/ Colored like a finely washed ivory,/ In which I beheld twin apples."[20] It seems in fact that Dosso has deliberately painted her breasts as part of the fruit bowl. The still life details of beans and cherries in the foreground, which evoke the imagery of Bernesque poetry, may also have sexual implications as Gibbons suggests.[21] Gibbons, who provided us with the basic interpretation of Dosso's painting, went too far, it would seem, when he suggested that "It is possible to perceive a certain pairing of the two women, the demure one standing more on the side of heavenly and virtuous love, the lusty one obviously representing the earthly variety."[22] He sees the painting as having to do with "the notion of moral choice." There is a long tradition in art and literature of Hercules' choice between virtue and vice, but there is no evidence of this choice in Dosso's painting. The woman who is supposedly related to heavenly love is hardly

16. Max J. Friedlaender and Jacob Rosenberg, *Die Gemälde von Lucas Cranach*, pls. 223–36.

17. Bert Meijer, "Esempi del comico figurativo nel rinascimento lombardo," p. 261, fig. 1.

18. Philip Sidney, *Complete Works*, p. 151.

19. This tradition is fully discussed by Mark Rose, "Sidney's Womanish Man," pp. 353–63.

20. Jacques Bosquet, *Mannerism*, p. 85.

21. The possible allusion to Bernesque poetry is noted by Donald Posner, *Annibale Carracci*, 1:11.

22. Gibbons, "Two Allegories," p. 495.

Figure 8–6. Lucas Cranach. *Hercules and Omphale*. Herzog Anton Ulrich-Museum, Braunschweig.

demure; she has a coy smile on her lips, and like the other figures, satirizes Hercules. To see the choice of Hercules in Dosso's painting, or even the faintest allusion to it, is as unlikely as reading, for example, Folengo's parodic *Orlandino* as a moralizing work. Dosso's painting is close to the ironic tone of Rabelais, who warns his readers against looking too hard for allegory where it may not exist: "But do you faithfully believe that Homer, in writing his Iliad and Odyssey, ever had in mind the allegories squeezed out of him by Plutarch, Ponticus, Eustathius, and Phornutus, and which Politian stole from them in turn? If you do, you are not within a hand's or a foot's length of my opinion."[23]

It is worth dwelling for a moment on Rabelais's words, because they raise a central problem in the study of Italian Renaissance iconography. While allegory was a pervasive literary and pictorial mode in the sixteenth century, some twentieth-century art historians, who could almost be the target of Rabelais's satire, tend to find allegory where it does not exist, where it may exist but was not taken seriously by the artist or patron, or where this allegory was alluded to ironically. Take, for example, Correggio's *Jupiter and Io*, one of the voluptuous Loves of Jupiter done for Federigo Gonzaga. Although Hartt's assertion that the painting represents the moment of orgasm may be taken as somewhat rhetorical, Correggio's work is nevertheless one of the most erotic works in Western art.[24] The beholder vicariously participates in the seduction, witnessing the gradual relaxation of Io's muscles as she yields herself to the forceful yet delicate cloud descending to envelop as well as penetrate her body. Now it has been shown that in the foreground of the painting there is a detail of a stag drinking water and that this image was a conventional symbol of the desire for God (*desiderio verso Iddio*).[25] But are we to suppose that the stag in Correggio's painting meant the same thing as when it appeared in a medieval manuscript illumination along with an Evangelist? Given the subject of the painting we might well suppose that the symbol refers to the pleasurable desire of Io for Jupiter. But if we take the symbol in a serious moralizing and allegorical sense, are we not in the strained position of having to interpret Jupiter as the Christian deity? Even St. John of the Cross and Santa Theresa, who did express their religious feelings in erotic terms, might have joined Rabelais in smiling at such an unlikely religious allegory in Correggio's painting. We have also seen that Bronzino's *Venus, Cupid, Folly, and Time* (see Figure 6-3) was probably not the serious moralizing work that Panofsky supposed but was rather an ironic play on conventional moralizing symbols. And returning, finally, to Dosso, although there may well be an allusion to the allegory of idleness in his *Bambocciata*, it remains an open question whether he or his patron took this allegory seriously. The gross and facetious tone of the painting makes it difficult for one to suppose, so simply, that it was done even in playful seriousness. After having considered the attitudes of courtly

23. François Rabelais, *The Histories of Gargantua and Pantagruel*, trans. J. M. Cohen, p. 38.

24. Hartt, *History of Italian Renaissance Art*, p. 515 and pl. 624.

25. Egon Verheyen, "Correggio's *Amori di Giove*," p. 186.

Figure 6-3, p. 146

patrons in the sixteenth century such as Leo X and Cosimo de' Medici, we can imagine Duke Ercole's presumed laughter at the picture (if it was indeed done for him). But are we to imagine the duke reflecting deeply on the dangers of his own idleness as he looked at Dosso's painting?

Just a few years after the death of Dossi, the highly imaginative Bolognese painter and master of the mock-heroic, Pellegrino Tibaldi, painted a fresco cycle from Homer's *Odyssey* in the palace of Cardinal Poggi in Bologna (Figure 8–7). Tibaldi's brilliantly witty and fantastic work reflects his earlier experience in Rome, where he also decorated the villa of Poggi. It is perhaps still one of the most underestimated works of the sixteenth century, although its "almost Ariostesque and fabulous irony" has been celebrated by Briganti.[26] Briganti only intimated that Tibaldi's cycle was a parody of Michelangelo, but more recently Antoine Schnappner has spoken of Tibaldi's "reminiscence buffone" of Michelangelo's *Ignudi* and slaves in which Michelangelo's drama is transformed into comedy.[27] In an elaborate illusionistic scheme, which may owe something to Raphael's loggia of Cupid and Psyche as well as Giulio's Mantua decorations, Tibaldi painted a series of *Ignudi* capriciously modeled on Michelangelo's Sistine ceiling figures, who twist and turn in strained postures and who are a travesty of the heroic ideal and *terribilità* in Michelangelo's work. Tibaldi's figures kick, twist, and stretch in some of the most comical and exaggerated postures imaginable, and one can understand why their parodic wit was not to be overlooked later by the young Annibale Carracci.

The parody here, which is perhaps even more explicit than in Giulio's giants, again brings to mind the pervasive literary parody of the period to be found in Ariosto, Berni, Rabelais, Shakespeare, and Cervantes. Tibaldi's decoration is a farce; in the original sense of the word (from *farcire*), it is stuffed with delightful details of wit and caricature. In his scene of Ulysses and Circe, the men transformed into animals by the latter are presented with amusing and fantastic animal heads grotesquely placed on human bodies. Tibaldi depicts a rather ridiculous Cyclops, who does not observe the fleeing men of Ulysses, and he portrays a comically bombastic wind god, flanked by allegories of wind, who have funny puffed cheeks. In his scene of Ulysses on the island of the Sun God, Tibaldi shows us one of Ulysses' men holding his finger to his lips, silencing the beholder as the oxen are stolen. The bulging eyes of this figure are a joke, a parody of the expression of one of the terrified, damned souls in Michelangelo's *Last Judgment*. Tibaldi also gives to one of the oxen on the island a similar expression that makes the frightened face of Michelangelo's damned soul seem even more ridiculous. By making bizarre caricatures from Michelangelo's art, Tibaldi is not only parodying the great artist's work but he is also turning the Homeric narrative into farce. His frenetic parody of the Homeric epic, expressed by ridiculous *furia* and *terribilità*, can

26. Giuliano Briganti, *Il Manierismo e Pellegrino Tibaldi*, p. 79 and pls. 114ff.

27. Antoine Schnapper, "Les salles d'Ulysse au Palazzo Poggi," pp. 3ff.

Figure 8–7. Pellegrino Tibaldi. *Adventures of Odysseus* (detail). Palazzo Poggi, Bologna.

Figure 5-19, p. 137

28. Bernice Davidson, "Drawings by Perino del Vaga for the Palazzo Doria, Genoa," pp. 315–26.

29. Ibid., fig. 14.

30. Ibid., fig. 9.

31. Wilhelm Suida and Bertina Suida Manning, *Luca Cambiaso: la vita e le opere*, pls. 2ff.

32. Ibid., pls. 74–75.

33. Gibbons, *Dosso and Battista Dossi*, pls. 161ff.

34. Domenico Scaglietti, "La maturità di Amico Aspertini e i suoi rapporti con la maniera," pp. 21ff.

be compared to Ariosto's romantic parodies of heroic fury in the *Orlando furioso* and the contemporary travesty of romance in Folengo's *Orlandino*.

Tibaldi's superb decoration is representative of a kind of mock-heroic tradition found throughout North Italy in the sixteenth century down through the early work of Carracci in the late cinquecento, many of these influenced by Raphael and Michelangelo. We have already considered Giulio Romano's mock-heroic *Fall of the Giants* (see Figure 5-19), for example, and if we look to Genoa, we find that another follower of Raphael, the elegant and highly accomplished Perino del Vaga, included various humorous details in his fresco decorations of the Palazzo Doria. These frescoes celebrate the power of the great Genoese admiral, Andrea Doria, who was allied to the Holy Roman Emperor, Charles V.[28] In Perino's *Fall of the Giants*, which has been subjected to the most minute formal analysis, the nude giants, evocative of Michelangelo, are cast across the surface of the fresco in bizarre and topsy-turvy postures that are rather ridiculous.[29] Even more bizarre are some of the ancestors of Doria, done by Perino in the loggia of the villa that faces the seas dominated by Admiral Doria; most notable is the elderly figure who seems to be sliding off his seat on to his shield.[30] Perino's influence in Genoa was considerable, and he strongly influenced Luca Cambiaso, who did a series of mock-heroic decorations in the Palazzo Doria-Spinola.[31] His mock-heroic *Battle of Hercules and Amazons*, which again recalls the *furia* of the mock-romance tradition, includes a comically crushed horse in the foreground which is not unlike some of Tibaldi's bizarre creatures. Cambiaso's mock-heroic battle, like those of Ariosto, Rabelais, Cervantes, and others, is to be seen against the various heroic battle paintings of the Renaissance by Raphael, Titian, and Tintoretto, celebrating the great heroes of Italy. Just as Perino made the ancestors of Doria, in all their military pomp (evoking the Medici Chapel), seem a bit eccentric, Cambiaso makes the image of war seem somewhat ridiculous. Cambiaso also did other delightful and amusing works, including the strikingly illusionistic *Diana and Satyr* in the Villa Pallavicini and the *Venus* (now in the Villa Borghese) who is surrounded by charming pop-eyed dolphins.[32]

Mock-heroic elements abound in countless other fresco decorations done in North Italy during the cinquecento. Dosso Dossi traveled north to Trento where he included some wonderful comic passages in his allegorical decorations of the Castello del Buonconsiglio, a work that may have been influenced by Parmigianino's Fontanellato frescoes.[33] A delightful, comic cycle was painted in this period in Emilia by the energetic and eccentric Amico Aspertini, who decorated the Castello Isolani at Minerbio.[34] Aspertini's decorations, which reflect Dosso's Trento work, consist of strange caryatids and bizarre allegories as well as caricatural images of Mars and Hercules. Like Tibaldi's

Poggi frescoes, Aspertini's work, as Scaglietti has put it, has a "power of fantasy" as his strangely grotesque figures seem to pulsate throughout the Sala di Marte and the Sala di Ercole. Perhaps one of Aspertini's most delightful inventions occurs in the Sala di Astronomia where a female figure (Astronomy?) seems to be weighed down by the symbolic sphere that she is supposed to be holding.[35] At Novellara, in Emilia, Lelio Orsi designed a number of notable and fantastic facade decorations, filled with mock-heroic effects, related especially to Giulio's work at Mantua. An especially appealing example is the drawing in Princeton for the facade of his own house (Figure 8-8). In the Louvre there is also a series of drawings by Orsi that appear to be for a fresco decoration of a mythological subject, although the frescoes are no longer known to us.[36] Like so many of the works we have been discussing, they caricature some of their mythological subjects. One delightful sheet by Orsi shows Apollo rushing urgently forward in his chariot, which is pulled by bizarre and hilarious horses, who belong to the story of equestrian humor that we have already noted. In another sheet we find a *repoussoir* figure ludicrously pouring water on the flaming steeds of Apollo in a joke reminiscent of one of Giulio's (Figure 8-9). Turning to the far north of Italy, we find that the Lombard, Romanino, who like Dosso painted humorous work at Trento, painted some amusing caricatures of mythological subjects in his native Brescia. As part of his Palazzo Bernari (formerly Lechi) decorations, he included an amusing, plump Bacchus, as well as some bizarre nudes and female allegories.[37] He painted other laughable gods and exceptionally fine satyr heads in the Palazzo Averaldi.[38] These satyrs are charming in their caricatural ugliness and along with Veronese's satyr heads above the doors at Maser they are among the most splendid of the cinquecento.

Romanino's humorous mythological decorations stand out against other comic Lombard works of lesser quality. Many of these paintings portray *villani* with caricatural expressions, reflecting a coarse humor like that of the various Northern *villanelle* written in dialect. These anonymous paintings seem to depend both on Leonardo's caricatures and on the Northern works of Metsys. Related to these Lombard paintings but of higher quality is Niccolò Frangipane's satirical painting of the performance of a madrigal (Chateau of Leefdael).[39] In this work by the Friulian master, who was influenced by Venetian art, especially Titian's, we see a delightful band of figures reminiscent of Dosso's characters in the *Bambocciata*, singing or keeping time to a madrigal that can be identified in the score held by a figure to the left. It is the *Bella guerriera mia* of Orlando di Lasso, which is based on a Petrarchan sonnet by Bembo. The highly idealized and refined Petrarchan sentiments of Bembo are subjected to a delightful satire here as they are sung about by grossly salacious characters (including a satyr). We can perhaps imagine what

35. Ibid., fig. 38.

36. Jacob Bean, *Italian Renaissance Drawings from the Musée du Louvre*, nos. 38–39.

37. Maria Luisa Ferrari, *Il Romanino*, pl. 101.

38. Ibid., pls. 104–5. The caricature of Romanino's work is noted by Ferrari.

39. Bert Meijer, "Harmony and satire in the work of Niccolò Frangipane: problems in the depiction of music," pp. 94–112. Similar material is discussed in the previously cited "Esempi del comico figurativo" by Meijer and in Barry Wind, "*Pitture ridicole*: Some Late Cinquecento Comic Genre Paintings," pp. 25–35.

Figure 8–8. Lelio Orsi. *Design for the Facade of the Artist's House*. The Art Museum, Princeton University.

Figure 8–9. Lelio Orsi. *Study of the Chariot of Apollo*. Cabinet des Dessins, Louvre, Paris.

Frangipane's painting sounds like by comparing its satire to the highly face-tious and parodic madrigals of Banchieri and Vecchi. By depicting the singers of the Petrarchan madrigal as crude types Frangipane quite literally makes a travesty (from *travestir*). The spirit of the painting is similar to so much Renaissance literature in which Petrarchan conventions are spoofed.

Perhaps the most distinguished pictorial humorist of the late cinquecento, Annibale Carracci, assimilated much of the Northern Italian tradition that we have been considering. His early fresco decorations in the Palazzo Fava and the Palazzo Magnani in Bologna include witty caricatures reminiscent of Tibaldi's fantastic decorations for Poggi, and his *Laughing Man* is in the tradi-tion of Dosso's caricatural types.[40] Carracci did a number of caricatural draw-ings, and he made a composition for an etching of Jupiter and Antiope, which is a rather ludicrous exaggeration of the kind of voyeurism we have seen in various works, especially by Titian.[41] This kind of voyeurism is delightfully exploited by Annibale in an early work (Figure 8–10). Here a satyr offers a bowl of fruit to Venus at the same time that he is pulling a drapery away from her body. With a touch of wit Carracci identifies Venus through the bracelet she wears, depicting the Three Graces, who were her hand maidens. The amusing, good-natured satyr who approaches her has an imploring smile on his face. There is an incongruity in this situation in that a satyr is not simply propositioning an ordinary nymph but the goddess of love herself. To a society highly conscious of class distinctions, as seen in the mockery of yokels by Rabelais, Bruegel, and Shakespeare, the audacity of the crude satyr would

40. Posner, *Annibale Carracci*, 2: pl. 10.

41. Maurizio Calvesi and V. Casale, *Le incisioni dei Carracci*, no. 206.

Figure 8–10. Annibale Carracci. *Venus and a Satyr*. Uffizi, Florence.

almost certainly have been amusing. At the left side of the painting a *putto* clutches Venus's leg and sticks his tongue out. We also saw this good-humored thrusting of the tongue in a more delicate form in Botticelli's *Mars and Venus* (see Figure 2-12). And even though the definitive iconography of the tongue-thrust has yet to be written, it would seem that the thrusting of the tongue had a sexual meaning in the Renaissance. Even as late as the nineteenth century it had a sexual meaning in *The Gilded Age* of C. W. Warner and Mark Twain, "Her intimacy with Selby was open gossip, and there were winks and thrustings of the tongue in any group of men when she passed by."[42] As we have seen in other works the comic theme of Carracci's painting is expressed playfully. The humor here is also based on voyeurism. Venus is shown with her back to us, and we cannot see the tantalizing "fruits" that are revealed by the satyr. The little *putto* on the left almost seems to tease the beholder, for as he clutches Venus's leg, he makes us aware of what is so close, but alas, outside of our field of vision.

Carracci's humor is sometimes rather coarse in the manner of earlier Northern works. His *Butcher's Shop* is closely related to Domenico Passeroti's more overtly comic painting of the same subject (Palazzo Barberini) in which the hideous butchers are meant to be laughable in their ugliness (Figure 8-11).[43] Carracci's painting seems, however, more subtle in effect. Although Martin's identification of Carracci's painting as a family portrait is tenuous, he was no doubt right in recognizing its satirical qualities, especially its parodic references to Michelangelo. As we have already noted, parody subjects the art of others to ridicule, but at the same time this mockery is frequently of an artist held in high regard. There is something delightfully ridiculous about the transformation of figures from Michelangelo's *Sacrifice of Noah* into those of a butcher shop. But at the same time it would seem that Carracci also admired the style of Michelangelo which he mockingly adapted.

Carracci's *Bean Eater* is also indebted to the coarse naturalism of the North, especially in Lombard painting (Figure 8-12). In particular his subject has been related to Vincenzo Campi's *Family of Fishmongers*, which includes a comical figure eating beans.[44] Done with bravura brushwork, Carracci's picture reveals the same fascination with gluttonous appetites and boorish manners that is found in Renaissance literature. We are reminded again of Pulci's Margutte, who is comically gluttonous, and of Folengo's Griffarosto, who had a ready throat ("la gola pronta") and who lived in a monastery that became a sort of tavern: "fuise claustrum quod nunc est taberna."[45] We are also reminded of Giovanni della Casa's boorish and comical antitheses to the man of manners, the gluttons who "we sometimes see with their snouts buried readily in their plates, like pigs, never raising their faces or lifting their eyes, still less their hands, from their food. They eat, or rather gobble with both cheeks bloated as though they were sounding a trumpet or

42. Mark Twain and C. W. Warner, *The Gilded Age*, p. 400.

43. John Rupert Martin, "The Butcher Shop of the Carracci," pp. 263–66. For a more recent discussion of the painting, see Barry Wind, "Annibale Carracci's 'Scherzo': The Christ Church *Butcher Shop*," pp. 93–96.

44. A. W. A. Boschloo, *Annibale Carracci in Bologna: Visible Reality in Art after the Council of Trent*, pp. 71–72.

45. Teofilo Folengo, *Orlandino*, in *Opere italiane*, ed. Umberto Renda, 1:128.

Figure 2–12, p. 39

Figure 8–11. Annibale Carracci. *The Butcher's Shop.* Christ Church Picture Gallery, Oxford.

Figure 8–12. Annibale Carracci. *The Bean Eater*. Galleria Colonna, Rome.

blowing the fire."[46] These gluttons are like Rabelais's Gargantua, who "shat, pissed, spewed, belched, farted, yawned, spat, coughed, hiccuped, sneezed, blew his nose like an archdeacon, and breakfasted, to protect himself from the dew and bad air, on fine fried tripes, good rashers grilled on the coals, delicate hams, tasty goat stews, and plenty of early morning soup."[47] Their boorish ways are idealized in the philosophy of table manners proclaimed by Sancho Panza: "And to tell the truth, even if it's only bread and onion that I eat in my corner without bothering about table manners and ceremonies, it tastes

46. Della Casa, *Galateo*, p. 98.

47. Rabelais, *Gargantua*, p. 82.

48. Miguel Cervantes, *The Adventures of Don Quixote*, trans. J. M. Cohen, p. 83.

Figure 3–9, p. 72

49. Ludwig H. Heydenreich and Wolfgang Lotz, *Architecture in Italy: 1400–1600*, pp. 324–26.

50. John Rupert Martin, *The Farnese Gallery*.

51. Charles Dempsey, " 'Et Nos Cedamus Amori': Observations on the Farnese Gallery," pp. 363–74; followed by Posner, *Annibale Carracci*, 1:83.

to me a great deal better than turkey at other tables where I have to chew slowly, drink little, and wipe my mouth often, and where I can't sneeze and cough when I want to, nor do any of those other things which solitude and freedom allow of."[48] This kitchen humor, which has antecedents in medieval literature, is also found in the North in the works of Bosch and Bruegel and later in the paintings of Hals, Steen, Brower, and Ostade.

At the end of the cinquecento, Annibale Carracci and another great North Italian artist, the Lombard genius, Caravaggio, traveled to Rome where they created some of the finest and most important works of the period. In most histories of art the work of these two masters (combining the naturalism and classicism of cinquecento art) is interpreted as the foundation of the new baroque epoch. Yet we can also look at them as continuing the humorous tradition in the sixteenth century, especially that of cinquecento Rome. When both Carracci and Caravaggio arrived in Rome, mannerist artists such as Federico Zuccaro were still working, and the satirical tradition of the early cinquecento, which we saw in the works of Raphael, Michelangelo, Rosso, Parmigianino, and Giulio, still persisted in their work. We should in fact recall Zuccaro's recent *Porta Virtutis* of 1580 which mocked the artist's critics in the papal court (see Figure 3–9). When Zuccaro, who became the president of the Roman academy of art, built his magnificent palace on the Pincio, he had the front door made into a witty mouth of hell, a bizarre invention related in spirit to the monstrous creatures at Bomarzo, and the grotesques of Michelangelo.[49]

Annibale Carracci's great satirical work in Rome is the decoration of the Farnese gallery. This sensuous decoration, which depicts various mythological subjects and celebrates the triumph of love, was discussed in Neoplatonic terms by Bellori in the seventeenth century, and there may be a Neoplatonizing allusion intended in the decoration as Martin has recently suggested.[50] But as Dempsey has also recently observed, Annibale's frescoes are a tour de force of satirical wit.[51] If it was done for a Farnese wedding as Dempsey supposes, this decoration would belong to the long tradition of matrimonial comedy that we have seen or suspected in works by Botticelli, Mategna, Raphael, Sodoma, and Rosso. Carracci's frescoes relate to the great mock-heroic cycles in North Italy that we have discussed and to Raphael's loggia of Cupid and Psyche, which had influenced these North Italian decorations. In addition to his mythological scenes, including the playful *Triumph of Bacchus* in the center of the ceiling, Carracci filled his decoration with comic masks, capricious *putti*, and bizarre nudes, evoking Tibaldi's imaginative inventions at Bologna. Near his Jupiter and Juno, to take but a single example, Carracci has painted a nude who eccentrically covers his head with drapery (Figure 8–13). Below this scene a mask leers at us, and to the right little *putti* play with the skull of

Figure 8-13. Annibale Carracci. *Jupiter and Juno*. Farnese Gallery, Rome.

an ox. The playful commentary throughout the decoration on the loves of the gods belongs to the long and delightful tradition that we have traced back to Botticelli and Mantegna in the quattrocento. The witty and lifelike caryatids and *Ignudi* of Carracci's decoration are also related to the illusionistic wit we have seen in works by Mantegna, Filippino, Peruzzi, and others.

Carracci's great contemporary and rival in Rome, Caravaggio, is also known for his satirical character. Perhaps one of the most familiar expressions of Caravaggio's satirical bent is his *Amor* (Berlin) which makes a mockery of Baglione's *Divine Love* for Marchese Giustiniani (Figure 8-14).[52] Caravaggio's coyly erotic Cupid is evocative of Parmigianino's creature, and the theme of his painting, the triumph of love over war (symbolized by the armor on the ground) is still in the tradition of Botticelli's *Mars and Venus*, although clearly in a different key. Caravaggio's sense of humor is also apparent in his less frequently discussed *Sleeping Cupid*, which in its coarseness is in the tradition of Bronzino's *Morgante* or Dosso's *Bambocciata* (Figure 8-15). Caravaggio is playing here on the famous Hellenistic sculpture that was imitated by the

52. Walter Friedlaender, *Caravaggio Studies*, cat. no. 23.

Figure 8–14. Caravaggio. *Amor*. Gemäldegalerie, Berlin.

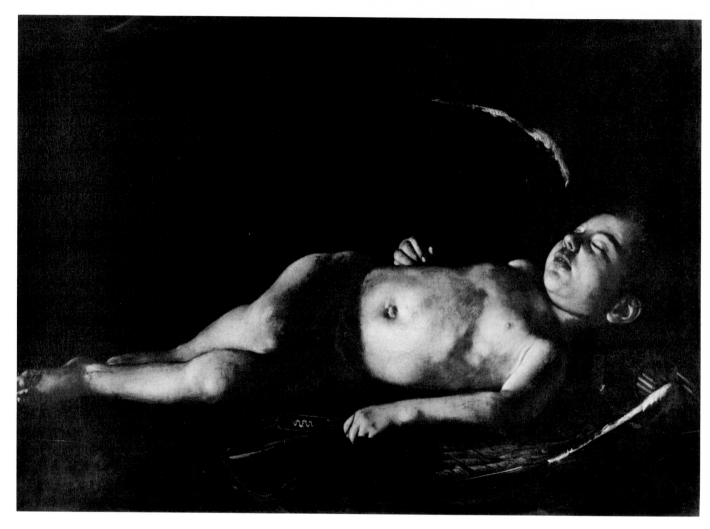

Figure 8–15. Caravaggio. *Sleeping Cupid*. Palazzo Pitti, Florence.

young Michelangelo and which Tintoretto adapted in his *Vulcan and Venus*. His little creature is a deliberate parody of the idealizing tendency in the ancient sculpture and in the various classicizing Cupids of the cinquecento (by Raphael, Giulio Romano, and Iacopo Zucchi, for example), including his own lovely, if facetious, Berlin *Amor*. This creature, instead, is something of an *Amor alla romana* with thick lips, a fat nose, and puffed cheeks. His gentle travesty of the classical god, which in many respects anticipates the similar but more explicit burlesque in the work of Velasquez (for example, the *Borracchos*), might also be compared to Shakespeare's affectionate mockery in *Love's Labor's Lost* of the god of love: "This whimpled, whining, wayward boy,/ This senior-junior, giant-dwarf, Dan Cupid."[53]

53. Shakespeare, *Love's Labor's Lost*, act III, scene i, ll. 168–69.

IX. *Love, Laughter, and Revelry*

Then, heigh-ho, the holly. This life is most jolly.—William Shakespeare, *As You Like It*

In the previous chapters we have surveyed a full range of playfulness in the art from Giotto through Caravaggio, and in doing so, we have encountered various senses of humor and manifestations of wit. Further study would show that the art of Giotto and his contemporaries emerges from a rich tradition of humor in medieval art, and similarly the comic tradition in art persists long after the Renaissance into the baroque and later periods. We have, for example, enjoyed the suave wit of Botticelli and Raphael, and relished the more macabre and anguished humor and wit of Michelangelo. Some artists discussed above were sardonic in their wit and humor, especially Rosso and Parmigianino, while others such as Bronzino transformed their witticisms into the most highly polished and *ricercato* pictorial jokes. At times we have seen how artists could range from extreme delicacy in their humor to vulgar comedy. This shift was especially apparent in the work of Dosso Dossi, whose Jupiter painting butterflies expresses gentle pathos, while his *Bambocciata* or satire of Hercules is coarse (see Figure 8–5). These Renaissance artists relied heavily on various devices including incongruity and ambiguity, especially in their *grotteschi* and *bizzarrie*, and their playful illusionism, and its general tone, like that of much literature of the period, may ultimately be characterized as ironic.

I have been less concerned in this essay with exploring the specific intentions of works of art than with associating the tone and imagery of these works with humorous writings of the Renaissance. We have seen that the works of Raphael, Botticelli, Michelangelo, and others can be related in theme and tone, and sometimes in terms of common literary sources, to the writings of the period, both the Italian literature of Aretino, Castiglione, and Ariosto, and the continental literature of Erasmus, Rabelais, Montaigne, and Shakespeare. Similarly we have noted affinities between the humor of Northern and Italian art.

In recent years art historians have questioned the extent and character of Neoplatonic influence on Italian Renaissance art, which was once considered to be overwhelming. In pursuing this issue I have tried to show that the sexual comedy in certain works might either be ironic or related to the pervasive anti-Platonic current of the period, which is a counterpart of the more widely discussed anti-Petrarchan poetry of the period. We have looked at a variety of works that can be called satires or parodies, and it should become even more apparent in time that the satirical and parodic currents of Renaissance art, as

Figure 8–5, p. 191

Figure 8–10, p. 201

Figure 7–1, p. 159

Figure 6–3, p. 146

well as irony, were more pervasive than has previously been supposed. Similarly, there are topics that we have scarcely touched on here that are in need of further research; for example, the iconographical connections between comic madrigals and other humorous musical offerings and comic or witty art. A wealth of information, both published and unpublished, pertaining to music for Renaissance festivities, exists to sustain such an investigation. We have noted only in passing that much of the playful and facetious art of the Renaissance has been connected to nuptial celebrations. It is indeed surprising that although marriage and the family are fashionable historical subjects at present, the most recent books on the social history of Renaissance art have scarcely mentioned the function of nuptial art.[1] Yet works by artists such as Botticelli, Mantegna, and Raphael should eventually be recognized as part of a tradition of nuptial festivities. We have noted how various humorous or witty works were made for loggias, bedrooms, *saloni*, and baths, and no doubt further study of the function and context of works of art will enrich our understanding of their significance.[2] In addition to the masterpieces by the greatest artists of the Renaissance that I have discussed, there is also a vast body of art by lesser masters, especially in prints, which should be further used to explore the iconology of humor and wit in the Renaissance. Some of these prints, along with poetry of the period, may eventually provide us with clues concerning aspects of popular festivities such as carnival celebrations.

Of all the themes touched upon or explored, perhaps the most dominant one is the humor in classical or mythological subject matter: the playfulness, laughter, and mockery of the gods and classical heroes. The frequent mockery of the gods especially recalls Lucian, who influenced artists such as Raphael,

1. Peter Burke, *Culture and Society in Renaissance Italy: 1420–1540.*

2. The introduction to E. H. Gombrich, *Symbolic Images.*

Figure 7–2, p. 162

Figure 7–3, p. 163

Botticelli, and Rosso Fiorentino, just as he influenced the leading writers of the period including Machiavelli, Erasmus, and Rabelais. As principal performers in comic Renaissance art, the gods and goddesses mirror the humorous foibles and weaknesses of humanity. So very often this satire pertains to the theme of love. Dossi's Hercules is ridiculous when tamed by Omphale, just as the Mars of Botticelli, Piero di Cosimo, and others is laughable when subdued by Venus. Raphael's Jupiter is laughable as he kisses Cupid; Bellini's image of the Olympian deity in a state of inebriation is delightfully funny, and Dossi's image of Jupiter painting butterflies is touching in its gentle playfulness. The puckish and capricious Cupid repeatedly provokes laughter, or elicits a smile. His legions of *amorini* mirthfully celebrate the triumph of love in countless works from Botticelli to Carracci. Cupid's own love life is teasingly presented by Raphael in his loggia of Cupid and Psyche. Cupid is disguised, so to speak, as Genius in Donatello's statue. He is devilishly amusing in Parmigianino's painting where the theme of love and pain is evoked, and he is humorously coy as his mother's lover in Bronzino's *Venus, Cupid, Folly, and Time* (see Figure 6–3). As the goddess of love, Cupid's mother dominates the love life of Olympus. The story of her comic affair with Mars is playfully told and retold by Renaissance artists. In Peruzzi's fresco she is a coquette, and in Raphael's frescoes for Chigi she is teased for her jealousy of Cupid's lover, Psyche. She is the subject of much playful voyeuristic art as in Carracci's *Venus and a Satyr* (see Figure 8–10) and Giovanni da Bologna's statue of Venus (see Figure 6–8). Bacchus, who is frequently associated with Venus, elicits our smiles and laughter in countless Renaissance works. His entourage, consisting of laughable satyrs and his lieutenant, the "thickset old man with a big belly," Silenus, amuse us time and again in the works of Raphael, Carracci, and others. Silenus seems to be ubiquitous in the art of the cinquecento. He is reborn as the Medici dwarf, Morgante; and Shakespeare's "fat paunch," Falstaff, presiding as a master of misrule over the food, drink, lust, and laughter of Eastcheap, is seemingly Silenus reincarnate.

Perhaps of all the works discussed above, the ensemble of works done by Bellini and Titian for the *camerino* of Alfonso d'Este most clearly epitomize the sensuality, playful exuberance, and humor so pervasive in the Renaissance (see Figures 7–1, 7–2, 7–3). In Bellini's *Feast of the Gods* we enter into a voluptuous dream world, where we are amused by the tipsy gods and the abortive seduction of Lotis by Priapus. Titian injects a more dynamic exuberance into the cycle, which builds up to a crescendo. The rhythms of the dancing Andrians are dynamic, but harmoniously controlled, whereas the boisterous frolic of the *amorini* in the *Festival of Venus* is more explosive. Finally, a peak of frenetic intensity is reached by the leaping Bacchus in the pulsating *Bacchus and Ariadne*.

An uncommonly sympathetic and profound appreciation of Titian's *Bac-*

chanal of the Andrians appears in Ortega y Gasset's "Tres Quadros del Vino," an essay that is largely ignored by art historians even though it appeared over fifty years ago (see Figure 7–3).[3] Ortega's appreciation of the painting might be extended to the entire ensemble. The beauty and intuitive strength of his analysis cannot be readily summarized, but something of its force can be appreciated from his remark: "Men and women have chosen this peaceful corner of the universe to enjoy existence; they drink, laugh, talk, dance, caress one another, and sleep. Here all the biological functions appear dignified and with equal rights." Following Nietzsche, Ortega observes that the Andrians, having drunk, now "perceive with real clairvoyance the ultimate secrets of the cosmos. These people have not been initiated in the rhythmic mystery of the universe by external study; wine, who was a wise god, has given them a momentary intuition of the greatest secret of all." It is probably significant that the apex of the painting is the carafe of wine held up by one of the Andrians. Although it is tilted, suggesting intoxication or the movement of the dance, or both the figure who holds it is gazing in rapt veneration.

Although there presumably is no specific program for this group of paintings, which was commissioned over a number of years, there are nevertheless basic themes.[4] In three of the four paintings the joyful effects of wine are celebrated, and Bacchus appears in at least two of these paintings, the *Feast of the Gods* and the *Bacchus and Ariadne*. Perhaps these paintings, like other Bacchic works of the Renaissance such as Michelangelo's *Bacchus* (see Figure 3–1), conjured up the famous *In vino veritas*, a pervasive theme in the literature of the period. As Rabelais put it, drink "has the power to fill the soul with all truth, all knowledge, and all philosophy"—a thought possibly evoked by the raised carafe and seeming veneration of it in Titian's *Andrians*.[5] In virtually all of the paintings we find expressions of that universal force presided over by Venus, who is celebrated in the *Festival of Venus*. We witness the loves of the gods, of men and women, of satyrs and nymphs, and the union of Bacchus and Ariadne. Music, which is so intimately associated with love in the Renaissance, is evoked by the instruments in the *Feast of the Gods*, and in the *Bacchus and Ariadne*, and is most explicitly expressed by song and dance in the *Andrians*. The setting of these scenes is woodlands, sometimes dense as in the *Feast of the Gods* and sometimes more open with fields as in the *Festival of Venus*. This is the realm of satyrs, companions of Bacchus and Venus, who appear in three of the paintings. It is the realm of playful satire.

Alfonso's paintings are related to various aspects of art and life in the Ferrarese court. The themes of love, music, and drinking in these works recall similar concerns in the frescoes done earlier in Ferrara by Cossa and others for Borso d'Este. It is especially worth noting that the paintings for Alfonso describe food and eating as well as drinking; the apples in Titian's *Festival of Venus*, and the magnificent fruits in the *Feast of the Gods*. Just as the Raphael

3. José Ortega y Gasset, *Velasquez Goya and the Dehumanization of Art*, pp. 14ff.

Figure 3–1, p. 53

4. The themes of love and wine have recently been stressed by Philipp Fehl, "The Worship of Bacchus and Venus in Bellini's and Titian's Bacchanals for Alfonso d'Este," pp. 37–95.

5. François Rabelais, *The Histories of Gargantua and Pantagruel*, p. 705.

loggia of Cupid and Psyche, with its marriage banquet of Cupid and Psyche and its sumptuous festoons of fruits and vegetables, evokes the magnificent banquets of Chigi, and just as the splendid banquet of Cupid and Psyche done by Giulio Romano evokes the banquets of Federigo Gonzaga, the eating and drinking in these paintings by Bellini and Titian suggest the possibility that the *camerino* might have been used for similar entertainments. The actual playfulness, laughter, and wit of courtly conversations, and the pleasures of food, music, and drink at the Ferrarese court seem almost to reverberate in these paintings. In their playful sensuality and brilliant wit the paintings for Alfonso also bring to mind the comedies written for and performed at the court of Ferrara by Ariosto. The dense forest setting of these paintings and the magical joy of existence in them also evoke the delights of the enchanted and sensuous forests in Ariosto's *Orlando*, enjoyed at Ferrara. The *camerino* might be seen as a pictorial romance, its sensuality, *terribilità* satire, parody, and wit comparable to the rich romantic literary tradition fostered by the Ferrarese court in the works of Boiardo and Ariosto. The music that is made in these paintings, especially the amusing French drinking song in the *Andrians*, also evokes the rich musical life at Ferrara, which received such notable composers as Adrian Willaert. The playful aspects and facetiousness of these paintings help us to imagine the foolery of dwarfs and buffoons who populated the court of Ferrara. As we gaze at the cavorting *putti*, satyrs, and rustic gods in these works we recall fools like Matta, who was so dear to her "Fonso," as she called him, that the duke could not part with her.[6]

If the paintings for Alfonso can be associated with life at the court of Ferrara, they can also more generally be related to the art and literature of the period. We have already seen that the playful *putti* who appear in these works are related to the capricious creatures painted in the same period by Mantegna, Sodoma, Raphael, Correggio, Parmigianino, Giulio, and others. The *camerino* celebrates Bacchus, the humorous subject of much Renaissance art and literature; Lorenzo de' Medici's poetry, Piero di Cosimo's painting, and Michelangelo's *Bacchus*. Venus, the other principal divinity of the *camerino*, was also prominent in the comic work of Peruzzi and in the humorous work by Raphael for Bibbiena and Chigi. We should not fail to recall that Raphael had originally planned a *Triumph of Bacchus* for the *camerino*. Among the principal Bacchic characters in the *camerino* we find Silenus and satyrs, characters that we have repeatedly seen in comic works by Piero di Cosimo, Peruzzi, and Carracci, among others. Priapus, who appears in Bellini's painting, is representative of the pervasive priapean impulses that pervade so much of the humorous Renaissance art and literature, as seen in the priapean codpieces, keys, and needles of Rabelais, Bruegel, Giulio, Raphael, and Berni. As works adjacent to Alfonso's bedroom they can be compared to other comic-erotic boudoir decorations by Sodoma and Parmigianino and to other works that

6. Enid Welsford, *The Fool*, p. 135.

may originally have hung in bedrooms, especially works done in Venice. Although the *camerino* paintings seemingly do not celebrate a marriage, they nevertheless remind us of much humorous and erotic art by Botticelli, Raphael, Carracci, and others done as part of wedding celebrations. Of all the paintings in the *camerino* Bellini's is most representative of the satire and facetiousness in Italian Renaissance art. Bellini's humorous rustic image, which surprisingly is not dissimilar in theme to the humorous image of bucolic Virgilian gods painted by Pontormo for Leo X at Poggio a Caiano, gently mocks the gods.

The sensual abandon and satirical tone of these works for Alfonso also evoke the writings of Titian's friend, Pietro Aretino, whose witty letters acknowledge the benevolence of the d'Este house. Aretino has appeared in more than one of the situations that we have thus far discussed. We encountered him as a young man ("quasi garzone") in the Chigi household and writing a mock-will for Pope Leo's elephant in the period when Raphael was decorating the bath of Leo's friend, Bibbiena, and the villa of the pope's friend, Chigi. We discovered him composing funny and erotic sonnets, which were playfully illustrated in Rome by Giulio Romano, in the period when the satirical Rosso, Parmigianino, and Cellini were about town; and later we noted his observations concerning the decoration of the Sala di Psiche in the Palazzo del Te. During the later Venetian phase of his career we saw him commissioning and possibly creating the idea for the *Mars and Venus* by Rosso (see Figure 5–6), a composition probably intended for Francis I, who was to be Rosso's future patron. In Venice we also found Aretino cavorting with courtesans, writing facetious dialogues, exchanging ironical letters with Michelangelo concerning the *Last Judgment*, and jesting with his friend, Titian, who by the way, portrayed Aretino in two portraits with Rabelaisian brio. Aretino knew so many of the patrons, artists, and writers we have encountered; Chigi, Francis I, and Duke Cosimo were his patrons, Berni was his literary enemy, Giulio and Rosso were his collaborators; and Michelangelo was his uncomfortable correspondent. The recipients of his letters, which he had published, reads like a *Who's Who* of the cinquecento. There is a grain of truth in his ridiculous and Rabelaisian self-adulation:

> I am a second Alexander, Caesar, Scipio. Nay more: I tell you that some kinds of glasses they make at Murano are called Aretines. Aretines is the name given to a breed of cobs—after one Pope Clement sent me, and I gave to Duke Federico. They have christened the little canal that runs beside my house the Canalazzo, Rio Aretino. And to make the pedants burst with rage, besides talking of the Aretine style, three wenches of my household, who have left me and become ladies, will have themselves known only as Aretines. So many lords and gentlemen are eternally breaking in upon me with their importunities, my stairs are worn with their feet like the Capitol with wheels of triumphal chariots. I have come to be the Oracle of Truth, the Secretary of the universe: everybody.[7]

Figure 5–6, p. 114

7. Vincent Cronin, *The Flowering of the Renaissance*, pp. 190–91.

8. The term *Aretinian* is applied to Giulio Romano's work by Gombrich, *Symbolic Images*, p. 227, n. 40.

9. Jacob Burckhardt, *The Civilization of the Italian Renaissance*, p. 124.

Aretino was the self-appointed secretary of the Italian cinquecento, and his playfulness, jesting, and sensuality are closely related not only to the tone of the *camerino* but to much of the art of the period. We might aptly speak of the "Aretinian" spirit in the works of Rosso, Parmigianino, Bronzino, as well as of Titian.[8]

Mention of Aretino also brings to mind Rabelais, and we might note that Burckhardt compared Aretino at his best to the great French writer.[9] The paintings for Alfonso celebrate the two divinities, Bacchus and Venus, who are similarly invoked in Rabelais's magnificent literary banquet. Titian's paintings for Alfonso celebrate the physical and creatural aspects of man in a eulogy to his biological functions like that in Rabelais's writings. All of these paintings invite the participation of the beholder's senses, as we taste the wine in the *Feast of the Gods* and the *Andrians*, as we taste and smell the apples in the *Festival of Venus*, and as we taste the fruits in Bellini's painting. We hear the cosmic music and see its rhythms in Titian's *Andrians* and listen to the pulsating, frenzied music of the *Bacchus and Ariadne*. In all of these paintings our sense of touch is heightened as we gaze upon lovers who caress and stroke each other or *amorini* who hug and wrestle. Finally, our eyes feast on the brilliant and glittering brushwork with which these painters have presented to us their pageant of the senses. There is an exuberance, a joyful physical freedom expressed in these paintings, as in the *Festival of Venus*, where an *amorino* dives in total abandon into a group of his fleshy companions, conveying an almost oceanic sense of oneness with nature. Throughout these works the theme "drink" is invoked as it is in the French drinking song of the *Andrians* and in Rabelais's verdict of the Bottle.[10] The sensuality and playful comedy of the chattering *putti*, facetious satyrs, and rustic gods in these paintings might almost be called Rabelaisian. In short, love, music, wine, and laughter are the major themes of the paintings as they are for Rabelais, who sings in a delightfully humorous, priapean, and nearly goliardic poem on Venus and Bacchus:

10. Rabelais, *Gargantua*, pp. 704–6.

> Come, trink, by Bacchus let us tope
> Ho, ho, for now I truly hope
> To see some round and juicy rump
> Well tickled by may carnal stump
> And stuffed with my humanity.
> For what says my paternity?
> My paternal heart tells me
> That not only shall I be
> Soon comfortably wedded,
> But when wife is bedded
> She'll love the sport. By Venus
> What bouts there'll be between us![11]

11. Ibid., p. 705.

Bellini's and Titian's paintings for Alfonso are a celebration of life and its pleasures, which like the writings of Aretino and Rabelais, evoke the mythic world of the gods and the sensual and facetious literature of antiquity. Both Venus and Bacchus are divinities who symbolize the annual re-creation or restoration of the world, and it might be said that like the pagan rites of antiquity and the carnival celebrations of the Middle Ages and Renaissance, which annually celebrated this regeneration through playful and sensual imagery, the paintings for Alfonso are a similar celebration.[12] Through them the patron, his court, and his guests might be imagined as momentarily restored. They were made for the duke's recreation, reminding us of the original sense of this word. The paintings for Alfonso are still imbued with the romantic ideals of the Middle Ages, which as we noted lived on in the writings of Ariosto and which persisted in the pastoral comedies of Shakespeare. One might well imagine the courtly protagonists of Shakespeare's *As You Like It* in the pastoral setting of these paintings, in this Golden Age where time has stopped; and as in the comedies of Shakespeare, we can speak of them as having with their tragic implications (the Bacchus myth) a happy ending or resolution. The duke's momentary recreation in these mythologies, free from the responsibilities of political life, might also be compared to Prince Hal's youthful escape into the Dionysiac world of Eastcheap, where the prince cavorts with the Shakespearean Silenus, Falstaff. As improbable as it at first seems, one might even associate the restorative virtues of these paintings with the life-enhancing celebrations in Bruegelian dances. If the spiritual *paradiso* of Botticelli's *Primavera* (see Figure 2–9) and the analogous poetry of Lorenzo de' Medici were meant to restore the viewer's spirit, or elevate it, infusing it with heavenly splendor and the *spiritus mundi*, these paintings for the duke of Ferrara were seemingly intended to restore their viewer physically to a oneness with nature. The laughter and play in them, as in so many works of the Renaissance, contribute to our recreation in the deepest sense. For a moment we can sing, "Then, heigh-ho, the holly./ This life is most jolly."[13]

12. These remarks are influenced in general by the following: C. L. Barber, *Shakespeare's Festive Comedy*; Mikhail Bakhtin, *Rabelais and His World*; and Northrop Frye, *Anatomy of Criticism*.

Figure 2–9, p. 32

13. William Shakespeare, *As You Like It*, act II, scene vii, ll. 182–83.

Bibliography

PRIMARY SOURCES

Alberti, Leon Battista. *Ecatonfilea*. In *Opere volgari*, edited by Cecil Grayson, vol. 3, pp. 199ff. Bari, 1973.

Aretino, Pietro. *Aretino's Dialogues*. Translated by Raymond Rosenthal. New York, 1971.

———. *Il primo libro delle lettere*, edited by Fausto Niccolini. Bari, 1913.

Arlotto, Piovano. *Motti e Facetiae*. In *Novelle del Quattrocento*, edited by Aldo Borlenghi. Milan, 1962.

Beccadelli, Antonio. *Hermaphroditus*. In *Poeti Latini del Quattrocento*, edited by Francesco Arnaldi, pp. 6ff. Milan-Naples, 1964.

Berni, Francesco. *Rime facete*. Milan, 1959.

———. *Opere burlesche*. 2 vols. London, 1723.

Bibbiena, Bernardo Dovizi da. *La Calandria*. In *Commedie del Cinquecento*, edited by Nino Borsellino, vol. 2, pp. 16–97. Milan, 1967.

Bisticci, Vespasiano da. *The Vespasiano Memoirs*. Translated by William George Waters and Emily Waters. London, 1926.

Bronzino, Il (Allessandro Allori). *Li Capitoli Faceti*. Venice, 1822.

Bracchi, Alessandro. *Carmina*, edited by Alessandro Perosa. Florence, 1944.

Bracciolini, Poggio. *The Facetiae of Poggio*. Translated by Edward Storer. London, 1928.

Brantôme, Seigneur de. *Recueil des Dames*. Paris, n.d.

Burchiello, Il. *Sonnetti del Burchiello del Bellincioni e d'altri poeti fiorentini alla burchiellesca*. London, 1757.

Calmo, Andrea. *I piacevoli et ingegnosi discorsi*. Venice, 1542.

Caro, Annibale. *Gli Straccioni*. In *Commedie del Cinquecento*, edited by Nino Borsellino, vol. 2, pp. 202–79. Milan, 1967.

Castiglione, Baldesar. *The Book of the Courtier*. Translated by Charles Singleton. Garden City, N. J., 1959.

Cellini, Benvenuto, *The Life of Benvenuto Cellini*. Translated by John Addington Symonds. New York, 1930.

Cervantes, Miguel. *The Adventures of Don Quixote*. Translated by J. M. Cohen. Baltimore, 1964.

Cleveland, John. *The Anti-Platonick*. In *The Metaphysical Poets*, edited by Helen Gardner, p. 218. Baltimore, 1957.

Coryat, Thomas. *Coryat's Crudities*. 2 vols. Glasgow, 1905.

Della Casa, Giovanni. *Galateo*. Translated by R. S. Pine-Coffin. Harmondsworth, 1958.

D'Aragona, Tullia. *Della Infinità di Amore*. In *Trattati d'Amore del Cinquecento*, edited by Giuseppe Zonta, pp. 187–248. Bari, 1912.

Doni, Anton Francesco. *I Marmi*. Vol. 1. Bari, 1928.

———. *La mula la chiave e madrigali satirici del Doni fiorentino*. Bologna, 1968.

———. *Pistolotti amorosi*. Venice, 1585.

Domenichi, Ludovico. *La nobilità delle donne*. Venice, 1555.

Elyot, Thomas. *The Boke Named The Governour*. New York, 1907.

Erasmus. *The Colloquies*. Translated by C.R. Thompson. Chicago, 1963.

———. *The Julius exclusus of Erasmus*. Translated by P. Pascal. Bloomington, 1968.

———. *The Praise of Folly*. Translated by John Wilson. Ann Arbor, 1968.

Facezie e Motti del secc. XV e XVI ined. Bologna, 1968.

Fedeli, Vincenzo. *Relazione*. In *Relazioni degli ambasciatori veneti al Senato*, edited by Arnoldo Segarizzi, vol. 3, part 1, pp. 123–74. Bari, 1916.

Firenzuola, Agnolo. *Ragionamenti d'amore*, edited by Bartolomeo Rosetti. Rome, 1966.

Folengo, Teofilo. *Orlandino*. In *Opere italiane*, edited by Umberto Renda, vol. 1, pp. 7ff. Bari, 1911.

Franco Niccolò. *Dialoghi piacevoli*. Venice, 1542.

Garzoni, Tommaso. *La piazza universale di tutte le professioni del mondo*. Venice, 1666.

Gelli, Giovanni Battista. *The Circe*, edited by Robert Adams. Ithaca, 1963.

Gottifredi, Bartolomeo. *Specchio d'Amore*. In *Trattati d'Amore del Cinquecento*, edited by Giuseppe Zonta, pp. 251–302. Bari, 1913.

Grazzini, Anton Francesco. *Le Cene*. Florence, 1857.

Jonson, Ben. *Selected Masques*, edited by Stephen Orgel. New Haven and London, 1975.

———. *The Works of Ben Jonson*. Boston, 1853.

Manetti, Antonio. *Novella del Grasso Legnaiuolo*. In *Novelle del Quattrocento*, edited by Aldo Borlenghi, pp. 343–89. Milan, 1962.

Machiavelli, Niccolò. *The Chief Works and Others*. Translated by Allan Gilbert. 2 vols. Durham, 1965.

Medici, Lorenzo de'. *Opere*, edited by Attilio Simoni. Vol. 2. Bari, 1914.

———. *Carnival Song*. In *Lyric Poetry of the Italian Renaissance*, edited by L. R. Lind, pp. 223–27. New Haven and London, 1954.

Michelangelo Buonarroti. *Complete Poems and Selected Letters of Michelangelo*. Translated by Creighton Gilbert and Robert N. Linscott. New York, 1963.

Montaigne, Michel de. *The Complete Essays of Montaigne*. Translated by Donald Frame. Stanford, 1968.

Nietzsche, Friedrich. *Mixed Opinions and Maxims*. In *The Portable Nietzsche*, edited by Walter Kaufmann, pp. 64–67. New York, 1960.

Ovid. *Metamorphoses*. Translated by Horace Gregory. New York, 1958.

Peachem, Henry. *Minerva Britanna*. Leeds, 1966.

Philo-Puttanus. *The Whore's Rhetoric*. New York, 1961.

Piccolomini, Alessandro. *La Raffaella*, edited by Dino Valeri. Florence, 1944.

Poliziano, Angelo. *Odae*. In *Poeti Latini del Quattrocento*, edited by Francesco Arnaldi, pp. 1050ff. Milan-Naples, 1964.

———. *Tutte le poesie italiane*, edited by G. R. Ceriello. Milan, 1952.

Pontano, Giovanni. *Eridanus*. In *Poeti Latini del Quattrocento*, edited by Francesco Arnaldi. Milan-Naples, 1964.

Rabelais, François. *The Histories of Gargantua and Pantagruel*. Translated by J. M. Cohen. Baltimore, 1963.

Sansovino, Francesco. *Ragionamento*. In *Trattati d'Amore del Cinquecento*, edited by Giuseppe Zonta, pp. 153–243. Bari, 1912.

———. *Venetia città nobilissima et singolare*. Venice, 1968.

Sanzio, Raffaello. *Letter to Count Baldasarre Castiglione*. In *Italian Art: 1500–1600*, edited by Robert Klein and Henri Zerner, pp. 32–33. Englewood Cliffs, 1966.

Shakespeare, William. *The Works of Shakespeare*. 3 vols. London, 1950.

Shirley, James. *Cupid and Death*. London, 1951.

Sidney, Philip. *The Defense of Poesie*. In *Complete Works*, edited by Robert Kimbrough, pp. 102–58. New York, 1969.

Siqüenza, Fra José. *History of the Order of St. Jerome*. In *Bosch in Perspective*, edited by James Snyder, pp. 34–41. Englewood Cliffs, 1973.

Twain, Mark, and Warner, C. W. *The Gilded Age*. Hartford, 1874.

Thomas, William. *History of Italy (1549)*, edited by George B. Parks. Ithaca, 1963.

Vasari, Giorgio. *Le vite dè più eccellenti pittori scultori et architettori*. Edited by Gaetano Milanesi. 8 vols. Florence, 1906.

———. *The Lives of the Most Eminent Painters, Sculptors, and Architects*. Translated by Gaston Du C. De Vere. 10 vols. London, 1912–1914.

SECONDARY SOURCES

Books

Ackerman, James S. *The Architecture of Michelangelo*. Harmondsworth, 1971.

Adelman, Janet. *The Common Liar: An Essay on "Antony and Cleopatra."* New Haven, 1973.

Ancona, Paolo d'. *The Schifanoia Months at Ferrara*. Milan, 1954.

Ariès, Philippe. *Centuries of Childhood*. Translated by Robert Baldick. New York, 1962.

Auerbach, Erich. *Mimesis*. Translated by Willard R. Trask. Princeton, 1957.

Baccheschi, Edi. *L'opera completa del Bronzino*. Milan, 1973.

Bakhtin, Mikail. *Rabelais and His World*. Translated by Helene Iswolsky. Cambridge, Mass., 1968.

Baldass, Ludwig. *Hieronymus Bosch*. London, 1960.

Barber, C. L. *Shakespeare's Festive Comedy*. Princeton, 1959.

Barfucci, Enrico. *Lorenzo dei Medici e la società artistica del suo tempo*. Florence, 1964.

Bartsch, Adam. *Le Peintre Graveur*. Vol. 15. Leipzig, 1867.

Battisti, Eugenio. *Antirinascimento*. Milan, 1962.

Baxandall, Michael. *Painting and Experience in Fifteenth Century Italy*. Oxford, 1974.

Bean, Jacob. *Italian Renaissance Drawings from the Musée du Louvre*. New York, 1974.

Bean, Jacob, and Stempfle, Felice. *Drawings from New York Collections I: The Italian Renaissance*. New York, 1965.

Berenson, Bernard. *Italian Pictures of the Renaissance: Venetian School*. 3 vols. London, 1957.

Berti, Luciano. *Pontormo*. Florence, 1966.

Borsook, Eve. *A Companion Guide to Florence*. London, 1966.

Boschloo, A. W. A. *Annibale Carracci in Bologna: Art after the Council of Trent*. The Hague, 1974.

Bosquet, Jacques. *Mannerism*. New York, 1964.

Bovero, Anna. *Tutta la pittura del Crivelli*. Milan, 1961.

Brendel, Otto. "The Scope and Temperament of Erotic Art in the Greco-Roman World." In *Studies in Erotic Art*, edited by Theodore Bowie and Cornelia V. Christenson, pp. 3–108. London and New York, 1970.

Briganti, Giuliano. *Il Manierismo e Pellegrino Tibaldi.* Rome, 1945.

Burckhardt, Jacob. *The Civilization of the Italian Renaissance.* New York, 1954.

Burke, Peter. *Culture and Society in Renaissance Italy: 1420–1540.* New York, 1972.

Bush, Virginia. *The Colossal Sculpture of the Cinquecento.* New York, 1976.

Calvesi, Maurizio, and Casale, V. *Le incisioni dei Carracci.* Rome, 1965.

Casagrande, Rita. *Le cortigiane veneziane nel '500.* Milan, 1968.

Chastel, André. "Cortile et Théatre." In *Le Lieu Théâtral à la Renaissance,* edited by Jacques Jacquot, pp. 41–47. Paris, 1968.

Cipriani, Renata. *All the Paintings of Mantegna.* 2 vols. New York, 1964.

Clements, Robert J. *The Poetry of Michelangelo.* New York, 1963.

Cleugh, James. *The Divine Aretino.* London, 1965.

Cochrane, Eric. *Florence in the Forgotten Centuries.* Chicago, 1973.

———. "A Case in Point: The End of the Renaissance in Florence." In *The Late Renaissance,* edited by Eric Cochrane, pp. 43–73. New York, 1970.

Colacicchi, Giovanni. *Antonio del Pollaiuolo.* Florence, 1943.

Colie, Rosalie. *Paradoxica Epidemica: The Renaissance Tradition of Paradox.* Princeton, 1966.

Cronin, Vincent. *The Flowering of the Renaissance.* New York, 1969.

Cuttler, Charles. *Northern Painting.* New York, 1968.

Davies, Martin, *National Gallery Catalogues: The Earlier Italian Schools.* London, 1961.

De Campos, Redig. *The "Stanze" of Raphael.* Rome, 1957.

De Tolnay, Charles. *Michelangelo.* Vol. 5. Princeton, 1970.

Douglas, Langton. *Piero di Cosimo.* Chicago, 1944.

Dussler, Luitpold. *Raphael: A Critical Catalogue of his Pictures, Wall-Paintings, and Tapestries.* London and New York, 1971.

Einem, Herbert von. *Das Program der Stanza della Segnatura im Vatikan.* Opladen, 1971.

Einstein, Alfred. *The Italian Madrigal.* 3 vols. Princeton, 1949.

Ferrari, Maria Luisa. *Il Romanino.* Milan, 1961.

Fiocco, Giuseppe. *L'Arte di Andrea Mantegna.* Venice, 1959.

Fischel, Oskar. *Raphael.* London, 1964.

Frame, Donald. *François Rabelais.* New York and London, 1977.

Freedberg, Sydney J. *Andrea del Sarto.* 2 vols. Cambridge, Mass., 1963.

———. *Painting in Italy: 1500–1600.* Harmondsworth, 1971.

———. *Painting of the High Renaissance in Rome and Florence.* 2 vols. Cambridge, Mass., 1961.

Frey, Dagobert. *Manierismus als Europäische Stilerscheinung.* Stuttgart, 1968.

Friedlaender, Max, and Rosenberg, Jacob. *Die Gemälde von Lucas Cranach.* Berlin, 1932.

Friedlaender, Walter. *Caravaggio Studies.* New York, 1969.

———. *Mannerism and Anti-Mannerism in Italian Painting.* New York, 1965.

Frommel, Christolph. *Baldasarre Peruzzi als Maler und Zeichner.* Vienna, 1967–1968.

Frye, Northrop. *Anatomy of Criticism.* Princeton, 1973.

Galli dè Paratesi, Nora. *Semantica dell'Eufemismo.* Turin, 1964.

Gibbons, Felton. *Dosso and Battista Dossi.* Princeton, 1968.

Glück, Gustaf. *Pieter Breughel the Elder.* Vienna, 1936.

Gombrich, E. H. *Symbolic Images.* London, 1972.

Gombrich, E. H., and Kris, Ernst. *Caricature.* Harmondsworth, 1941.

Graf, Arturo. *Attraverso il Cinquecento.* Turin, 1926.

Haraszti-Takács, Marianna. *The Masters of Mannerism.* Budapest, 1968.

Hartt, Frederick. *Giulio Romano.* 2 vols. New Haven, 1958.

———. *History of Italian Renaissance Art.* Englewood Cliffs, 1969.

———. "The Meaning of Michelangelo's Medici Chapel." In *Essays in Honor of Georg Swarzenski,* pp. 145–55. Chicago, 1951.

———. *Michelangelo: The Complete Sculpture.* New York, 1968.

———. *Michelangelo Drawings.* New York, 1970.

Hayum, Andrée. *Giovanni Antonio Bazzi-"Il Sodoma."* New York, 1976.

Held, Julius. "Flora, Goddess and Courtesan." In *De artibus opuscula XV: Essays in Honor of Erwin Panofsky,* edited by Millard Meiss, vol. 1, pp. 201–18. New York, 1961.

Heydenreich, Ludwig H., and Lotz, Wolfgang. *Architecture in Italy: 1400–1600.* Harmondsworth, 1974.

Huizinga, Johan. *Homo Ludens.* Boston, 1964.

———. *The Waning of the Middle Ages.* New York, 1954.

Janson, H. W. *Apes and Ape Lore in the Middle Ages and the Renaissance.* London, 1952.

Kaiser, Walter. *Praisers of Folly: Erasmus, Rabelais, Shakespeare.* Cambridge, Mass., 1963.

Klein, H. A. *Graphic Worlds of Peter Bruegel The Elder.* New York, 1963.

Kolve, V. A. *The Play Called Corpus Christi.* Stanford, 1966.

Kristeller, Paul. *Andrea Mantegna.* London, 1901.

Kristeller, Paul Oskar. *The Philosophy of Marsilio Ficino.* New York, 1943.

———. *Renaissance Thought.* New York, 1961.

Künzle, Paul. "Raffaels Denkmal für Fedro Inghirami auf dem letzten Arazzo." In *Mélanges Eugène Tesserant*, pp. 499ff. Città del Vaticano, 1964.

Lehmann, Phyllis, and Lehmann, Karl. *Samothracian Reflections.* Princeton, 1973.

Lessing, Gotthold. *Laocoön.* Translated by E. Frothingham. New York, 1969.

Levenson, Jay; Oberhuber, Konrad; and Sheehan, Jacquelyn L. *Early Italian Engravings from the National Gallery of Art.* Washington, D. C., 1973.

Levey, Michael. *Painting at Court.* New York, 1971.

———. "Sacred and Profane Significance in Two Paintings by Bronzino." In *Studies in Renaissance and Baroque Art Presented to Anthony Blunt on His 60th Birthday,* pp. 30ff. London and New York, 1967.

Linfert, Carl. *Hieronymus Bosch.* New York, 1971.

Lucie-Smith, Edward, and Jacquiot, Aline. *The Waking Dream: Fantasy and the Surreal in Graphic Art: 1450–1900.* New York, 1975.

Marlier, Georges. *Erasme et la peinture flamande de son temps.* Brussels, 1954.

Martin, John Rupert. *The Farnese Gallery.* Princeton, 1965.

Meiss, Millard. *The Painter's Choice.* New York, 1976.

Minor, Andrew C., and Mitchell, Bonner. *A Renaissance Entertainment: Festivities for the Marriage of Cosimo I, Duke of Florence, in 1539.* Columbia, Mo., 1968.

Mitchell, Bonner. *Rome in the High Renaissance.* Norman, Okla., 1973.

Muecke, D. C. *Irony.* London, 1970.

Nagler, A. M. *Theatre Festivals of the Medici, 1539–1637.* New Haven, 1967.

Nelson, John Charles. *Renaissance Theory of Love.* New York, 1958.

Oberhuber, Konrad. *Die Kunst der Graphik IV: Renaissance und Barock.* Vienna, 1968.

Ortega y Gasset, José. *Velasquez Goya and the Dehumanization of Art.* London, 1972.

Panofsky, Erwin. *Idea: A Concept in Art Theory.* New York, 1968.

———. *Problems in Titian, Mostly Iconographic.* New York, 1968.

———. *Renaissance and Renascences in Western Art.* New York, 1960.

———. *Studies in Iconology: Humanistic Themes in the Art of the Renaissance.* New York, 1962.

Passavant, Günter. *Verrocchio.* London, 1969.

Pastor, Ludwig. *The History of the Popes.* Vol. 8. London, 1950.

Paulson, Ronald. *William Hogarth: His Life, Art and Times.* 2 vols. New Haven, 1971.

Perella, Nicholas James. *The Kiss Sacred and Profane.* Berkeley, 1969.

Pittaluga, Mary. *Filippo Lippi.* Florence, 1949.

Popham, A. E. *Correggio's Drawings.* London, 1957.

———. *The Drawings of Parmigianino.* New York, 1953.

Popham, A. E., and Wilde, Johannes. *The Italian Drawings of the XV and XVI Centuries . . . at Windsor Castle.* London, 1949.

Posner, Donald. *Annibale Carracci.* 2 vols. London, 1971.

Quintavalle, Augusta Ghidiglia. *Gli affreschi giovanili del Parmigianino.* Milan, 1961.

Randall, Lilian. *Images in the Margins of Gothic Manuscripts.* Berkeley, 1966.

Rearick-Cox, Janet. *The Drawings of Pontormo.* 2 vols. Cambridge, Mass., 1964.

Robb, Nesca. *Neoplatonism of the Italian Renaissance.* New York, 1935.

Robertson, D. W. *Preface to Chaucer.* Princeton, 1962.

Rochon, André, editor. *Formes et Significations de la "Beffa" dans la Littérature Italienne de la Renaissance.* Paris, 1972.

———. *Formes et Significations de la "Beffa" dans la Littérature Italienne de la Renaissance (Duxième Série).* Paris, 1975.

———. *La Jeunesse de Laurent de Medicis.* Paris, 1963.

Saxl, Fritz. *Lectures.* 2 vols. Vienna, 1957.

Schneider, Laurie. *Giotto in Perspective.* Englewood Cliffs, 1974.

Shapley, Fern Rusk. *Paintings from the Samuel H. Kress Collection.* 2 vols. London, 1968.

Shearman, John. *Andrea del Sarto.* 2 vols. Oxford, 1965.

———. *Mannerism.* Harmondsworth. 1967.

Suida, Wilhelm, and Manning, Bertina. *Luca Cambiaso: la vita e le opere.* Milan, 1958.

Symonds, John Addington. *Renaissance in Italy.* 2 vols. New York, 1935.

Tietze-Conrat, Erica. *Dwarfs and Jesters in Art.* New York, 1957.

Verheyen, Egon. *The Paintings in the Studiolo of Isabella d'Este at Mantua.* New York, 1971.

Walker, John. *Bellini and Titian at Ferrara*. New York, 1956.

Warburg, Aby. *Gesammelte Schriften*. Nendeln-Liechtenstein, 1969.

Welsford, Enid. *The Fool*. Cambridge, 1935.

Wethey, Harold. *Titian*. 3 vols. London, 1969–1975.

White, Christopher. *Recent Acquisitions and Personal Gifts, National Gallery of Art*. Washington, D. C., 1974.

Wind, Edgar. *Bellini's Feast of the Gods*. Cambridge, Mass., 1948.

———. *Pagan Mysteries in the Renaissance*. New York, 1968.

Winternitz, Emanuel. *Musical Instruments and Their Symbolism in Western Art*. New York, 1967.

Wittkower, Rudolph, and Wittkower, Margot. *Born under Saturn*. New York, 1963.

Woefflin, Heinrich. *The Art of the Italian Renaissance*. New York, 1963.

Wright, Thomas. *A History of Caricature and Grotesque in Literature and Art*. New York, 1968.

Periodical Articles

Adhémar, Jean. "Aretino: Artistic Adviser to Francis I." *Journal of the Warburg and Courtauld Institutes* 17 (1954) :311–18.

Alpers, Svetlana. "Breughel's Festive Peasants." *Simiolus* 6 (1972–1973) :163–76.

———. "Realism as a comic mode: low life painting seen through Bredero's eyes." *Simiolus* 8 (1975–1976) :115–44.

Brendel, Otto. "The Interpretation of the Holkham Venus." *Art Bulletin* 38 (1946) :65–75.

Brown, Clifford M. "New Documents of Andrea Mantegna's Camera degli Sposi." *Burlington Magazine* 114 (1972) : 861–63.

Cropper, Elizabeth. "On Beautiful Women, Parmigianino, *Petrarchismo*, and the Vernacular Style." *Art Bulletin* 58 (1976) :374–96.

Davidson, Bernice. "Drawings by Perino del Vaga for the Palazzo Doria, Genoa." *Art Bulletin* 41 (1959) :315–26.

De Jongh, E. "Erotica in Vogelperspektief." *Simiolus* 3 (1968–1969) :22–74.

Dempsey, Charles. " 'Et Nos Cedamus Amori': Observations on the Farnese Gallery." *Art Bulletin* 50 (1968) :363–74.

———. "*Mercurius Ver*: The Sources of Botticelli's *Primavera*." *Journal of the Warburg and Courtauld Institutes* 38 (1968) :251–73.

Dollmayr, Hans. "Lo Stanzino del Cardinal Bibbiena." *Archivio storico dell'arte* 3 (1890) :272–80.

Ettlinger, L. D. "Hercules Florentinus." *Mitteilungen des Kunsthistorischen Institutes* 16 (1972) :119–42.

Fehl, Philipp. "Raphael as Archeologist." *Archeological News* 4 (1975) :29–48.

———. "The Worship of Bacchus and Venus in Bellini's and Titian's Bacchanals for Alfonso d'Este." *Studies in the History of Art: National Gallery of Art* 6 (1974) : 37–95.

Ferruolo, Arnolfo B. "Botticelli's Mythologies, Ficino's *De Amore*, Poliziano's *Giostra*: Their Circle of Love." *Art Bulletin* 37 (1955) :17–25.

Freedberg, S. J. "Observations on the Painting of the Maniera." *Art Bulletin* 47 (1965) :187–97.

Friedlaender, Walter. "La tintura delle rose." *Art Bulletin* 20 (1938) :320–24.

Frye, Northrop. "The Nature of Satire." *The University of Toronto Quarterly* 14 (October 1944) :75–89.

Gilbert, Allan. "Review of Erwin Panofsky, *Studies in Iconology*." *Art Bulletin* 22 (1940) :172–74.

Gilbert, Creighton. "Antique Frameworks for Renaissance Art Theory: Alberti and Pino." *Marsyas* 3 (1946–1947) : 87–106.

Gibbons, Felton. "Two Allegories by Dosso for the Court of Ferrara." *Art Bulletin* 47 (1965) :493–99.

Gnoli, Domenico. "Raffaello alla corte di Leone X." *Nuova antologia* 14 (1888) :571–610.

Gombrich, E. H. "Huizinga and 'Homo Ludens.' " *Times Literary Supplement* (4 October 1976) :1083–89.

Hamill, Alfred E. "Letter to the Editor." *Art Bulletin* 29 (1947) :65.

Hayum, Andrée. "A New Dating for Sodoma's Frescoes in the Villa Farnesina." *Art Bulletin* 48 (1966) :215–17.

Heikamp, Detlef. "La Grotta Grande del Giardino di Boboli." *Antichità Viva* 4 (July–August 1965) :27–43.

Holderbaum, James. "A Bronze by Giovanni da Bologna and a Painting by Bronzino." *Burlington Magazine* 98 (1956) :439–45.

Hutchinson, Jane Campbell. "The Housebook Master and the Folly of the Wise Man." *Art Bulletin* 48 (1966) : 73–78.

Hyman, Isabel. "Notes and Speculations on S. Lorenzo, Palazzo Medici, and an Urban Project by Brunelleschi." *Journal of the Society of Architectural Historians* 34 (1975) :98–120.

Janson, H. W. "Review of Erwin Panofsky, *Studies in Iconology*." *Art Bulletin* 22 (1940) :174–75.

Kaufmann, Thomas Da Costa. "Arcimboldo's Imperial Allegories." *Zeitschrift für Kunstgeschichte* 39 (1976) : 275–96.

Kinkead, Duncan. "An Iconographic Note on Raphael's

Galatea." *Journal of the Warburg and Courtauld Institutes* 33 (1970):313–15.

Lord, Carla. "Tintoretto and the *Roman de la Rose*." *Journal of the Warburg and Courtauld Institutes* 33 (1970):315–17.

Martin, John Rupert. "The Butcher Shop of the Carracci." *Art Bulletin* 45 (1963):263–66.

Marutes, Harry. "Personifications of Laughter and Drunken Sleep in Titian's 'Andrians.'" *Burlington Magazine* 115 (1973):518–25.

Mattingly, Garrett. "Machiavelli's Prince: Political Science or Political Satire." *The American Scholar* 27 (1958):482–91.

Meijer, Bert. "Esempi del comico figurativo nel rinascimento lombardo." *Arte Lombarda* 16 (1971):259–66.

————. "Harmony and satire in the work of Niccolò Frangipane: problems in the depiction of music." *Simiolus* 6 (1972–1973):94–112.

Middeldorf, Ulrich. "Letter to the Editor." *Art Bulletin* 29 (1947):65–66.

Moxey, K. P. F. "Erasmus and the Iconography of Pieter Aertsen's *Christ in the House of Martha and Mary* in the Boyman van Beuningen Museum." *Journal of the Warburg and Courtauld Institutes* 34 (1971):335–36.

Panofsky, Erwin. "Erasmus and the Visual Arts." *Journal of the Warburg and Courtauld Institutes* 32 (1969):200–227.

Panofsky, Erwin, and Panofsky, Dora. "The Iconography of the Galerie François I at Fontainebleau." *Gazette des Beaux-Arts* 52 (1958):113–90.

Reff, Theodore. "The Meaning of Titian's *Venus of Urbino*." *Pantheon* 21 (1963):359–66.

Rose, Mark. "Sidney's Womanish Man." *The Review of English Studies* 15 (1964):353–63.

Sale, Roger. "An Iconographic Program by Marco Parenti." *Renaissance Quarterly* 27 (1974):293–99.

Scaglietti, Domenico. "La maturità di Amico Aspertini e i suoi rapporti con la *maniera*." *Paragone* 20 (July 1969):21–43.

Schapiro, Maurice L. "Donatello's *Genius*." *Art Bulletin* 45 (1963):135–42.

Schnapper, Antoine. "Les salles d'Ulysse au Palazzo Poggi." *L'Oeil* no. 133 (January 1966):3–9.

Shearman, John. "Die Loggia der Psyche in der Villa Farnesina und die Probleme der letzten Phase von Raffaels graphischem Stil." *Jahrbuch der Kunstsammlungen in Wien* 24 (1964):59–100.

Smith, Webster. "On the Original Location of the *Primavera*." *Art Bulletin* 57 (1975):31–40.

Spini, Giorgio. "Architettura e Politica nel Principato Mediceo." *Rivista storica italiana* 83 (1971):792–845.

Spitzer, Leo. "Die Wortbildung als stilistisches Mittel exemplifiziert an Rabelais. . . ." *Beihefte zür Romanische Philologie* 29 (1910).

Steinberg, Leo. "Michelangelo's Florentine *Pietà*: The Missing Leg." *Art Bulletin* 50 (1968):343–53.

Summers, David. "Michelangelo's Architecture." *Art Bulletin* 54 (1972):146–57.

Verheyen, Egon. "Correggio's *Amori di Giove*." *Journal of the Warburg and Courtauld Institutes* 29 (1966):160–92.

————. "Die Malereien in der Sala di Psiche des Palazzo del Te." *Jahrbuch der Berliner Museen* 14 (1972):33–68.

Wickhoff, Franz. "Die Hochzeitsbilder Sandro Botticelli." *Jahrbuch d. K. Preussische Kunstsammlungen* 27 (1906):198–207.

Wind, Barry. "Annibale Carracci's 'Scherzo': The Christ Church *Butcher Shop*." *Art Bulletin* 58 (1976):93–96.

————. "*Pitture ridicole*: Some Late Cinquecento Comic Genre Paintings." *Storia dell'Arte* 20 (1974):25–35.

Wind, Edgar. "A Note on Bacchus and Ariadne." *Burlington Magazine* 92 (1950):82–85.

Winner, Mathias. "Pontormos Fresko in Poggio a Caiano." *Zeitschrift für Kunstgeschichte* 35 (1972):153–97.

————. "Raffael malt einen Elefanten." *Mitteilungen des Kunsthistorischen Institutes* 11 (1965):71–109.

Zeri, Federico. "Major and Minor Artists in Dublin." *Apollo* 99 (January 1974):88–103.

Index

References to illustrations are
indicated in italic type.